UNIVERSITY OF MICHIGAN PUBLICATIONS
LANGUAGE AND LITERATURE
VOLUME XXVIII

WASHINGTON IRVING
AND
GERMANY

Washington Irving New York
1 Feby 1823

Washington Irving

AND

Germany

BY

WALTER A. REICHART

ANN ARBOR

THE UNIVERSITY OF MICHIGAN PRESS

Library of Congress Catalog Card No. 57–7102

Publication of this book was made possible by a grant from the Horace H. Rackham School of Graduate Studies.

Printed in The United States of America

FOR RUTH

Preface

Most readers are probably aware of Washington Irving's close contact with Spain as the author of the romantic tales and sketches *The Alhambra,* and later as Envoy Extraordinary and Minister Plenipotentiary to the Court at Madrid, but it may come as something of a surprise to see Irving's name associated with Germany. Yet only a few years before Irving set foot on Spanish soil and immediately after the prestige of *The Sketch Book* and *Bracebridge Hall* had made him famous in England, he set out for Germany with a specific purpose: to collect material for a "German Sketch Book." To examine how he came to make such plans, how he toured Germany and Austria in 1822–23 and spent half a year in Dresden before returning to the onerous task of writing the *Tales of a Traveller,* and how much these travels influenced his work is the purpose of this study. Of interest is the fact that both "Rip Van Winkle" and "The Legend of Sleepy Hollow," two masterpieces of the American short story, are indebted to German literature for much of their substance. Although it may be surprising and disappointing to know that these narratives with their Catskill and Hudson Valley scenes, considered so genuinely American, were in part suggested to Irving by his German reading, such information explains his eagerness to continue his German studies and to proceed to that land where "the rich mine of German literature holds forth abundant reward."

Tabulations of Irving's extensive and varied contacts with German literature, the identification of virtually all the theatrical performances he witnessed in his travels, a list of German titles that he recorded in his notebooks, and a catalogue of his German books in the Irving Memorial at Sunnyside, Tarrytown on the Hudson, are included as an appendix to this study.

In the preparation of this volume I have incurred all too many obligations to acknowledge individually, but the most important I must list. Twenty years ago, when I first began this study, Professor Henry A. Pochmann had just published the results of his basic investigation of Irving's German sources. He generously gave me the benefit of his spadework and urged me to continue while he turned to other subjects. The late Professor Stanley T. Williams, whose definitive *Life and Work of*

Washington Irving has become the guidebook for Irving scholarship, not only encouraged me at every turn, but patiently answered numerous queries and placed much valuable source material at my disposal. Professor Percival R. Kirby of the University of Witwatersrand, South Africa, who discovered the manuscript of the Irving-Livius adaptation of Weber's comic opera *Abu Hassan,* made this text available. Mrs. Louis Dupont Irving of New York City invited me to visit Sunnyside when it was still the property of the Irving family, so that I could examine the collection of German books which Washington Irving had brought back to America.

My careful retracing of Irving's footsteps in Dresden, fortunately completed before World War II destroyed the Saxon capital, would have been impossible without the cordial assistance of the Director of the Sächsische Landesbibliothek, the late Dr. Martin Bollert. He not only provided me with working space in the library—an almost unheard of privilege in European libraries—but found the proper channels to help my research. Through his negotiations I was received by Prince Johann Georg, a brother of the last King of Saxony, whose family archives yielded some evidence of Irving's associations with the royal family during his winter in Dresden. Permission to reproduce for the frontispiece of this volume the Vogel von Vogelstein pencil sketch of Irving, practically unknown in this country, was given by the Dresden Museum.

No one can work in the field of Irving scholarship without being indebted to the New York Public Library, where the largest collection of Irving manuscripts is available. Other libraries have loaned books and journals generously, but I cannot express my gratitude individually. The Reference Division of the University of Michigan Library, however, must be singled out. The enthusiastic and untiring efforts of the staff to locate and make available to me the out-of-the-way items for which I continually asked helped me greatly and have been deeply appreciated. Finally, I am grateful to my friend and colleague, Professor C. D. Thorpe, for many helpful suggestions in the preparation of the manuscript.

W.A.R.

Ann Arbor
October, 1956

Contents

WASHINGTON IRVING

AND

GERMANY

1

In England

IN THE SUMMER OF 1822 Washington Irving left London for the Continent in the hope of effecting a cure for a cutaneous complaint that had troubled him for almost a year. In February of that year he had been considering the baths at Aix-la-Chapelle,[1] but the final work of preparing the manuscript of *Bracebridge Hall* and seeing it through the press had demanded his presence in London. These obligations fulfilled, he could set out upon the journey to that yet unexplored realm of romantic Germany that had beckoned to him ever since he had heard of Thomas Campbell's travels in Germany and had witnessed Walter Scott's enthusiasm for German literature, an enthusiasm shared by English readers for more than two decades.

The publication of *The Sketch Book* had made Irving "the most fashionable fellow of the day"[2] in England, and literary men as well as Hyde Park society eagerly sought his company. Irving, gratified and flattered, readily accepted such a welcome. His fondness for society and literary gossip, already a characteristic of his New York days, had increased with the years. Though he was dazed by such unexpected fame and adulation, he was no more astonished than his hosts, who had to acknowledge that here was an American who could write like an Englishman. Irving was welcomed to John Murray's drawing room and soon felt at home in the circle of prominent men of letters who met there regularly. He relished the intimate friendship of Francis Jeffrey and Walter Scott, he enjoyed the company of the genial Thomas Moore and the witty Sydney Smith, and he was dazzled by the brilliant company at Holland House. Gradually, however, the gaiety of the social whirl with its irregular hours and demands upon his time and energy began to tire him; he actually longed for a quiet interlude of travel and study to refresh his mind and body. On June 11, 1822, he wrote to his friend Brevoort:

> . . . I am nearly killed with kindness, for I have not a moment to myself and am so fatigued with company and dinners and evening parties, that I find it impossible to regain a perfect state of health but am still troubled with lameness & inflammation in the ancles, the lingering of my tedious malady. I shall however, soon leave this scene of bustle & dissipation and go to a watering place on the continent (Aix la Chapelle) where I hope thoroughly to reinstate my health. Within these two months past I have given myself up to society more than I have at any time since I have been in Europe, having for the last four or five years been very much shut up & at home. I was determined this spring to give myself a holiday & make use of the opportunity presented me of seeing fashionable life. I have done this to a considerable degree, though I have suffered much draw back on account of the indifferent state of my health.
>
> The success of my writings has given me ready access to all kinds of society—and I have been the round of routs, dinners, operas, balls, & blue stocking coteries. I have been much pleased with those parties in which rank & fashion and talent are blended; and where you find the most distinguished people of the day in various departments of literature, art & science brought into familiar communion with leading statesmen and ancient nobility.[3]

The choice of Irving's destination was not accidental. He had been dissatisfied with the progress of his convalescence and with the advice of his London physician,[4] so he was willing to attempt his own cure. Having heard of famous watering places in Germany, he decided to combine the advantages of such treatment with the pleasures of foreign travel. His curiosity and impatience to see the land whose literature had already served as a source for some of his most popular tales in *The Sketch Book* determined his itinerary. *Bracebridge Hall,* despite its good reception in England, showed clearly that Irving was exhausting his English environment and needed new scenes and new anecdotes that could be metamorphosed into respectable literary sketches. He was ready for one of those romantic interludes of travel that recurred regularly in Irving's life and usually preceded a period of composition. He was hoping to explore Germany—a little hurriedly, perhaps, since he expected to return to Paris in autumn[5]—in order to relish her medievalism and to read enough of her folklore to spur his imagination and to enable him to produce a "German Sketch Book."

Irving liked to travel after completing a volume of sketches, as, contrary to the widely held view, writing was always an exhausting process for him.[6] His *Journals,* with their minute details concerning the laborious composition and revision of his work, constantly reflect Irving's eager efforts to overcome the limitations of a mediocre mind. The task of writing worried him and left his nerves on edge.

It was neither a scholar's zeal nor intellectual curiosity, therefore, that took Irving inside the German borders, as was the case of his countrymen George Ticknor, Edward Everett, George Bancroft, and Henry Wadsworth Longfellow, who studied at Göttingen in order to understand German life, literature, and civilization.[7] Irving was thirty-nine years old, hardly an age to set out upon his *Wanderjahre;* he was not eager or young enough to be receptive to the varied influences of foreign travel and study. Eighteen years earlier Irving had seen Europe for the first time with the buoyant exuberance of youth, excited by the landscapes and the exotic customs; even then he had not made a great effort to acquire new ideas or to extend his mental horizon, and now his thought patterns were set. Outwardly, Irving seemed satisfied with his world and was prone to contemplate every foreign scene with almost an air of English condescension.[8]

Before proceeding to Irving's actual experiences in Germany, it may be well to recall his earliest contacts with German culture and to establish the degree of his familiarity with the language in order to explain his eager anticipation of travel in Germany. His childhood and youth had given him only a desultory education with no systematic training in foreign languages. He had still heard Dutch spoken in church and market place so that he had acquired a smattering, but aside from some routine Latin, which helped him somewhat in later years with his French, Spanish, and Italian studies, he had had no real experience with a foreign tongue in his school days.[9] Not until after his arrival in England in 1815 was Irving tempted to begin the study of German—once he had really become aware of the recent influence of this foreign literature on English letters.

Irving's early enthusiasm for the theatre, which made him a "hanger-on" at stage doors and in the greenrooms even in London a score of years later,[10] may well have brought him into contact with

German drama in English translation on the New York stage. William Dunlap, who had assumed the management of the Park Street Theatre in 1798, had translated a number of original dramas from the German: his version of Zschokke's *Abällino, der grosse Bandit* was first performed in 1801 and maintained its popularity for years. Kotzebue, whose vogue was world-wide, led all foreign productions in America, and Schiller's *Die Räuber* was performed at intervals and reprinted four times.[11] More definitely established is the likelihood of Irving's acquaintance with some magazine articles that touched upon German literature and philosophy. If he read the *Literary Magazine and American Register* or the *Port Folio* or any other American magazines between 1806 and 1813 he could not fail to see constant references to the work of Klopstock, Wieland, and Goethe, and to articles containing general observations about German life.[12] Moreover, established as "the most eminent New York man of letters,"[13] Irving was persuaded late in 1812 to assume the editorship of *Analectic Magazine,* formerly *Select Reviews,* a monthly which furnished American readers with a selection of foreign materials. Irving was more than a nominal editor and contributed at least eleven articles during the following two years.[14] Hence he must have read and even selected some of the copy, which included a number of significant items bearing upon German literature.

In the November, 1813, issue appeared an "account of C. M. Wieland," a glowing and sentimental tribute upon the occasion of the poet's death, which characterized him as "equally eminent as a poet and a prose writer, as a moralist and a philosopher, as a translator and an author of the most brilliant originality and invention."[15] Such unrestrained praise reflected the popularity of Wieland in England after the middle of the eighteenth century, rivaled only by that of Gessner.[16] William Sotheby's translation of *Oberon* had appeared in 1798 and was reprinted in America in 1810 from the third London edition.[17] Only a few years later Irving made this entry in his notebook: "light tales in the manner of Wieland,"[18] a reminder, perhaps, to try to emulate the facile pen of this popular author. After a preliminary notice of the publication of Mme de Staël's *De L'Allemagne,* also in the November, 1813, issue, the *Analectic Magazine* of April, 1814, reprinted from the *Edinburgh Review* a twenty-four page discussion of it. This article must have aroused Irving's interest and supplied him with much literary information. The review traced the growing importance of German literature in the eighteenth century and its reception in England, and made the observation that Germany "possesses a greater number of laborious scholars and of useful books than any other country."[19] What could have proved more enticing to Washington Irving? Though there is no definite proof that Irving read *De L'Allemagne,* it seems likely in view of its international reputation. If he did not have access to the American edition he probably came to know the work during his English residence after 1815.[20] Irving's fondness for literary associations could not have allowed him to forget that he had made the personal acquaintance of Mme de Staël at the house of (Karl) Wilhelm von Humboldt on his first journey to Europe. Obviously it had been a red-letter day for Irving, and in his journal he made the following entries:

> [March 30, 1805.] We also presented a letter of introduction from Mr. Degen of Naples to the Baron Humbolt [*sic*], minister for the Court of Prussia at Rome. He recieved [*sic*] us very politely and we passed half an hour with him in an agreeable & interesting manner. He is brother to the celebrated Humboldt who has made such an extensive tour in America—and informs us that he expects his brother in Rome in a few days when he will make us acquainted with him. The Baron is said to be a very literary man and bears an amiable character in other respects.
>
> [April 4.] In the evening we visited the Prussian Minister Baron Humbolt. We found there Madam De Sta[ë]l the celebrated authoress of Delphine &c. She is a woman of great strength of mind & understanding by all accounts—we were in company with her but a few minutes.
>
> [April 7.] In the evening we accompanied the Baron de Humboldt to the conversazione of the Marquis [*blank*], Minister imperial at the Court of Rome. Here we found a crowded assembly, . . . consisting of the first nobility of Rome and several foreigners of distinction. The company was very brilliant, as usual they mingled together for an hour or so conversing together till the assembly was formed . . .
>
> [April 10.] In the evening we were to a private conversazione at the Baron De Humboldts.[21]

Whether Irving met the famous scientist Alexander von Humboldt at this time is not certain, but he came to know him later in Paris[22] and could say upon hearing of his death, "I met Humboldt often in society in Paris. A very amiable man. A great deal of bonhommie."[23] Irving's nephew recorded concerning Mme de Staël that "*Delphine* was the only one of her productions which Mr. Irving had then read" and that he seemed, "by what he once stated to me, to have been somewhat astounded at the amazing flow of her conversation, and the question upon question with which she plied him."[24] It is unthinkable that Wilhelm von Humboldt, who had lived in Jena as a close friend of Goethe and Schiller, would fail to speak to Mme de Staël, who had just visited Weimar in 1803, of his own experiences there, and surely Irving must have listened carefully. The announcement of the publication of *De L'Allemagne* must have awakened fond memories in Irving and have led him to an early perusal of this important estimate of German culture.

The first tangible evidence of Irving's awareness of the prevailing enthusiasm for German literature is revealed in a biographical sketch which he wrote in 1810 as an introduction to an American edition of Thomas Campbell's poetical works. With the factual details furnished by Campbell's brother Archibald, who was living in New York, Irving made a polite attempt at a critical estimate.[25] He praised "the exquisite little poems" in sentimental platitudes and superficial verbiage but without a semblance of analysis or incisive criticism. Campbell's interest in German letters Irving accepted as characteristic of the age: "About this time the passion for German literature raged in all its violence in Great Britain, and the literary world was completely infatuated by the brilliant absurdities of the German muse . . . The universal enthusiasm with which this new species of literature was admired, awakened in the inquiring mind of our author a desire of studying it at the fountain head." This passion for German literature, which eventually gripped Irving as it had gripped Campbell, sent them both to Germany. Irving quoted further without comment a revealing passage from Campbell's own reactions as recorded in one of his letters from Germany:

> My time at Hamburgh was chiefly employed in reading German; and, I am almost ashamed to confess it, for *twelve successive weeks* in the study of Kant's philosophy. I had heard so much of it in Germany, its language was so new to me, and the possibility of its application to so many purposes, in the different theories of science and Belles Lettres, was so constantly maintained, that I began to suspect Kant might be another Bacon, and blamed myself for not perceiving his merit. Distrusting my own imperfect acquaintance with German, I took a disciple of Kant's for a guide through his philosophy, but found, even with all his fair play, nothing to reward my labors. His metaphysics are mere innovations upon the received meaning of words, and the coinage of new ones, and convey no more

> instruction than the writings of Duns Scotus and Thomas Aquinas. In Belles Lettres, the German language opens a richer field than in their philosophy. I cannot conceive a more perfect Poet than their favourite Wieland.[26]

Such second-hand information was supplemented in the summer of 1817 when Irving was living in England and visited Thomas Campbell at Sydenham. Campbell had first gone to Germany in 1800, hoping "to see Schiller and Goethe—the banks of Rhine—and the mistress of Werter."[27] Actually, at Hamburg he saw Klopstock (who impressed Campbell greatly and inspired a poem), found the material for his best-known lyric "Hohenlinden," and formed a life-long friendship with August Wilhelm Schlegel. Campbell returned to Germany again in 1814 and in 1820, visited Heidelberg, and traveled along the Rhine and down the Danube to Vienna, an itinerary not unlike the one that Irving was to follow.

Most important among Irving's literary associations in Great Britain was his staunch friendship with Walter Scott. In 1813 Henry Brevoort had delighted Scott with a copy of Knickerbocker's *History of New York*,[28] and when, in August, 1817, Irving was traveling through Scotland, the land of his forefathers, and he appeared at Abbotsford with a letter of introduction from Thomas Campbell, "the glorious old minstrel himself came limping to the gate,"[29] took him by the hand, and promptly made him a member of the household. Already familiar with much of Scott's work, Irving came now completely under the influence of Scott's romanticism and was definitely directed toward German letters. In a sense, however, the Gothic romances of Walpole and Mrs. Radcliffe, the grotesque tales of M. G. Lewis, and even the writings of his own countryman, Charles Brockden Brown, had prepared him for the new fashion in literature. The style of Goldsmith and Sterne, of Addison and Steele, in short the literary tradition of the eighteenth century under whose tutelage he developed, had left their mark upon his writing, but the library of Abbotsford impressed Irving with the untapped resources of German romance and medieval lore. Scott himself had been struck by the German fever that had spread through England two decades earlier;[30] he had plunged into the study of German so that by 1794 a certain facility in reading the language was his and he was able to begin to translate Bürger's "Lenore," a ballad that became the rage in England and appeared in five translations in 1796.[31] Scott completed it and "Der wilde Jäger" and published both poems anonymously under the titles "William and Helen," and "The Chase."[32] In 1798 he translated Goethe's *Götz von Berlichingen,* the historical drama which influenced the direction of his own literary development.[33]

When Irving arrived at Abbotsford, Scott was at the beginning of his great creative period, and the identity of the "Great Unknown" was still something of a mystery to the public. He was writing the drama *The Doom of Devorgoil,* in which "the story of the ghostly barber" admittedly is based upon the legend "Stumme Liebe," by Musäus.[34] *The House of Aspen,* written immediately after translating *Götz* though not published until 1827, and the novel *Anne of Geierstein* include the motif of the Vehmgericht, which Goethe's drama had used and which was the subject of Veit Weber's *Die heilige Vehme,* a volume which both Scott and Irving came to own. The vast library at Abbotsford, "well stored with books of romantic fiction in various languages, many of them rare and antiquated,"[35] caught Irving's interest. German literature was well represented, and here Irving probably examined for the first time editions of Goethe, Schiller, Wieland, Bürger, Tieck, Fouqué, and Musäus. Scott's interest in history, legends, and wondrous tales explains the abundance of medieval historical accounts, tales of magic and necromancy, folklore, and fairy stories that he continued to acquire even in later years (as indicated by the dates of publication), when his enthusiasm for German literature was waning. More than three hundred German titles are listed in Scott's library, and the majority of these volumes were on his shelves when Irving visited him.[36] The period of his own German studies already lay behind Scott, but it is fair to assume that he encouraged Irving in his new German interests. Washington Irving's acquisition of the poems of Bürger, a folklore collection of Büsching, some volumes of Goethe, tales and legends collected by Gottschalck, the Grimm brothers, Wieland, Musäus, and Tieck, his purchase of the dramas of Müllner and Schiller, and even of seven volumes of *Sagen der Vorzeit* by Veit Weber, an author to whom Scott acknowledged his own indebtedness in the foreword to *The House of Aspen,* can hardly be coincidental.[37] At Abbotsford Irving's eyes were opened to the vast possibilities in such sources. Scott's conversation strengthened Irving's resolve to write, to study the fascinating history of folklore, and to direct his narrative talent toward themes of the romantic and the miraculous. He had found a sympathetic mentor whose wise talk of legend and writing Irving kept turning over in his mind. No one else had ever spoken to him so understandingly of his lifelong interests.[38]

The trip through Scotland completed, Irving returned to Liverpool and to the office of the family firm of P. and E. Irving, which was tottering on the brink of bankruptcy. Business affairs had grown steadily worse since the autumn of 1815, when Washington Irving, hoping to avert complete disaster, had first participated actively in the management of the firm. Finally, bankruptcy proceedings offered the only way to wind up the tangled financial affairs. In the face of such humiliation and in the vague hope of making himself independent through his pen, Irving began his serious study of German. "At this time he had shut himself up from society, and was studying German, day and night, in the double hope that it would be of service to him, and tend to keep off uncomfortable thoughts; and I have heard him say," noted his nephew, "that while waiting for the examination [in bankruptcy court] he was walking up and down the room, conning over the German verbs."[39] Irving himself wrote: "For months I studied German day & night by way of driving off horrid thoughts."[40] He set to work learning the declensions of the German adjective. *Guter Wein, gute Milch, gutes Bier* served as paradigms, and a full page of declensional endings are recorded in his notebook.[41] Rabenhorst's *Pocket Dictionary of the German and English Languages* (1814), Schiller's *Don Carlos* in an English translation (1798) and *Die Räuber* (1816), and Wieland's *Die Abentheuer des Don Sylvio von Rosalva* (1772), which he purchased in Liverpool, are still preserved at Sunnyside and testify to Irving's serious purpose.

The last-mentioned novel reflects a change in technique that had a strong appeal for Irving. Walpole's genre, the Gothic novel emphasizing supernatural elements, had gained ground so rapidly that tales of horror and terror soon became commonplace. Clara Reeve then varied the formula a little and introduced what Walpole called the "tame ghost." She managed at the end of a work to explain away all apparitions, unearthly voices, mystifications, and occult experiences as misapprehensions or coincidences, though often the explanations were as difficult to accept as the mysterious occurrences. Wieland's narrative, also veering from the straight ghost story, with wit and a spirit of enlightenment, struck a satirical note. The subtitle of the English translation (1773), "Reason Triumphant Over Fancy; Exemplified in the Singular Adventures of Don Sylvio de Rosalva. A History in Which Every Marvellous Event Occurs Naturally," emphasized this aspect. Such a description would attract Irving, whose own predilection for the rational explanation of *diablerie* was to be the touchstone of his most successful tales. *Don Quixote* had made fun of the antiquated romance of knighthood and adventurous chivalry; *Don Sylvio* was a satire upon the fairy tales, superstitions, and sentimentalism so popular in Wieland's day.

Never before had Irving worked so hard. The leisurely dabbling in literature which had produced his earlier work, a distillate of satire and good-natured humor reflecting the conscious sophistication of a growing urban center, lay behind him. His brothers' failure provided the necessary economic pressure to advance his literary apprenticeship, and Scott gave him confidence in a firm determination to support himself by his writings. In August, 1817, some nine sketches lay unfinished in his portfolio,[42] but it was almost a full year before he could rid himself of all feelings of despondency and lethargy in order to write his masterpiece, "Rip Van Winkle." This interval was filled with long hours of study to acquire a working knowledge of German. Only his unpublished Notebook gives further hints of this preoccupation and lists a few additional German phrases like *Das schwartze Pferd, Das deutsche Schifferhaus, Auchs bequemes Lager & Mittagessen,*[43] and some book titles, among which Wagener's *Die Gespenster,* Laun's *Erzählungen* (with a price of seven shillings indicated), and Lafontaine's *Kleine Romane* represent German material. Whether these volumes were acquired to advance his reading skill cannot be ascertained, but the entry of a cost price supports this assumption, as any expenditure—even the price of two shillings and six pence for the little red morocco volume that served as the Notebook of 1818—is recorded in it. More easily established is the fact that such reading left no tangible evidence in his own compositions and probably served only as exercise material. But Irving was reading with a purpose and kept his eyes open for any bits of lore that might furnish bone and sinew for a tale. How much Irving was reading about Germany in English publications lies in the realm of conjecture, but some notations in his Notebook of 1818 are significant. The cryptic phrase "light tales in the manner of Wieland," written at a time when Irving had probably read, at least in translation, some of this affable but discursive raconteur, does not necessarily promise great familiarity with the work of this author—Irving's transcription reveals his struggle with the name—but looks more like a reminder to himself to cultivate a similar vein of writing. In the earlier part of this Notebook Irving had made extracts from Riesbeck's *Travels through Germany* that have some bearing on the story of "Rip Van Winkle." (Actually, Riesbeck's work contained enough praise of Wieland to warrant Irving's favorable notation.[44]) By far the most striking extracts are those from the fourteenth travel letter of Riesbeck, dealing with the romantic environs of Salzburg. Here Irving may have found the lodestar that directed him toward "Rip Van Winkle." He carefully copied almost verbatim—though sometimes shortened or paraphrased—

the essence of such lore as might serve him later as material for a tale. In the following quotation, entirely from his Notebook, the phrases in parentheses were supplied by Irving to give context and meaning to his citations; the text in italics (mine) is particularly pertinent for the source of the story of "Rip Van Winkle":

> Watzman (Mountain in Bavaria where it is said) the Emperor Charles the Great and all his army are confined until Doomsday, (near Saltzburg—a) *cleft of the mountain from whence you hear a dull rumbling like a distant thunder*—probably the mountain has some lake in its bosom.
>
> On a certain day of the year about midnight the Emperor is to be seen with his whole train of ministers & generals going in procession to the cathedral of Saltzburg.—
>
> From the cleft whence the spirit of the great Charles issues to walk by night, the stream precipitates itself with a loud noise and falls in a variety of cascades down the deep and narrow gully which it seems to have dug itself in the hard marble.
>
> I am a lover of mountain scenes. The pulse of nature beats strongly here. Everything discovers more life & energy and emphatically speaks an almighty power at work. The stream which without knowing the path it must pursue, meanders thro the plain, works thro the mountain & grows impetuously in its course, the motions of the clouds, the revolutions of the sky and the peals of thunder are all more strong & animated.
>
> The vallies in the fair season of the year are filled with finer perfumes of flowers & herb than those of the plains. Nature is here more varied & picturesque, (man more vigorous, fanciful, imaginative, meditative).
>
> *Wizards whose white beards have grown—ten or 20 times around the table on which they sit sleeping in the mountain—and of hermits a thousand years old who have led stray goat-hunters through subterranean passages and shown* them fairy palaces of gold and precious stones.[45]

The bulk of *The Sketch Book,* in which "Rip Van Winkle" first appeared, consists of literary essays in the manner of eighteenth-century English authors and reflects the style in which Irving had schooled himself, but there is also a new note of romanticism. This concession to the age by the very impressionable New Yorker is attributable to a number of influences and literary contacts, not the least of which was his growing acquaintance with German literature. His urbane manner, the dignity and grace of his descriptive writing—humorous yet tinged with a faint touch of good-natured irony or a nostalgic longing for the passing romance of English country life—endeared him at once to readers on both sides of the Atlantic. Irving's success was immediate, first in America and a little later in England: abroad because of the gracious and flattering attitude of an American toward the mother country, at home because of a natural pride in the international success of a native son and also because of the vogue for a genteel and somewhat romanticized approach to life. Today most of the essays are forgotten. They read like pages from the memory books of an ancient past. A few like "Westminster Abbey," "Stratford-on-Avon," or "The Mutability of Literature" have not lost their charm. They can be read with full enjoyment and seem hardly touched by the passage of time; but the artificiality, the dullness and pedantry of "Rural Funerals," of "Roscoe," of "The Pride of the Village" reveal Irving's most serious shortcomings. He was not a great or original talent; he was able to embellish rather than to create. Hence he sought to relieve the monotony of the literary essays filled with bookish lore, assembled at the Athenaeum in Liverpool or at the British Museum in London, with fictional narratives. Irving had neither great inner resources nor a stock of learning to draw on, and was dependent upon literature not only to furnish the necessary stimulation for writing, but actually to yield the materials that could be molded into finished literary products.

Obvious proof of Irving's fortuitous reading as a momentous factor in the composition of *The Sketch Book* is revealed in the numerous quotations, often from almost forgotten Elizabethans, traceable to thirty-seven English writers.[46] Such a study of books, reflected in his notes, included the reading of much contemporary writing, particularly the new literature by Byron, Scott, and Moore.[47] Equally significant were the numerous publications translated or adapted from the popular literature of Germany. Available were *Tales of Wonder, Tales of Terror,* and *The German Museum, or Monthly Repository of the Literature of Germany, the North & the Continent in General* (1800–1801), which attempted to give the British a survey of what was newest in the German language, and translated many tales of Wieland and Musäus.[48]

Irving was well aware of what was being printed, reprinted, and imitated concerning German literature in English books and magazines, but he was also making laborious efforts to find in this foreign literature original stories that might be suitable for his purpose. The opportunities were great and fortune smiled on Irving. His German studies had not been in vain. He found legends and folklore that gave substance to his work and furnished the plots for his best known short stories, a genre acknowledged as an American contribution to literature. "Rip Van Winkle" and "The Legend of Sleepy Hollow" set the pattern for a type of fiction so successful and popular in its appeal that Irving utilized it in his later collections of tales in place of the more conventional literary sketch. However, he never surpassed—in fact never equaled—his initial achievement. These two stories, hailed more than twenty years later as "perhaps the finest pieces of original fictitious writing that this century has produced next to the works of Scott,"[49] have kept *The Sketch Book* alive. Such praise was not uncommon throughout the nineteenth century, and their popularity even today has suffered little when compared to the fate of the bulk of the essays, whose faded charm and bookish flavor are only too apparent. In these two stories Irving achieved something of immortality.

What enhanced the appeal of these stories was their acceptance as original, indigenous literature, reflecting the spirit of early American life. His depiction of the intimate details of the domestic scene, realistically portrayed against an American background, of the local color and atmosphere, done with whimsical humor—elements always characterized as typically native—gave Irving a deserved reputation as the first American man of letters. In England the immediate reaction to the publication of *The Sketch Book* was one of hearty approbation; the laudatory appraisals revealed amazement at "the work of an American, entirely bred and trained in that country . . . , written throughout with the greatest care and accuracy, and worked up to great purity and beauty of diction, on the model of the most elegant and polished of our native writers."[50] Not until after the publication of *Bracebridge Hall* and *Tales of a Traveller* was Irving subjected to frequent criticism for a lack of originality in his writing and for a dependence upon literary materials which he refurbished before publishing as his own. Some inquiring voices were raised and even Irving's most successful story, "Rip Van Winkle," did not completely escape criticism. General legends of enchanted sleep were sometimes mentioned,[51] as were the story of Epimenides as told by Diogenes Laertius,[52] the account of the haunted glen of Thomas the Rhymer, to which Scott had called Irving's attention—"a fine old story, said he, and might be wrought up into a capital tale"[53]—and, most important of all, the Kyffhäuser stories of the Harz Mountains. In reference to these last stories, which are of special significance for this study, Irving found it necessary to defend his position in a footnote at the end of the essay "The Historian," in *Bracebridge Hall*:

> I find that the tale of Rip Van Winkle, given in the Sketch Book, has been discovered by divers writers in magazines, to have been founded on a little German tradition, and the matter has been re-

vealed to the world as if it were a foul instance of plagiarism marvelously brought to light. In a note which follows that tale, I had alluded to the superstition on which it is founded, and I thought a mere allusion was sufficient, as the tradition was so notorious as to be inserted in almost every collection of German legends. I had seen it myself in three. I could hardly have hoped, therefore, in the present age, when every ghost and goblin story is ransacked, that the origin of the tale would escape discovery. In fact, I had considered popular traditions of the kind as fair foundations for authors of fiction to build upon, and made use of the one in question accordingly. I am not disposed to contest the matter, however, and indeed consider myself so completely overpaid by the public for my trivial performances, that I am content to submit to any deductions, which, in their afterthoughts, they may think proper to make.[54]

Irving had made no claim to originality and had, as he said, indicated his source for "Rip Van Winkle" at the end of his narrative. Here he stated succinctly, before indulging in his customary Knickerbocker flourish of substantiating the veracity of the tale by vowing that he himself even talked with old Rip Van Winkle, that "The foregoing tale, one would suspect, had been suggested to Mr. Knickerbocker by a little German superstition about the Emperor Frederick *der Rothbart,* and the Kypphäuser mountain."[55]

Such similarities in plot were recognized in Irving's own day without much investigation. In 1822 an anonymous author contributed to the American magazine the *Port Folio* a complete translation of "Peter Klaus" and in a brief note identified Büsching as Irving's source and recounted the basic Kyffhäuser legend.[56] In time, the matter was so completely lost sight of that no investigator has referred to it since.

In 1868 Bayard Taylor and in 1883 J. B. Thompson named "Peter Klaus" as Irving's source without, however, revealing and emphasizing the full extent of such indebtedness.[57] The first scholarly investigation was made in Germany (1901) by Professor Sprenger,[58] who printed the text of "Peter Klaus" from Grässe's *Sagenbuch des preussischen Staats,* fully aware that this story was first printed in Otmar's *Volkssagen*[59] in 1800 and is a composite of a series of Kyffhäuser legends. (For that reason, presumably, the Brothers Grimm who included eighteen items from Otmar's twenty-four in their famous *Deutsche Sagen* (1816) did not include "Peter Klaus";[60] it lacked the simplicity of genuine folklore and reflected the technique of a professional narrator.) Sprenger collated the texts of "Rip Van Winkle" and "Peter Klaus" and showed such similarities of phrase and idiom that he clearly established Irving's dependence upon this German source. He listed further German legends of lost herds, mysterious games of nine-pins, and prolonged periods of supernatural sleep which Irving might have known, but erred in believing that Irving's travels through the Harz region took place before the writing of "Rip Van Winkle." Sprenger's article remained practically unknown because it was printed in an annual school report of a German *Gymnasium*, but was discovered by Professor Pochmann in 1930, when he was making a broader study of the German sources in *The Sketch Book*.[61]

Irving had found the story of a simple herdsman who followed his straying goats into a subterranean cave, where he was pressed into service as pin boy in a mysterious game of nine-pins. The man partook of the fragrant wine that was available, and when he awoke he was alone in the meadow, his dog and his herd were gone. Somewhat puzzled and with a feeling of strangeness in an environment that should have been familiar, he returned to his village. Everything had changed: his beard had grown a foot, people whom he had never seen before stared at him, his own hut was dilapidated, and his wife and children had disappeared. Strangers questioned him, but finally he recognized a woman, a former neighbor suddenly grown old and senile. When a young woman with two small children appeared, whose resemblance to his wife startled him, he asked her name and her father's. Then followed the recognition and his sudden realization that he had been gone twenty years.

Irving did more, however, than merely expand the story to four times its original length. With his unique style he provided a picturesque setting of a small Dutch community in the Catskill Mountains. The goatherd of the legend became the good-natured, indolent Rip Van Winkle, beloved by all in the village, a special favorite among the children to whom he was a willing companion and playmate, but hopelessly henpecked at home. His only refuge from the tart temper and the sharp tongue of Dame Van Winkle was the woods, into which he strolled, gun in hand and his faithful dog Wolf at his side, whenever flight from the wrath of his spouse became advisable. Under such circumstances Rip fell into the company of odd-looking personages who, instead of being knights of the Kyffhäuser, were cronies of Hendrick Hudson and lineal descendants of Irving's Knickerbocker clan. The rest of the story followed naturally within the framework of such a milieu. Rip Van Winkle's return home, his bewilderment at the political changes, his confusion at having lost his identity and at finding the precise counterpart of his youth standing before him reveal masterly touches of the narrator's technique. The final recognition of his son and daughter is skillfully motivated by the appearance of a young mother whose infant becomes frightened by his disheveled appearance. She tries to reassure her offspring with a "hush, Rip, hush you little fool; the old man won't hurt you," and in a flash he senses the situation. And when he hears that his termagant wife had burst a blood-vessel in a fit of passion, he can contain himself no longer, and embraces his daughter and her child. "I am your father!" cried he,—"Young Rip Van Winkle once—old Rip Van Winkle now!—Does nobody know poor Rip Van Winkle?"

Having accepted Irving's dependence upon Otmar, Pochmann was somewhat puzzled by the curious reference in the author's note to "the Emperor Frederick *der Rothbart,* and the Kypphäuser mountain." It seemed a misleading suggestion to direct the reader "to 'Der verzauberte Kaiser'—which incidentally, is the legend that immediately follows 'Peter Klaus' in Otmar's collection,"[62] but has no immediate bearing upon the plot of "Rip Van Winkle." It is merely the legend of the great Emperor, his red beard growing through the stone table, sleeping in his subterranean castle. This version does not even include the popular motif of the Emperor rousing himself every hundred years to ask whether ravens still fly on the mountain and, after an affirmative reply, relapsing into sleep for another century, awaiting a call to deliver his people from their enemies.

In all essential points "Rip Van Winkle" is the story of Otmar's "Peter Klaus," but Irving did not use Otmar as his source. He depended upon Büsching's[63] collection of German folklore. This volume of *Volks-Sagen, Märchen und Legenden,* still among the books at Sunnyside, contains eight main geographic categories subdivided into eighty-four groups of legends and fairy tales, whereas Otmar printed only twenty-four separate stories. Both Otmar and Büsching group "Peter Klaus" and the Kyffhäuser stories among "legends of the Harz," a designation that Irving used in reference to "Rip Van Winkle" in a notation among his manuscripts.[64] But only Büsching's arrangement and sequence of legends explains Irving's notations: Under section VII, "Sagen und Mährchen vom Harz" (pp. 303–70) there is a collection of six stories as item 69, entitled "Der Kyffhäuser." The fourth of these, "Der Ziegenhirt," is the story of "Peter Klaus," the sixth is "Der verzauberte Kaiser," which is again subdivided into four separate stories of Emperor Frederick. Hence it was perfectly logical and proper for Irving to refer to his source for "Rip Van Winkle" as the "little German superstition about the Emperor Frederick *der Rothbart,* and the Kypphäuser mountain." These stories both belong to the same cycle of legends and he had found the Emperor Frederick stories grouped together with the "Peter Klaus" story. His sincere protest against any innuendoes of plagiarism was justified by his awareness of the prevalence of this traditional legendary material. He had seen it in three different collections; precisely which the three were cannot be established, but Otmar, Büsching, an anonymous volume of *Volkssagen* (Eisenach, 1795), Gustav's *Volkssagen* (1806), and Behrens' *Hercynia curiosa* (1712) contain some phases of the Kyffhäuser legends.

The only remaining problem, which can be discussed but hardly solved, pertains to the extent of Irving's knowledge of German at the time he composed "Rip Van Winkle." William Roscoe's translation of "Peter Klaus" was still eight years off.[65] With his limited training in foreign languages, once Irving had determined to learn German it demanded will power and determination to cling to his purpose, but on May 19, 1818, he could write:

> I have been some time past engaged in the study of the German language, and have got so far as to be able to read and *splutter* a little. It is a severe task, and has required hard study; but the rich mine of German literature holds forth abundant reward.[66]

In view of his difficulties with German during his travels on the Continent three years later, some doubt is justified about his familiarity with the idiom, but his claim at this time is modest enough. Excluding the possibility that Irving received some assistance in the matter of translating (he knew the Roscoe family in Liverpool and had probably seen Scott's own copy of Büsching at Abbotsford, or had found a ready-made translation in an out-of-the-way magazine, no longer available), it is fair to assume that his studies had progressed sufficiently far by the summer of 1818, when he was writing "Rip Van Winkle," that with the aid of a dictionary he could make a tolerable translation of simple material. And "Peter Klaus" is written in plain, unadorned, straightforward German. Its vocabulary is simple, the sentence structure easy, the narrative brief and without bombast or syntactical difficulties: the sort of task that might be set today for a freshman in college German. Normally, translating might have been a dull and monotonous chore for Irving, but this time he had both purpose and determination. His brothers had lost only their money in the failure of their business enterprise, but he had lost more. The dark clouds that settled over his usually happy temperament smothered his creative talents. His ability to work gone, his prospects as a writer were dim. His German studies, prosaic and uninspiring in themselves, served at least as an intellectual exercise and filled this barren period. Eventually Washington Irving was aroused from this lethargy and stimulated artistically by Henry Van Wart, who recalled their happy youth in the Sleepy Hollow area with "the oddest characters of the valley, the ridiculous legends and customs, habits, and sayings" of those quaint Dutchmen.[67] Irving's imagination was fired, and suddenly boyhood memories and German legends coalesced. His efforts at language study bore fruit as he fused personal recollections and folklore materials into the story of Rip Van Winkle, his finest tale.

The writing of "The Legend of Sleepy Hollow" followed the pattern of "Rip Van Winkle," and it is also indebted to German literature for much of its plot. Irving had sketched the outline for the story while visiting his sister at Birmingham in the fall of 1818, after hearing his brother-in-law's recollections of his early days at Tarrytown on the Hudson and the story of one Brom Bones, a wild blade who boasted of having once met the devil on a return from a nocturnal frolic.[68] The rest of the descriptive setting followed easily. As in "Rip Van Winkle," it is a romantic and sequestered region, this time along the Hudson, with its inhabitants predominantly descendants of early Dutch settlers. This prosperous rural community, in which Mynheer Van Tassel's comfortable home was situated, was set apart from all other communities of the sort by an abundance of haunted spots and twilight superstitions. In fact it boasted of a very special apparition, the galloping ghost of a Hessian trooper whose head had been carried away by a cannonball during the Revolution—the Headless Horseman of Sleepy Hollow. The happy domestic scene at Baltus Van Tassel's, the contemplated quilting frolic, the schoolhouse of Ichabod Crane, and his luckless wooing of the beautiful Katrina give the story an American setting so genuine and realistic as to place it, with "Rip Van Winkle," into almost every collection of American short stories; yet the climactic episode of Ichabod Crane's encounter with the Headless Horseman—a typical Knickerbocker caper—is taken directly from a German source. The comic relief that clears the atmosphere of terror and fear, that explains the weird and supernatural events as a simple mad-cap prank, distinguishes this tale from a more serious effort like Burns's "Tam O' Shanter." This parallel has been drawn before and there are external similarities: the haunted church, the romantic pursuit that terminates in or near a stream with a bridge over which, according to the belief of both Tam and Ichabod, fiends may not cross.[69] These similarities, however, do not touch the crux of the source problem. In all likelihood Irving was familiar with the poem of Burns and in a general sense may have drawn upon it, as he no doubt also was aware of the legend of the ruthless huntsman of Bürger's ballad, "Der wilde Jäger," which Scott had translated. But the fantastic adventure at midnight, the headless horseman who threw his detached head at Ichabod's skull, the unexpected denouement that implicates a disguised rival, and the hurled pumpkin, in short, the climax of Ichabod's unhappy adventure, were borrowed by Irving from the fifth of the "Legenden von Rübezahl" in the collection of *Volksmärchen* by Musäus.

Pochmann, in his previously mentioned article,[61] gave convincing citations from the German source, but was unaware of an English translation available to Irving. In 1791 two volumes of *Popular Tales of the Germans,* containing about half the stories in Musäus, had been published anonymously (though the translation is now ascribed to William Beckford, the author of *Vathek*). The second volume included five chapters of Rübezahl legends under the title "Elfin Freaks; or, the seven legends of Number-Nip."[70] This was the first and perhaps the most significant collection of German romances and tales to appear just before popular taste in England created an insatiable demand for German translations or for imitations of this kind of story, encompassing the gruesome, the uncanny, the fantastic, and the horrible. An absurd musical adaptation of the first "Number-Nip" story, presented at the Covent Garden Theatre, October 6, 1819, attests to the popularity of these legends.[71] Irving, the inveterate patron of the theatre, was in London at that time and may have seen it. John Miller, who was Irving's first publisher in England, distributed it. No evidence points toward any translation of Musäus other than the anonymous one available to Irving at this time despite the reference of Walter Scott to works of Musäus, "of which Beddoes made two volumes."[72]

In transferring the episodes in "The Legend of Sleepy Hollow" from the Riesengebirge of Silesia to his own native haunts along the Hudson, Irving repeated the procedure he had used in writing "Rip Van Winkle." He used a setting similar to the original to provide the necessary background of haunted woods, superstitious fears, and spectral apparitions, but converted the adventure of a simple-minded and credulous coachman into a real American tale of local color and native humor.[73] The hair-raising experience of the coachman had served Musäus only as introductory material for one of his fairy tales, tales that delighted eighteenth-century readers because they maintained a kindly though skeptical attitude toward the fanciful qualities of folk legends. He elaborated a mock-serious appraisal of the severed head:

> The examination of the head was committed to the physician. However, without subjecting it to his anatomical knife, he instantly recognized it for an huge hollowed out gourd filled with sand and stones,

> and worked up into a very grotesque figure, by the addition of a wooden nose, and a long flax beard.[74]

Irving emphasized the nocturnal adventure and concluded the story with a sly Knickerbocker touch. The disillusioning discovery of the shattered pumpkin and Brom Bones's knowing laugh at all references to the unhappy Ichabod reveal Irving's human understanding.

Among the other writings in *The Sketch Book,* the numerous sketches of English life afford a curious blend of fact and fiction. Irving was realizing the dreams of his childhood in observing at first hand historic scenes in the land of his fathers, but he ignored the wretched poverty engendered by the increasing conflict between new industrialism and an established agrarian economy and fixed his mind's eye on the subdued elegance and glamour of the historical past, or on things like the patriarchal setting of a squire's country hall. Here he found England, or at least the England that he sought. He had come to Europe "to escape from the commonplace realities of the present, and lose myself among the shadowy grandeurs of the past,"[75] and he remained faithful to his purpose. The Old World was for him completely a world of romance and enchantment.

"The Spectre Bridegroom," the third of *The Sketch Book* stories indebted to German sources, differs in its setting as well as in its spirit from "Rip Van Winkle" and "The Legend of Sleepy Hollow." Here is a tale based entirely upon literary sources. The background of the story, the romantic scenery of the Odenwald in Germany, the names of places and characters lay completely outside of Irving's experience. Hence it was impossible to give intimate and lifelike portrayals of persons or scenes. Irving had not yet reached the borders of Germany and depended solely upon his imagination or his booklore for the creation of his setting. Therefore he avoided descriptive details and was content to create the impression of familiarity with the environment through a casual use of German phrases. The designation of the great family of Katzenellenbogen (a name that Irving explained with pretended seriousness in a footnote), judicious references to the tender ballads of the *Minnelieder* or the chivalric wonders of the *Heldenbuch,* actual preference for German terms like *Rhein-wein* and *Ferne-wein,* and even the somewhat ill-chosen appellation of *Saus und Braus* to characterize the reception of the distinguished guest, are examples of an effort to create atmosphere. It might be argued that the effort seems studied and forced, that this foreign phrase, conveying the meaning of "riotous living," is inappropriate to characterize the good fellowship and hospitality which are implied here. But the impression created, and certainly borne out by the concluding episodes of the story, argues that Irving was slyly and humorously satirizing not only the romantic and supernatural trappings dear to him and his contemporaries, but also the solemn and ponderous style of the German stories of the time.

The climax of the story is reached in the sudden realization of the wedding company that the pale and gloomy bridegroom, who already had caused annoyance and consternation by his delayed arrival, was leaving without his bride, gravely and precipitously, immediately after the banquet:

> "I must away to Wurtzburg [*sic*] cathedral—" "Ay," said the baron, plucking up spirit, "but not until tomorrow—tomorrow you shall take your bride there."
>
> "No! no!" replied the stranger, with tenfold solemnity, "my engagement is with no bride—the worms! the worms expect me! I am a dead man—I have been slain by robbers—my body lies at Wurtzburg—at midnight I am to be buried—the grave is waiting for me—I must keep my appointment!"
>
> He sprang on his black charger, dashed over the drawbridge, and the clattering of his horse's hoofs was lost in the whistling of the night.
>
> The baron returned to the hall in the utmost consternation, and related what had passed. The ladies fainted outright, others sickened at the idea of having banqueted with a spectre. It was the opinion of some, that this might be the wild huntsman, famous in German legend.[76]

The consternation of the company was surpassed only by the indignation of the baron and the dismay of the bride, widowed even before she was married; but the return of the ghostly lover two nights later and the disappearance of the bride the succeeding night, presumably abducted by the goblin and borne away to his tomb, wrung the full measure of grief and terror from the hearts of the great family of Katzenellenbogen. Preparations for the pursuit of the spectre bridegroom were being made when the lovers returned and the mystery was solved. The handsome cavalier, suspected of being a spectral apparition, revealed his identity as Sir Herman Von Starkenfaust. He had originally come to the castle with grievous news: his friend, whose marriage was to be celebrated, was dead, killed by robbers. The betrothal had been arranged by the two families and the young people had not yet met. Sir Herman fell in love with his friend's betrothed at sight, but fearing the hostility of her family, failed to clarify a confused situation. After his unseemly departure from the wedding festivities as a ghost, he returned to woo and to win the fair bride. Fear and laments turned to joy as the old count embraced a substantial son-in-law instead of a wood-demon who promised perchance a troop of goblin grandchildren. Everyone was happy except one of the aunts who "was particularly mortified at having her marvelous story marred, and that the only spectre she had ever seen should turn out a counterfeit."[77]

In "The Legend of Sleepy Hollow" Irving had explained away the mystery that had inspired fear and terror in Ichabod Crane in terms of natural phenomena and had made sly thrusts at the extravagances of the narrative. In "The Spectre Bridegroom" he went a step further. Instead of a facetious twist at the end of the story, which gives a burlesque touch to a Gothic theme, Irving unfolded in mock seriousness an entire story. His whimsical humor and Knickerbocker flourishes constantly reassure the reader, despite an atmosphere of ominous foreboding. Actually what he had written was a parody upon the famous German ballad "Lenore." This poem of August Bürger, first printed in 1773 in the *Göttinger Musenalmanach* for 1774, took England by storm in the nineties and fired Scott's imagination. His translation, or more accurately, adaptation, "William and Helen," was obviously known to Irving. He probably had read some of the other versions also. His reference in "The Spectre Bridegroom" to "the history of the goblin horseman that carried away the fair Leonora; a dreadful story, which has since been put into excellent verse, and is read and believed by all the world,"[78] implies as much since only Stanley, Spencer, and Beresford used the spelling "Leonora."[79] The atmosphere of this dramatic ballad and its haunting melody assured its immediate success in a romantic and sentimental age. "Lenore" relates a folk legend of a brave soldier who falls in battle while his sweetheart vainly awaits his return. Her bitter grief and constant tears allow him no peace; such impious lamentation summons the spirit of her lover from his grave. He returns at night, claims his love, lifts her on his horse, and gallops away. The midnight hour reveals him as a skeleton.

Irving utilized the theme, but in his affable manner avoided any serious implications. The betrothal in his tale had been arranged by the parents. The appearance of Herman Von Starkenfaust in place of the expected but unknown lover proved soul-satisfying. There was no real grief, only consternation and dismay at the sudden disappearance of the ghostlike lover. Such temporary distress was quickly dissipated by the revelation of the true facts, and the playful and romantic mood, interrupted momentarily, could be resumed. The deft touch of a masterly narrator good-naturedly ridiculed the popular love of the grotesque and the supernatural.

In Irving's ghost stories the literary device of the humorous flourish which suddenly reveals the absurdity of the earlier mystification, is almost his trademark. It is also characteristically American. The New World lacked the ancient customs and traditions of Europe, where genuine and long-acclaimed ghosts were a part of the local heritage. Neither castle ruins nor prison vaults were available in America and once the primeval forests were cleared and the frontier pushed back, where was the necessary setting for acceptable tales of horror? The synthetic atmosphere which Irving effectively created had to be sustained by the narrative itself. Irving never intended to write fairy tales or stories of the supernatural, but used the spectral apparatus of these genres to make the reader the dupe of his genial wit.

The extent of Irving's contact with German materials before 1819 and their influence on *The Sketch Book* were virtually unknown when the book appeared, and such direct borrowing was an interesting but not the determining factor in its success. Its favorable reception depended upon the charm of the author's style, the purity and melody of his prose, as well as upon the content. Paradoxically, the stories based on German sources reveal more robust characterization of flesh and blood persons than many of the sketches based on Irving's observations and experiences in England. Irving did not create out of an inner abundance, but needed substance for the spinning of yarns, in which he was a master. Though he was delighted with the variety and richness of German inventions, he was careful to avoid the grotesque absurdities accepted at this time as the hallmark of German fiction. The elegance and ironic didacticism of Musäus, who could express in a playful or even jesting tone sound principles of human behavior, were closer to Irving's own spirit than the historical romances of Veit Weber or the overwrought terror of Grosse. Unfortunately, many of the ephemeral publications of the first two decades of nineteenth-century England have disappeared and only a small proportion of these once popular stories is available for examination. Here and there references to them can be found in collections of folklore still extant, even when not mentioned in Morgan's bibliographical compilation.[80] Irving recorded the price of a volume of Laun's *Erzählungen* in his "Notebook of 1818," at the very time that he was trying to master the German language. How much Irving knew about this prolific and popular Dresden author cannot be demonstrated, but Laun was acknowledged in England as "the historian of ghost-stories, which have really occurred but which have subsequently been capable of rational explanation," and three or four of his stories were published in English by Ackermann about this time.[81] Direct borrowing from German sources has been established in the three best-known stories of *The Sketch Book*, but the more intangible and elusive influence of Irving's wide and varied reading during his residence in England can only be surmised. His determined effort to read German and his eagerness to visit the regions where the folklore originated are perhaps the most acceptable tokens of his awareness of such sources.

The success of *The Sketch Book*, so complete in America, was not immediately duplicated in England. Irving had difficulties in finding a publisher, but once the book appeared, England too succumbed to its musical prose, its quiet humor, and its charming elegance. Murray, after having seen the printed numbers from America, refused at first to undertake its publication: "I do not see that scope in the nature of it which would enable me to make those satisfactory accounts between us, without which I really feel no satisfaction in engaging";[82] Irving was forced to seek help elsewhere. His determination to publish a British edition was intensified by the prospect of an unauthorized republication, a common practice at the time because of inadequate copyright protection. He turned to Scott and inquired whether Mr. Constable might be inclined to become his London publisher. The sincere encouragement of Scott's reply, his generous offer of the editorship of an Edinburgh periodical, and his "earnest recommendation to Constable to enter into the negotiation" came too late to save Irving from another disappointment. Irving "had determined to look to no leading bookseller for a launch, but to throw my work before the public at my own risk, and let it sink or swim according to its merits," a procedure that Scott warned against in another letter as "certainly not the very best way to publish."

The failure of Irving's publisher, J. Miller, after the first volume was put to press and "getting into fair circulation," had dashed any hopes of the successful distribution of *The Sketch Book* in England, when the intercession of Scott, now Sir Walter, saved the day. He prevailed upon Murray to take over. So the "Prince of Booksellers,"[83] as Irving called Murray a few years later, became his publisher, and the prestige of this firm and the support of friendly critics launched Irving's success abroad. Whereas *Salmagundi* amused and delighted only a small coterie of kindred spirits in New York and *A History of New York* gave Irving prestige at home as a distinguished American writer, *The Sketch Book* made Irving famous in England as well as in America. In fact his fame and popularity spread rapidly to the Continent so that three years later

French and German translations of his works greeted his eyes in the bookshops of Paris, Leipzig, and Dresden.

After a year's sojourn in France, Irving, intending to strengthen his reputation as a writer, began another series of sketches that eventually constituted *Bracebridge Hall.* It was a less spontaneous effort than *The Sketch Book.* Irving wrote incessantly without too clear a concept or a specific plan in mind, and finished the work only under the constant prodding of an impatient publisher. Thomas Moore, who was enjoying his enforced residence in Paris and knew all distinguished British visitors who crowded that metropolis after travel on the Continent had become possible again, had given Irving two practical suggestions: the idea for "the description of the booksellers' dinner,"[84] which furnished the underlying idea of "Buckthorne," a story that was expanded, rewritten, and finally included in *Tales of a Traveller,* and the hint to take "the characters in his 'Christmas Essay,' Master Simon, etc. etc., for the purpose of making a slight thread of a story on which to string his remarks and sketches of human feelings."[85] Irving avidly seized upon this suggestion for the skeletal structure of the new volume in order to give continuity to his sketches "of English house-keeping in something like the genuine old style."[86] Yet he found it difficult to keep such a long story alive without introducing separate narratives, somewhat in the manner of his most successful tales of *The Sketch Book.* Hence he resorted to the device of storytelling, "a good old-fashioned fireside amusement," as the Squire of the Hall termed it, in order to fill the two volumes expected by Murray.

Irving even attempted to recapture some of the grotesque humor and quaint background of the early Dutch settlements in New York by introducing a manuscript tale from the papers of the late Mr. Diedrich Knickerbocker, "Dolph Heyliger." Here Irving may have drawn again upon some German sources for part of his plot. A volume of English sketches hardly afforded many opportunities for utilizing legendary materials, ghosts and goblins, or ghoulish superstitions. Only one general reference occurs, a reference to "the wild huntsman, the favorite goblin in German tales,"[87] who had figured so prominently in "The Spectre Bridegroom." "Dolph Heyliger" boasts of a mysterious and learned Dr. Knipperhaus, who "had a secret belief in ghosts, having passed the early part of his life in a country where they particularly abound; and indeed the story went, that, when a boy he had once seen the devil upon the Harz Mountains in Germany,"[88] and actually owned a haunted farmhouse a few miles from town. There are references to "pistols loaded with silver bullets," reminiscent of the legend of *Der Freischütz,* and to "a spectre without a head."[89] The real kernel of the somewhat tedious and drawn-out story is the search for the buried treasure, which Dolph finally locates in the old well near the haunted house. To gain this prize Dolph had received on three successive nights a visitation from a ghostly Dutchman, had taken a journey up the Hudson under the influence of this apparition, was knocked overboard in a storm, and finally saw the phantom in a dream point out near the haunted house the well that held the treasure. This parallels rather closely the story of the man who shaved and is shaved by a ghost: The ghost directs him to someone who relates a dream in which he recognizes the location of a treasure in his father's garden. All this and a love story of the silent lover are related by Musäus in "Stumme Liebe," included in the collection of *Volksmärchen der Deutschen.*

The question of whether Irving might have read this hundred-page story in the original German, with all the elegance and stylistic locutions that Musäus delighted in, can be answered negatively. Even after his protracted residence in Germany Irving called upon his friends to read and translate this author for him.[90] "Stumme Liebe" was not included in *Popular Tales of the Germans* (1791) and was assumed unavailable in English translation ("The Spectre Barber") until 1823, when it appeared in the volume of *Popular Tales and Romances of the Northern Nations*—obviously too late for Irving's purpose. However, an examination of many tawdry and worthless collections of horror stories, ephemeral successes in England at this time, disclosed a volume of *Tales of the Dead*[91] which includes "The Spectre Barber" in a shortened and somewhat mutilated version. The essential elements of the plot are here, and it is easier to assume that Irving knew this source than to credit him with reading the original in German or even in French, where the title was the precise translation, "L'Amour Muet," hardly likely to attract a devotee of spectral research.

This collection of *Tales of the Dead* held much interest for Irving and his contemporaries. According to the "Advertisement" of the English edition, "the first four tales in this collection, and the last, are imitated from a small French work, which professes to be translated from the German."[92] Of these not only "The Spectre Barber" but "The Death Bride" and "The Family Portraits" bear some resemblance to stories of Washington Irving. The last of these will be discussed in connection with *Tales of a Traveller*. "The Death Bride" shows similarities to "The Spectre Bridegroom" in title and content, but it is the bride who assumes the form of a ghost. What lends real weight to the argument that Irving had read *Tales of the Dead* in England is the fact that the preface refers to Wagener's *Die Gespenster. Kurze Erzählungen aus dem Reiche der Wahrheit*, which "endeavors to explain apparitions by attributing them to natural causes."[93] This title was recorded by Irving in his Notebook of 1818 and must have attracted his attention particularly, as he favored natural explanations for his ghostly narratives. The notation was obviously for the future, one of the many isolated titles scattered throughout his journals and notebooks, recorded for use when his German studies had advanced.

The collection of *Tales of the Dead* must have been easily accessible, and Irving was not alone in his enthusiasm for such stories. Curiously enough, this identical volume in its French original[94] was read breathlessly by Byron, the Shelleys, and Polidori on June 18, 1816, at the Maison Chapuis on the shore of Lake Geneva,[95] and stimulated Mary Wollstonecraft Shelley to write her *Frankenstein*. She described this occasion and testified to the profound impression these stories made:

> But it proved a wet, uncongenial summer, and incessant rain often confined us for days to the house. Some volumes of ghost stories, translated from the German into French, fell into our hands. There was the story of the Inconstant Lover, who, when he thought to clasp the bride to whom he had pledged his vows, found himself in the arms of the pale ghost of her whom he had deserted. There was the tale of the sinful founder of his race, whose miserable doom it was to bestow the kiss of death on all the younger sons of his fated house, just when they reached the age of promise. His gigantic shadowy form, clothed, like the ghost of Hamlet, in complete armour, but with the beaver up, was seen at midnight, by the moon's fitful beams, to advance slowly along the gloomy avenue. The shape was lost beneath the shadow of the castle walls; but soon a gate swung back, a step was heard, the door of the chamber opened, and he advanced to the couch of the blooming youths, cradled in healthy sleep. Eternal sorrow sat upon his face as he bent down and kissed the forehead of the boys, who from that hour withered like flowers snapt upon the stalk. I have not seen these stories since then, but their incidents are as fresh in mind as if I had read them yesterday. "We will each write a ghost story," said Byron; and his proposition was acceded to.[96]

Today the volume seems dull and long-winded, but our taste has changed, and today *Bracebridge Hall* also seems lifeless. With one or two exceptions the characters are pale, shadowy figures that flit across the pages without coming to life. Irving's easy, good-natured humor becomes rather pedestrian and a little forced as it is spread over the many pages of a languishing narrative. There is no brilliance or sparkling wit, but much garrulity. Irving's contemporary critics were kinder. To be sure some reviewers recognized that Irving lived in the past rather than the present; one declared that "the great blemish of the work *Bracebridge Hall,* indeed is, that it is drawn not from life, but from musty volumes";[97] another that "no such beings exist now a days";[98] another that "the characters seem to dawdle and hang about without a purpose, while the title of the chapter is being fulfilled."[99] But "the quiet, gentle enthusiasm inspired by the modest English landscape in a genuine lover of nature"[100] and "the singular sweetness of the composition, and the mildness of the sentiments,"[101] to quote the influential Jeffrey, endeared the work to the English public. The British themselves were sentimental in their affection for their landscape, and of course Irving had the benefit of a friendly press. The beauty of his language and the cadence of his prose, the gentleness and urbanity of his own person achieved a tribute to the charm of English countryside and to the dignity of the traditions that remained forever Irving's delight. His own words are the best testimony:

> Having been born and brought up in a new country, yet educated from early infancy in the literature of an old one, my mind was early filled with historical and poetical associations, connected with places, and manners, and customs of Europe, but which could rarely be applied to those of my own country. To a mind thus peculiarly prepared, the most ordinary objects and scenes, on arriving in Europe, are full of strange matter and interesting novelty. England is as classic ground to an American, as Italy is to an Englishman; and old London teems with as much historical association as mighty Rome. . .
>
> I thought I never could be sated with the sweetness and freshness of a country so completely carpeted with verdure; where every air breathed of the balmy pasture, and the honeysuckle hedge. I was continually coming upon some little document of poetry in the blossomed hawthorn, the daisy, the cowslip, the primrose, or some other simple object that has received a supernatural value from the muse. The first time that I heard the song of the nightingale, I was intoxicated more by the delicious crowd of remembered associations than by the melody of its notes; and I shall never forget the thrill of ecstasy with which I first saw the lark rise, almost from beneath my feet, and wing its musical flight up into the morning sky.[102]

2

Arrival in Germany

The success of *The Sketch Book* was in part, at least, dependent upon those attractive stories in the Knickerbocker mood to which German materials had made a substantial contribution. Following *The Sketch Book, Bracebridge Hall* was adjudged somewhat repetitious; Irving's sentimental enthusiasm for the English landscape and its antiquarian aspects was losing its novelty. After all, he had written over eighty essays and sketches dealing with English life and English customs. He, as well as his readers, needed a respite. What was more logical, therefore, than to wish to proceed directly to the native haunts of his popular gnomes instead of digging through mountains of rubbish in British libraries for an occasional nugget? Irving had been lucky in his first contacts with German legends and was hopefully expecting to uncover a rich vein of high-grade ore in their native regions. Irving had nothing of the contemplative mood of Emerson, who eagerly turned his eyes inward in speculative meditation or critical self-examination, or of Thoreau's full satisfaction in solitary communion with nature. He was a restless and superficial observer, content to depict the picturesque trappings of the Old World in a haze of self-created romance. Travel meant new scenes, new stimuli, and, most important of all, new sketches, sketches to be distilled from the rambling jottings that always filled his journal or notebook, and to be based on "all those supernatural tales with which every mountain and valley in Germany abounds."[1]

Few European countries teemed with legend and superstition like Germany: the Rhine with its haunted castles, its Lorelei and Undine; the Harz with its innumerable phantoms and unearthly visitants; the Brocken as the rendezvous of witches; and all the Wild Huntsmen or ghostly White Ladies that could be found in almost every region. Hence Irving's journey to Germany was not merely a pleasure trip, as much of his travel had been on earlier occasions, when he characterized his tendency to roam as "the offspring of idleness of mind and a want of something to fix the feelings."[2] He was traveling for a double purpose: business and health. Perhaps the latter reason was the more immediate, as the discomforts and acute pain of his malady at times incapacitated him and had to be relieved before he could take pleasure again in travel. But his eager, perhaps naive, enthusiasm about finding literary material in Germany persisted. He expresses it in a letter to the Storrows: "I mean to get into the confidence of every old woman I meet with in Germany and get from her, her budget of wonderful stories."[3] This hopeful statement of anticipated procedure becomes more significant when it is realized that Irving's favorite, Musäus, was reputed to have used such a technique in compiling his *Volksmärchen*. In an English translation of Musäus, available since 1800, is the following description:

> He [Musäus] used to collect about him a number of old women with their spinning wheels, when seating himself in the midst of them, he listened patiently to their gossiping stories, which served him afterwards as foundations for those tales so much and so justly admired for their peculiar elegance and spirit. Often too would he call children out of the street, and becoming a child with them, learn some new legend or superstition which he repaid with a few half pence.[4]

Repeating on a more ambitious scale a technique that had proved fruitful and had yielded ample material for two successful books of travel sketches, Irving turned his back contentedly on England and looked hopefully toward the Continent.

Leaving London on July 6, 1822, for Rotterdam, Irving visited The Hague, Leiden, Haarlem, and Amsterdam before settling at Aix-la-Chapelle, where he arrived on July 18. He took up his residence at Meyer's Neues Bad where he identified himself in the guest list as a "merchant from New York."[5] Was it modesty that restrained Irving from claiming membership in the literary profession or was he still thinking of himself as a hapless member of the bankrupt firm of Peter and Ebenezer Irving? Actually Irving had never been a merchant, but perhaps his great loyalty to his family's mercantile reputation made him assume such a designation for want of a more proper title. He was seeking relief from a tormenting malady that made walking painful, and was content to travel unobtrusively and if necessary to conceal his identity.

Aix-la-Chapelle was a dull town and had historical significance only as the coronation city of the Holy Roman Empire of the German Nation until Frankfurt fell heir to that distinction. But memories of Charlemagne and his imperial residence still remained and attracted Irving's interest. He believed the stories that Charlemagne was born here and was impressed by the simplicity of Charlemagne's tomb in the cathedral.[6] As most spas do, Aix provided excitement and recreation for its visitors at the gambling tables. Irving watched the players at Rouge et Noir and wrote his observations to his sister. He noted with interest the peculiar costumes of the women, and the "military characters, in fierce moustaches and jingling spurs, with ribbons and various orders at their button-holes"; he was annoyed by the incessant smoking of the Germans, he found it "somewhat difficult to distinguish a gentleman from a common man among these northern people," and when he heard the watchman on the tower blow "as many blasts of his horn as there are strokes of the clock," he recorded that "the Germans are full of old customs and usages, which are obsolete in other parts of the world." But Irving was losing the enthusiasm with which he had anticipated his visit to Germany. His physical disorder demanded rigorous observance of a tedious routine and prevented a direct return to Paris. In the same letter to his sister, he revealed at length his unhappy frame of mind:

> I have now been here for upward of two weeks, and have had rather a lonely, uncomfortable time of it. For a greater part of the time I have been almost confined to my room, and have suffered extremely from the inflammation in my legs. I have been without any acquaintance and even without a disposition to make any; for my lameness and suffering almost unfit me for society. I am at times quite dispirited by this returning virulence of my complaint; it is so tedious of cure; it so completely alters all my habits of living and subjects me to such continual baths of a powerful kind, that I sometimes fear it may effect some injury to my constitution and prepare the way for other maladies . . . I am disappointed in Aix-la-Chapelle. To me it is a very dull place, and I do not find that others seem more pleased with it. The environs of the town are beautiful. There are public gardens that almost surround the walls, and very lovely country in every direction, but I have been unable to avail myself of the delightful walks, and have only once taken a drive in a carriage in the vicinity. . . .

> I think I shall make another push, and ascend the Rhine to Wisbaden, which is a more pleasant and fashionable watering-place; and where, from all I can learn, I think the waters will be more efficacious than here. At any rate, I shall then have seen the most beautiful part of the Rhine, and if I do not amend pretty readily in my health, I shall make for Paris at once, get in the neighborhood of a dry vapor bath, and then lay by until I make a perfect cure. It is extremely tantalizing to be here just on the frontiers of Germany, in the vicinity of some of the most beautiful and romantic scenery in Europe, and to be thus fettered and disabled.[7]

Irving's first impressions, therefore, were colored by alternate moods of high hope and deep dejection. He was miserable in solitude and longed for his London circle of friends with whom he might have whiled away the tedious hours in literary gossip. In short, he was not only ill in body, but depressed in spirit. Despite an occasional complaint about being "so harassed by society and by continual invitations,"[8] Irving enjoyed the diversions of the drawing room and needed companionship for perfect contentment. How completely his attitude changed with congenial company is revealed by his accidental meeting with an old friend, Thomas Brandram, a wealthy London merchant with whom he had traveled up the Hudson in 1803 and whom he had recently seen again in England.[9] His gloom vanished immediately as he eagerly accepted the invitation to ride in his friend's private carriage to Wiesbaden. They left August 5, stopping en route at Cologne that same night, and staying succeeding nights at Koblenz and Bingen.[10] Irving viewed with delight the picturesque castles and ruins of Ehrenbreitstein, Rheinfels, and Ehrenfels. The "Mouse Tower" near Bingen attracted his attention, and a little later he became concerned with the various brands and qualities of the local wines. He recorded carefully the names of red and white wines indigenous to this region, and affirmed that "the Johannisberg wine is the real 'nectar of the Rhine' as the Germans term it and is charged here within a few miles of the vineyard, seven florins a bottle (about 12 francs)."[11] Cheered by the companionship of his English friend and enjoying the unexpected luxury of traveling privately in style and comfort, Irving wrote his brother Peter enthusiastically about the same German scene that had previously failed to rouse his spirits:

> Away then we rolled; he had a charming light open carriage in which I could loll at full length; he was a capital traveller, took the management of every thing upon himself; had an excellent servant who was all attention to me, and in spite of my malady I made one of the pleasantest excursions possible. Though too lame to explore the

> curious old towns and the romantic ruins which we passed, yet I lolled in the carriage, and banquetted on fine scenery in Brevoort's favorite style. After all that I had heard and read, the Rhine far surpassed my expectations. Indeed, I am perfectly delighted with Germany.[12]

Irving stayed at Wiesbaden from August 8 to 21, lodged in room 49 at the magnificent Hôtel des Quatre Saisons,[13] and enjoyed excursions into the Taunus mountains in company with Mr. Brandram. But his pleasure was short-lived, as his friend left after three days, and Irving sank back into melancholy and loneliness. "I have been without a companion through the week; for at these watering places the people . . . are too taken up with their own parties and companions to trouble themselves with a stranger and an invalid, who cannot speak their language," he confessed to his sister,[14] and he appealed frantically to the Storrows for news of a friend. "I wish I could meet with Coolidge, for I am sadly in want of a companion . . . Has he given no directions where letters might find him?"[15] More than a week passed without a single entry in Irving's journals, though a letter to his sister reveals excursions into the forests and mountains of the Duchy of Nassau. He was restless and ill at ease in the limited freedom which his malady exacted and in no mood for literary composition.

Irving proceeded to Mainz (for which he always retained the French Mayence in his notebook) on August 21, in order to continue his treatments under what he hoped would be more favorable circumstances, yet he was somewhat regretful "at leaving the splendid hotel and pleasant environs of Wisbaden."[16] Irving was beginning to adjust himself to his new surroundings and started to study the habits of the people he observed, reporting upon their customs and traditions. Generally he reserved the more personal impressions and intimate details for his correspondence with his family and limited his journals to factual and historical details of his travels, upon which he might draw as source material. Hence his letters furnish the best indication of his thoughts and reactions, whereas his notebooks are a more accurate guide to his peregrinations. He wrote to his sister:

> I am very much pleased with the Germans; they are a frank, kind, well-meaning people, and I make no doubt were I in a place where I could become intimate, I should enjoy myself very much among them. The mode of living here is quite primitive in some respects, particularly as to hours. . . . The play goes in at six o'clock and comes out at nine. The balls begin at seven, or at most at eight o'clock, and are

> generally over between ten and eleven. Most commonly the good folks are all quiet and in bed by ten o'clock—after all, there is something very sensible and comfortable in this old-fashioned style of living, and it seems to be healthy too, for the Germans, in general, are a very hearty-looking people.[17]

Irving's delight in the informal intimacy of English inns was satisfied in Mainz by his residence at the "Hôtel de Darmstadt, ci-devant Hôtel de Paris" as he referred to it later in the introduction to his *Tales of a Traveller*. This hostelry of forty rooms abounded in "characters," not the least unusual of whom was its host, "a fat, jolly, waggish old Frenchman, a great Bonapartist in his heart."[18] He no doubt regaled Irving with harrowing tales of the ravaged city whose fate was comparable only to that of the unfortunate Miss Cunégonde in Voltaire's *Candide* who was ravished at every turn. Irving became quite one of the family and had daily lessons in French and German from one of his daughters.[19] It was *"La belle Catherine,* his youngest, about sixteen—very pretty and amiable—educated in a convent,"[20] who beguiled his weary hours as he convalesced from his tedious malady.[21]

Irving found the dry vapor baths too exhausting and decided to emphasize a more natural regimen, stressing moderate living, easy recreation, and more rest. This routine gave him more time for observing the quaint customs of the people and scrutinizing the numerous "originals" that suggested themselves for future essays. He watched the owner of the bath eagerly and wished to have "known the old gentleman a little earlier, he would have given me some excellent hints for my alchemist; as it is, I shall turn him to account some way or another, and mean to study him attentively."[22] Though physically still miserable, Irving was gratified by his surroundings and took numerous trips by land and by water to enjoy the beauties of the Rhine, which reminded him of the Hudson at its best.

> I cannot express to you how much I am delighted with these beautiful and romantic scenes. Fancy some of the finest parts of the Hudson embellished with old towns, castles and convents, and seen under the advantage of the loveliest weather, and you may have some idea of the magnificence and beauty of the Rhine.[23]

Frequently he met Englishmen, often former army officers, whom he welcomed as interesting fellow travelers. In such company Irving visited Frankfurt, where he was barely able to find lodgings at a shoemaker's because of the autumn fair. The motley crowds and picturesque sights amply repaid him for any inconvenience, however, and he described them in detail to his sister, cautioning her not to judge "from your fairs such an assemblage of merchants and traders from all parts of Germany, Holland, France, etc. who meet here to transact business . . ."[24] After three days he continued via Darmstadt (where he saw his first performance of Weber's *Der Freischütz*) and the Odenwald to Heidelberg. Eagerly Irving inspected the beautiful scenery of the Odenwald, remembering that here he had laid the scene of "The Spectre Bridegroom." A new note of optimism was sounded in a letter describing the progress of his journey:

> We came by what is called the Berg Strasse, or mountain road, a route famous for its beauty of scenery. Our road lay along the foot of the mountains of the Odenwald, which rose to our left, with vineyards about their skirts, and their summits covered with forests, from which every now and then peeped out the crumbling towers of some old castle, famous in German song and story; to our right spread out a rich plain as far as the eye could reach; with a faint line of blue hills marking the course of the distant Rhine. It is all in vain to attempt to describe the beauty of these scenes—the continual variety of romantic scenery that delights the eye and excites the imagination, and the happy abundance that fills the heart. . . .
>
> With all my ailments and lameness, I never have enjoyed travelling more than through these lovely countries. I do not know whether it is the peculiar fineness of the season, or the general character of the climate, but I never was more sensible to the delicious effect of atmosphere: perhaps my very malady has made me more susceptible to influences of the kind. I feel a kind of intoxication of the heart, as I draw in the pure air of the mountains; and the clear, transparent atmosphere, the steady, serene, golden sunshine, seems to enter into my very soul.[25]

Here lies the reason for Irving's decision to continue his tour into Germany instead of heeding Thomas Moore's flattering plea from Paris to rejoin his friends there.[26] As his health improved and he found congenial travel companions, Irving's wanderlust asserted itself again. In Heidelberg he called upon Count Jenison of Walworth, an expatriate Englishman to whom Irving had brought letters from friends in England. Irving stayed about two weeks,[27] though his entries conflict with the content of his letters, feeling greatly benefited by the baths and recovering rapidly from his lameness. During that time Irving enjoyed the friendship of the Jenisons, who entertained him and showed him a countryside that "abounds with old castles, famous in legend and goblin tale."[28] Once again Irving found himself welcomed hospitably into an English home of distinction, delighted to hear English spoken and enjoying the attentions bestowed upon him. He also made the acquaintance of a young Silesian prince and a young Saxon nobleman, Count S[c]hoenberg, both living in the same hotel with him, whose society gave him pleasure. Irving's plan to take up residence in Dresden, and his excursion from there into the Riesengebirge of Silesia, may well have been suggested by them. Three possible routes from Vienna to Dresden, including one "by the way of Breslau or a shorter way & thru the mountains from Neisse," were jotted down by Irving, undoubtedly upon their suggestion.[29]

In true tourist style Irving recorded historical bits of information: in Frankfurt the Römerplatz and city hall, where the Holy Roman Emperors had been crowned, interested him; in Erbach the armor of Götz von Berlichingen, Gustavus Adolphus, and Wallenstein were examined;[30] and a little later while at Baden-Baden he was fascinated by stories of the *Vehmgericht.* In Walter Scott's library Irving had seen historical treatises of the *Vehme;* now he welcomed the experience of examining underground passages and vaults that yielded such awe-inspiring details about mysterious, subterranean secret tribunals, the indispensable elements of a literary genre that had taken England by storm. At last he could see with his own eyes what he had previously only read about, or had boldly recreated in his imagination, and he recorded for his sister:

> Among the pine-covered mountains that overlook the town are the ruins of a grim old castle, and another protecting castle crests the hill on which the upper part of the town is built. . . . Underneath the castle we were shown subterraneous apartments that equalled the fabrications of novelists. They were chambers where the secret tribunal held its sittings, and where its victims were confined, and if convicted, tortured and executed. This was a mysterious association that, some centuries since, held all Germany in awe. It was a kind of Inquisition that took cognizance of all kinds of offences. Its sittings were held in secret; all its movements were wrapped in mystery. Its members consisted of all ranks, from the highest to the lowest; all sworn to secrecy; all forbidden to make known their being members; and all sworn by the most imposing oaths to inflict the punishment decreed by the tribunal, without regard to any tie of kindred or affection. A man, therefore, once condemned by the tribunal had no chance of escape. He knew not where to fly, or in whom to confide; his bosom friend, his very brother might be a member of the terrible tribunal, and, of course, obliged to be his executioner. The subterraneous apartments of the old castle of Baden was one of the places where the secret tribunal was held. The place was worthy of the institution. You can imagine nothing more dismal than the cells and

> dungeons of which it was composed. There was one vaulted room, black with the smoke of tapers, in which the judges of the tribunal had held their sittings. Narrow winding passages through walls of prodigious thickness led to the dungeons of the prisoners and the places of torture. All these were completely shut up from the light of day, and the doors were formed of immense blocks of stone that turned heavily on their pivots, groaning as they moved. There was one great pitfall, down which, we were told, prisoners were precipitated after execution; but enough of this gloomy picture.[31]

Regardless of whether the *Vehmgericht* had actually used these subterranean chambers as meeting places of the secret tribunal, Irving was naturally impressed by the romantic milieu.[32] The precise extent to which he had become acquainted with German tales of horror and sensationalism while in England can hardly be established, but we know that Irving was influenced by Walter Scott's enthusiasm for medieval lore. Perhaps Irving had already been allowed to read Scott's *The House of Aspen* in manuscript as well as his published translation of Goethe's *Götz von Berlichingen,* both of which include scenes portraying such secret tribunals. Moreover, Irving acquired the full set of eight volumes of Veit Weber's *Sagen der Vorzeit*—which contains *Die heilige Vehme,* the very source book of the genre—and eventually brought them back to America to his Sunnyside library. He also owned a German copy of *Götz von Berlichingen* and later witnessed a Dresden performance of Kleist's *Kätchen von Heilbronn,* whose opening scene portrays a session of this secret tribunal.

Leaving Heidelberg "on the 30th of September in company with Capt. Wemyss, the same young officer of dragoons that has travelled with me from Mayence to Frankfort, etc.,"[33] Irving stopped first at Karlsruhe and then proceeded through the fertile plains of Wurttemberg in order to cross the Rhine at Kehl for a day's excursion to Strassburg. Again the temptation to cut short his German tour presented itself when Irving found himself on French soil. "I assure you," he wrote in a letter to his sister, "I felt a kindly throb in finding myself in the territories of the gay nation; and I had several strong tugs of feeling that pulled me towards Paris. However, I resisted them all, and having looked at the noble cathedral of Strasbourg, and from its tower looked out over a magnificent reach of country, watered by the Rhine, I turned my back upon Strasbourg and France, and ordering post-horses at Kehl, bade a long and reluctant adieu to my summer friend and companion, the Rhine . . . I had bidden adieu to the gay borders of Germany that divide it from France, and was now about to penetrate into its interior."[34]

Had the melancholy mood induced by his ailment continued, or had he failed to find congenial companions like Brandram and Wemyss, Irving would surely have returned to Paris at this time. Instead, encouraged by the beauty of the German landscape and urged, perhaps, by his newly made friends, Irving determined to see more than the mere borders of romantic Germany. He stopped overnight in a small inn at Hausach in the Black Forest, in the valley of the Kinzig, entranced as "mine host sits by us at supper and entertains us."[35] He met in reality what he had until now always conjured up:

> [An inn such] as is sometimes shown on the stage, where benighted travellers arrive and meet with fearful adventures. We were shewn into a great public room wainscotted with wood, blackened by smoke, in which were waggoners and rustic travellers supping and smoking; a huge, rambling staircase led up to a number of old-fashioned wainscotted apartments. The hostess is dressed in one of the antique costumes of the country, and we are waited upon by a servant man in a dress that would figure to advantage in a melodrama; and a servant maid that is a Patagonian in size, and looks as to costume, as if she had come out of the ark. . . . The ruins of an old castle are perched upon a hill that rises just above the village, and may be seen from my window while I am writing. I can hear the owl hoot from the ruins of the castle, and the reply of some of his companions from the neighboring wood. Good night.[36]

Traveling through the Black Forest, at times glimpsing Lake Constance and then again the Danube, Irving continued to Ulm, where he saw among the painted windows in the cathedral the crest and motto of the noble family of Katzenellenbogen, and to Augsburg in Bavaria. His immediate goal was Munich, his real destination Vienna. On the way he saw the battlefields of Blenheim and reviewed the historical events that gave glory to Marlborough and Prince Eugene. Irving had now reached historical scenes of great interest to him though he was not aware that Hohenlinden, about which he had written somewhat glibly in his biographical sketch of Thomas Campbell,[37] was only a short distance away.

On October 8[38] Irving arrived at Munich a little after six in the evening and lost no time in attending the theatre, a pleasure which neither fatigue nor his limited understanding of German could curb. He had been an inveterate theatregoer in New York, London, and Paris, and the German stage was to prove equally attractive. He remained a week and indulged himself in the customary sight-seeing of the tourist. His notebooks reveal his tours of inspection; the palaces, the parks, the galleries, and even the prison are discussed in detail. With grim determination to miss nothing, Irving examined the rich collection of paintings and art treasures until he recorded wistfully and somewhat wearily the perennial lament of all tourists: "The misery of being walked thro' galleries of paintings. How sad that so many fine paintings should be doomed to be only glanced at by the world!"[39]

For the first time Irving was in an important German city that could boast of cultural advantages such as endeared Dresden to him a little later. Munich was still a small city, but under the benevolent regime of the art-loving Maximilian I, it was on its way to becoming the art center of South Germany. Irving admired the rich treasures of the library, the rare manuscripts and jeweled missals. The director was unusually attentive to his foreign visitor and showed him such rare items as a manuscript of the *Nibelungenlied,* probably the famous *Hohenems-Münchner Handschrift* acquired by the library in 1810. They talked of Dibdin, the noted English bibliographer and perhaps of Walter Scott, whose fame already had reached the continent. Irving recorded seeing *"Romance of Sir Tristan* by Sir Thomas of Erceldoune," but left uncertain whether he was referring to another rare medieval manuscript of Gottfried von Strassburg's epic or to a copy of Scott's bibliophile edition of *The Metrical Romance of Sir Tristrem* by Thomas the Rhymer (1804), considered at this time the possible source of the Tristan legend. All this reminded Irving of when, during his visit to Abbotsford, Scott had showed him the haunted glen of Thomas the Rhymer.[40]

Irving was delighted and astonished by the excellence of the performances witnessed at the theatre and the opera. Enthusiastically he wrote:

> This is a most charming capital. With a population of only about fifty thousand people, it combines more advantages than are to be met with in cities of three times its size. One of the finest libraries in Europe, a magnificent theatre, an Italian opera, a smaller theatre, splendid galleries of paintings, and princely palaces. There has been a grand fête on the king's birthday, which gave me a fine opportunity of seeing both the court and the populace. The king is a most amiable, worthy man, and extremely beloved by his people. . . .
>
> This place is quite remarkable for its musical resources. Mozart composed several of his best operas at Munich, and ever since the place has had a musical turn. The orchestra of the theatre is admirable. There is a female singer here [Madame Vespermann] that to my taste is preferable even to Catalani. We have music, morning, noon, and night, for there are three of the best military bands that I have

> ever heard, and one or other of them seems to be continually parading the streets.[41]

On October 17, in company with Captain Wemyss, Irving left Munich on his way to Vienna, but interrupted the journey the following day to remain in Salzburg. Though the visit there lasted only three days it yielded more information about folklore, as revealed in the extensive entries of the *Journals,* than had any other locality. Like most tourists Irving thought Salzburg one of the most romantic of places, but what delighted him more than the beautiful churches, the archbishop's palaces, or even the salt mines at Hallein with their elaborate underground passages and galleries that were illuminated on special occasions in fairylike splendor, were the picturesque Austrian peasant folk and their quaint costumes.

> People have the old-fashioned mode of kissing your hand when you confer a favor, i.e. the lower order—I have had my hand kissed for giving an old coat. High-crowned hats of peasants with gold band or bl[ac]k bands with gold tassels—little feathers in men's hats, trophies of birds they have killed—pretty flowers in hats of men and women—men with bl[ac]k leather breeches and embroidered girdles, some women with gold embroidered caps that cost twenty, thirty, sixty florins.[42]

Nor was it merely the quaint costumes or ingratiating manners of the peasants that thrilled this itinerant author. He had now left the beaten path of tourist travel and was getting acquainted with the native population and folklore. "These mountain regions are full of fable and elfin story; and I had some wonderful tales told me which I shall keep in mind. . . ,"[43] he wrote to his sister, and then proceeded to whet the appetites of the Storrow children in Paris:

> What stories I shall have to tell you when I get once more to Rue Thevenet!—By the way, put me in mind, when I see you, of the Emperor and his army shut up in the enchanted mountain—which mountain I have absolutely seen with my own eyes—Put me in mind of the little dwarf woman, with twenty rings on her fingers, who came nobody knows whence, and who went nobody knew whither—Put me in mind of the Black Huntsman and the enchanted Bullets. Put me in mind—but no matter . . . we'll have fine times I'll warrant you.[44]

For the first time Irving could record legends in his notebooks to be used later for the vaguely contemplated collection of tales! He was particularly interested in the anecdotes and stories associated with the famous

Untersberg, the legendary home of the sleeping monarch who would appear in time of national crisis to lead his people to victory. Irving had first found this superstition while reading Riesbeck in England; it is another version of the *Kaisersage* in which Charlemagne, Frederick Barbarossa, Frederick II, or even Charles V sometimes figure. He had already referred to it as the Kyffhäuser legend in his explanatory note at the end of "Rip Van Winkle." Five distinct stories of supernatural creatures appearing near the Untersberg are recorded without any reference to their source.[45] The titles which Irving jotted down a few pages further[46] include the *Brixener Volksbuch* of 1782, also entitled *Sagen der Vorzeit, oder ausführliche Beschreibung von dem berühmten Salzburgischen Untersberg oder Wunderberg* . . . , but these particular five stories are not printed in it. Nor are they included in similar collections, so that it seems likely that Irving actually heard them from some of the inhabitants, probably from the servants of the inn.[47] In fact it was the *valet de place* upon whom Irving leaned heavily for information. He quoted him frequently and it was from him that he received the inimitable characterization of those leisurely and unhurried people, the people for whom *gleich* [right away] means one hour, and *gleich, gleich,* two hours.[48]

Washington Irving arrived in Vienna on October 23, 1822, after traveling for more than three months through the picturesque and romantic regions of western and southern Germany. His lameness had finally yielded to treatment, so that he began to consider making winter quarters either in Vienna or Dresden. It would be wearisome to repeat the many effusions of delight with which Irving described his travels, but he summarized them best as he explained his plans in an unpublished letter to Thomas Moore:

> I was so much delighted with what I had seen of Germany, that on recovering sufficiently to venture again on long journeys, I set out in quest of adventures; like a true knight errant hardly knowing whither I should direct my course. In this way I travelled and travelled from Mayence to Frankfurt, from Frankfurt to Heidelberg; from Heidelberg above the Neckar of the Odenwald, then to Carlsruhe & Baden, then to Strassburg and then through the Black Forest to Ulm intending to visit the field of Battle of Blenheim; & afterward to push for Dresden, but from Blenheim I turned off in another direction, came to Munich, and having passed ten or twelve days here, seeing fêtes, operas and picture galleries, I am on the point of starting for Salzburg and then to the banks of the Danube and so to Vienna, where I shall repose some time after my ramblings. I do not know when I have enjoyed travelling more; the weather has been uncommonly fine; the countries through which I have passed abound with noble

> scenery and are full of story; and this desultory mode of wandering just suits my humour. The only drawback on all this pleasure is that I am burning the candle at both ends all this time. I am spending money, and my pen is idle—if I could only turn Pegasus into a post-horse, ye gods! How I should travel.[49]

His sojourn in Salzburg had been eminently satisfactory and his travels were becoming something of a business venture, a sort of investment to yield substantial dividends when he could find the necessary leisure and—what for Irving was even more important—when he could find the proper stimulus to work such bits of gold into the jeweled ornaments of a "German Sketch Book." No doubt Irving longed by this time for more social contacts, for literary salons and literary gossip which had made London and Paris dear to him. The prospect of similar happiness was not too distant, but its realization was not to be found in Vienna. For months Irving had sought American friends whom he might join in travel, but even his Vienna visit saw nothing of their scheduled arrival. "I have been disappointed in not meeting with Coolidge & Ritchie and now give them up," he wrote to Thomas Storrow just before leaving for Dresden.[50] Irving remained alone in Vienna, except for casual acquaintances on one excursion or another, yearning for the intimacy and sociability of the happy domestic circles of the Van Warts and the Storrows. He wrote Mrs. Van Wart:

> They [the letters] brought me at once into your dear little family circle, and made me forget for awhile that I was so far adrift from any home. These little tidings of the fireside, to a man that is wandering, are like the breezes that now and then bring to the sea-beaten sailor the fragrance of the land.[51]

For four weeks Irving remained in Vienna and visited the various palaces and art galleries, faithfully recording long lists of paintings. Nowhere else did he make such dull and uninteresting entries, enumerating the various schools of painting and numbering the pictures as if writing a catalogue. The sheer bulk of the art treasures exhausted his patience, until he finally was forced to use inclusive terms like "a room full of Vandykes" or "another room of Rubens."[52] Historical objects, armor and clothing of military heroes of earlier times exhibited in museums and palaces, were recorded in a matter-of-fact manner, but they no longer aroused his enthusiasm or curiosity. Even the imperial library with its priceless treasures could recall nothing more than a memory of Lord Byron's handwriting.

Only the landscape, the formal gardens, and the natural beauty of the Vienna Woods made his stay in the city tolerable.

Irving stopped off at the Hotel Stadt London on the Fleischmarkt, a hostelry in the heart of the city, not far from St. Stephan's Cathedral, which had been recommended along the way and was included in a hotel list jotted down in his notebook at the head of his Munich entries.[53] Always intrigued by picturesque personalities among his contemporaries, Irving eagerly recorded seeing "young Napoleon or the Duke of Reichstadt, as he is called," at the theatre and described his physiognomy as well as his behavior.[54] Such bits of historical information, which Irving liked to communicate to his correspondents, reveal not only a touch of didacticism but also a keen desire to revitalize contemporary history and to become, if possible, an actual participant in it. For Irving was the epitome of the traveling American in Europe, profoundly impressed by hallowed foreign customs and traditions, zealous to acquire that easy familiarity with historical scenes and personages that was the stock-in-trade of cultivated Europeans. Unfortunately for Irving, he was an outsider in Vienna and was forced to content himself with superficial observations of Viennese life and to restrict himself to endless rounds of sight-seeing.

The abundance of legends and myths that he was accumulating was arousing a new desire to write. His original plan for a "continental Sketch Book" was still in his mind. While walking in the Lichtenstein Palace Gardens he formulated a new plan: "In course of the walk tho[ough]t of preparing a collection of tales of various countries, made up from legends, etc., etc., etc."[55] Thus Irving soothed his conscience whenever the thought of his continued idleness troubled him. He even included a suitable setting for one of such tales and suggested the following introductory flourish: "As I was making my solitary supper on a woodcock and a glass of Hungary wine. . ."[56] The keynote was sounded, but Irving stopped. He probably hoped to utilize this phrase in the not too distant future, when his pen might move more readily. Instead, his restive spirit sought refuge in new scenes along the Danube. Irving made an excursion into the picturesque and romantic Wachau, a half day's journey upstream, where on both sides of the river, steep hills and vineyards remind the traveler of the Rhine country. Here too the rocky heights are crowned with melancholy ruins of castles that are intimately linked with history and legend.

This two-day tour with "an agreeable young Irish gentleman of the name of Brooke" for traveling companion took them to the famous Benedictine monastery at Göttweig, a fine example of Baroque architecture, where "the superior, a round, sleek, jolly looking friar," welcomed them politely. Irving saw "the library, which is very valuable, with many rare manuscripts, . . . the cabinet of natural history, . . . and the cellars as well stored with old wine as the library with old books."[57] They ascended the Danube a little farther and crossed the river to explore

> the old castle of Dürnstein where Richard Coeur de leon was confined. I presume you know the romantic story of his captivity; . . . [The castle] is built round the very peak of a high craggy rock, among stern dark mountains, and gloomy forests; with the Danube sweeping along below it. In one part of the ruins is the sweetest dark dungeon you can imagine; cut out of the solid rock; in which I'll warrant Richard was often put on bread & water, when he happened to be a little restive. I never saw a finer castle for a heroine to be confined in, or a ghost to haunt; though after the most diligent enquiry I could not find that the old ruins were haunted by a single goblin; which rather surprized me. The castles in Germany are generally very well off in that particular, and I have met with some that have had half a dozen ghosts to garrison them.[58]

This excursion was the high point in Irving's Vienna sojourn of almost a month, but it could not make up for the general disappointment that his routine sight-seeing engendered. His only acquaintances were Brooke and his neighbors at the hotel, "an Irish Col[onel]: rather advanced in life—who keeps a mistress partly thro' ostentation" and "a Dutch dandy who plays the piano and rides in the Prater."[59] In a sense they characterized for him the social life of Vienna. Obviously Irving was puzzled and gave full expression to his disappointment in a letter to his sister:

> This is one of the most perplexing cities that I was ever in. It is extensive, irregular, crowded, dusty, dissipated, magnificent, and to me disagreeable. It has immense palaces, superb galleries of paintings, several theatres, public walks, and drives crowded with equipages, in short, every thing bears the stamp of luxury and ostentation; for here is assembled and concentrated all the wealth, fashion, and nobility of the Austrian empire, and every one strives to eclipse his neighbor. The gentlemen all dress in the English fashion, and in walking the fashionable lounges you would imagine yourself surrounded by Bond street dandies. The ladies dress in the Parisian mode, the equipages are in the English style though more gaudy; with all this, however, there is a mixture of foreign costumes, that gives a very motley look to the population in the streets. You meet here with Greeks, Turks, Polonaise, Jews, Sclavonians, Croats, Hungarians, Tyroleans, all in the dress of their several countries; and you hear all kinds of languages spoken around you. . . . here the people think only of sensual gratifications.

> There is scarcely any such thing as literary society or I may say literary taste in Vienna.[60]

Was this an accurate picture of Vienna, the most cosmopolitan city in Europe, which less than ten years before had welcomed the august representatives of many nations to a political assembly that dictated the policies of Europe, and had dazzled all visitors by its brilliance and gaiety? At the time of Irving's arrival Vienna was a city of a quarter million inhabitants, one of the largest urban centers of Europe, enjoying something of a boom in the wake of political upheaval and the subsequent restoration to normalcy. After more than twenty years of revolution, political unrest, and actual warfare, which shattered the Holy Roman Empire of the German Nation and demoted the proud Hapsburgs to the humbler rank of "Emperors of Austria," peace with all its blessings smiled upon the land. The people of Vienna had twice seen the enemy within its gates, and the financial structure of the nation had collapsed in 1811. No one had been untouched by these catastrophes. The pleasure-loving Viennese had borne their burdens not without grumbling, to be sure, but with a full realization of the significance of events, and had steadfastly fixed their eyes upon the time when happiness and gaiety would again rule the day. The splendor of the Congress of Vienna had made amends for the tremendous sacrifices of the preceding decades. Peace had made the pursuit of happiness again the *raison d'être* of Vienna.

To a stranger the first look at this city, considered the metropolis of a great state, might well have been disappointing. Surrounded by about twenty-five suburbs in which the majority of the population lived, the heart of the town, the real "city," was still enclosed by substantial walls that had repeatedly protected Vienna and had actually been the last bulwark of Christendom against the victorious onslaught of the Turks. This medieval characteristic of the city was gradually adapted to a modern era by the removal of the fortified towers and the conversion of the military outworks and defenses into promenades that eventually became the famous Ring. An Englishman, visiting Vienna ten years after Irving, was still appalled to see the crowded conditions of this small inner space around which one could walk in fifty minutes, but which "contained almost every object of interest or importance: the imperial palace, the offices of government, the residences of all the higher classes, nobles, bankers, lawyers, etc.; all the superior shops; most of the public museums, libraries, and galleries; and with one exception all the good hotels."[61]

The absolutism of the age was fully reflected in the exclusive categories of the social hierarchy. At the top was the Court, which included the immediate families of the Royal House and a few hundred members of the highest nobility whose hereditary rights and privileges entitled them to the most important military and civil offices. Their wealth and influence made them all-powerful, and through a series of intermarriages over many generations they had become one large family. They patronized the arts, they attended the theatre and the opera, they participated in the chase, they visited various estates or watering places in season and remained in Vienna only through the winter months. They were a happy, carefree family living in a closed world, surrounded by their servants, blissfully ignorant of everyday problems. A second group, the petty nobility, included the army officers and public officials as well as financiers and manufacturers; these welcomed artists to their circles and became the hosts of the intelligentsia. The bourgeoisie and working classes led their quiet existence without much influence upon the times. Irving, who was never a friend of the outward manifestations of orthodox religious practices, may even have been repelled by the Jesuitical domination and clericalism which had been restored after the brief interlude of liberalism under Joseph II. Catholicism, which was already the state religion, had also become a popular cult through the zeal of the Romanticists.

Mme de Staël had noted the complete separation of high society and the realm of letters, unheard of elsewhere than Vienna.[62] She herself had had access to both when she arrived in Vienna with August Wilhelm Schlegel early in 1808. That was the occasion of Schlegel's delivery of his famous Lectures on Dramatic Art and Literature, from which Irving was to copy laboriously in 1825.[63] In London Irving, basking in the glory of his sudden fame, had divided his time among the literary groups in Murray's drawing room and the society that gathered around Lord and Lady Holland, the Earl Gray, and the Marquis of Landsdowne. Literature and society were intimately linked in London, and Irving had found the union pleasing;[64] but Vienna was different, and Irving had arrived unknown and without friends, without even a letter of introduction. Moreover, Vienna was too far south and east to attract many Englishmen or any Americans. It was the center of a variegated empire and its numerous crown lands contributed their representatives. Thoroughly German in spirit, it nevertheless bore the marks of its trade relations with the Balkans and the Near East. On the street Irving heard "all kinds of languages spoken," but none with which he was particularly familiar. Even the German that he heard, difficult to understand anywhere with his limited knowledge, must have seemed like a new language when heard in the vernacular of the streets of Vienna.

Irving's sojourn in Vienna was definitely a period of missed opportunities. He who loved the stage found himself in a city with five theatres catering to the varied tastes of the populace, where the Opera and the Burgtheater ranked with the best in Europe, and yet attended only a performance of Beethoven's *Fidelio,* which he disliked for its noise and melodramatic style, and a third-rate opera, *Raoul der Blaubart!* The Royal Theatre under the direction of Schreyvogel had been lifted so far above the level of other German stages that Tieck, upon coming to Vienna in 1825, praised the teamwork of the artists and the general quality of the performances as of an excellence to be found nowhere else.[65] Goethe had been forced to depend upon south German and Austrian actors when he had taken over the Weimar Theatre in 1791, and after that the vogue for Viennese plays had only increased.[66] The works of Collin, Castelli, Weissenthurn, Müllner, and Werner plus innumerable *Volksstücke* dominated the popular stages, and the great dramas of Franz Grillparzer were establishing a new reputation to be measured only in terms of Goethe's and Schiller's.

The enthusiasm for the theatre was greater than ever in this period,[67] and aristocrats and shopkeepers alike substituted the dramatic stage for the political arena as the subject of their conversations. And no one regretted the change. To be sure the worthless pieces were legion and a stranger might be bewildered, especially without an adequate knowledge of German. Perhaps that helps to explain Irving's nonattendance at operatic performances in Vienna.

In the light of Irving's later interest in Spanish literature, it seems unfortunate that he was unaware of being in a center for Spanish studies. When August Wilhelm Schlegel had delivered his Vienna Lectures on Dramatic Art and Literature in 1808 he had kindled a general enthusiasm for Spanish literature. The intimate relationship of the Austrian and Spanish dynasties and the rich treasures of the Royal Library naturally encouraged such interests. Schreyvogel, the secretary of the Burgtheater, translated from the Spanish and achieved his greatest success with an adaptation of Calderón's *La Vida es sueño,* first performed March 15, 1822.[68] Moreover, he had traveled the length and breadth of literary Germany in his youth, had lived in German cultural centers like Weimar and Jena, and had known Goethe, Schiller, and Wieland intimately. He had watched the flowering of the Weimar stage under Goethe's enthusiastic direction and had returned to Vienna determined to raise its theatre to a new level. Schreyvogel had edited a critical journal, written dramatic sketches ranging from spectacular *Ritterdramen* to sentimental *Rührstücke* and at the same time had the practical knowledge and business training absolutely essential for directing a theatre.[69] What it would have meant to Irving to have made his acquaintance!

Another phase of Viennese life that would have appealed to Irving he missed entirely because of his isolation: the Viennese society to be found in the salons of the upper middle class and the petty nobility. Irving, of course, loved literary society, but could not find it in Vienna. The most famous salon there was that of Caroline Pichler,[70] whose popularity as a writer had revived an institution first established by her mother, Charlotte Greiner, in the late 1770's. This court of the muses met in a suburb, the Alservorstadt, where gradually all visitors of importance called to pay their respects. Some dubbed her Vienna's Mme Récamier, others, like Mme de Staël, who had visited her as early as 1808, made a finer distinction in characterizing her as *la muse de Faubourg,* and between 1815 and 1824 her assemblies included artists, scholars, poets, musicians, and diplomats, all of whom participated eagerly in the old-fashioned pleasures of her drawing room. There were musicales, recitations, readings, and social intercourse, but by ten o'clock her guests were expected to return home. Here was the embodiment of *Biedermeier* life and literature, reminiscent of the diluted romanticism that Irving was to love in Dresden. Here was a home that had welcomed Mme de Staël, Ludwig Tieck, the Schlegels, Carl Maria von Weber, Adam Oehlenschläger, and Bertel Thorvaldsen on their visits to Vienna and was receiving Schreyvogel, Grillparzer, and Hammer-Purgstall at this time.

The nobility gathered at the home of Bernhard von Eskeles, the wealthy banker who had helped to establish the Austrian National Bank and who was the financial adviser of Emperor Francis I. His brilliant and witty wife and Fanny Arnstein, the wife of the other member of the firm of Arnstein and Eskeles, became the leading hostesses of the diplomatic and aristocratic circles at the time of the Congress of Vienna; Henriette von Arnstein, a friend of Mme de Staël who was married to the banker Pereia, continued her mother's famous salon. Thus, despite the political tyranny of the Restoration and the era of Metternich, the social life of the capital flourished and its legendary gaiety and sociability were in no sense impaired. Perhaps the realm of music offered even greater attractions. Haydn and Mozart were dead, but their music lived, and Schubert and Beethoven were frequently guests of the social circles described above. The homes of the Sonnleithner and the Fröhlich families, both intimately linked with Grillparzer, were musical centers, and these families counted Beethoven and Schubert among their intimate friends.

How proudly Irving would have written to his family of such contacts! Yet he remained unaware of the opportunities and failed to meet Caroline Pichler, whose enthusiasm for Walter Scott's work not only led her through his numerous publications but also strongly influenced her own historical novels. In 1819 she had translated and published a ballad from *The Lady of the Lake* and the following year she published her translation of Byron's *The Corsair*.[71] Only a few months before Irving's visit to Vienna, Carl Maria von Weber, the composer of Irving's favorite German opera, *Der Freischütz,* had arrived from Dresden with greetings from Tieck and Böttiger, who had both visited Caroline Pichler years before. It is revealing to compare Irving's experiences in Vienna with those of Böttiger, Irving's Dresden friend, who, on his arrival had promptly sought out Caroline Pichler and found himself at once in the literary circles of that city.[72]

It became, therefore, increasingly evident to Irving that Vienna was not the anticipated city where he might devote himself to the study of the German language and attempt the composition of another volume of tales amidst congenial surroundings. He determined to push on toward Dresden, whose beauty and charm beckoned more irresistibly than ever. In notifying his sister of his plans, he lauded the rumored advantages of Dresden over Vienna in no uncertain terms:

> I am beginning to think of leaving Vienna. I shall probably stay a week longer and then take my departure for Dresden, which will be my winter quarters. It is a more quiet and intellectual city than this: for here the people think only of sensual gratifications. There is scarcely any such thing as literary society, or I may say literary taste in Vienna. Dresden on the contrary, is a place of taste, intellect, and literary feeling, and it is the best place to acquire the German language, which is nowhere as purely spoken as in Saxony. Dresden is about three hundred miles from here by the shortest road, which lies through Moravia and Bohemia. I think it very probable that I shall make the journey alone, as there are few persons travelling for pleasure so late in the season; and I prefer travelling alone unless I can find a companion exactly to my mind.[73]

His enthusiastic estimate of Dresden must have been based, at least partly, upon specific information communicated to him. It may be remembered that at Heidelberg Irving had met a young Saxon nobleman, who no doubt spoke well of the attractions of Dresden. Its fame as an art center was renowned and Irving's general praise was well deserved. Only on one point, on his estimation of the relative merit of the German language in Saxony, is there room for doubt. Though it is true that excellent German was spoken in aristocratic circles, the tendency to interchange voiced and voiceless consonants in initial positions was already common practice. The notations of Irving and of Emily Foster, attempting to record phonetically what they heard, show some of the peculiarities.[74] This ridiculous aspect of

Saxon speech eventually made the Dresden vernacular the object of vaudeville humor. The Saxon vernacular, though stigmatized "a wretched speech," was heard even in prominent society, so that correct pronunciation came to be considered a mark of affectation.[75]

As far as Dresden's other qualities are concerned, Walter Scott, who had been greatly benefited in his German studies by the assistance of James Skene, who had spent several years in Saxony and obtained a thorough knowledge of the language there,[76] may well have recommended Dresden to his friend. Irving also received magazines and newspapers from America (he was still reading the *Analectic Magazine* early in 1819)[77] and may have seen two enthusiastic appraisals of Dresden—the home of the muses—that had appeared the preceding year:

> Would one become an amateur himself, I would counsel him, next to going to Italy, to make a pilgrimage to Dresden—where Winckelmann imbibed first nourishment of his enthusiasm—and attend the lectures of Mr. Böttiger, in the Hall of Antiques, in that beautiful city. I have yet met with nothing abroad, that gave me a deeper impression of the rich resources of European instruction, than the lectures I heard from this most learned and amiable man, in the hall of the Japan palace, surrounded by the monuments themselves of ancient art.[78]

Unexpectedly, Irving found another congenial traveling companion in the person of Willoughby Montagu, a First Lieutenant in the English Royal Artillery, with whom he left Vienna November 18. After touching Klosterneuburg, Znaim, Budwitz, Stannern, Iglau, Stecken, Deutsch-Brod, Czaslau, Kollin, and Böhmisch-Brod, they arrived in Prague four days later. The trip was somewhat tedious and uncomfortable. The "Austrian country towns [were] very uninteresting—whitewashed into uniformity" and Irving was "kept awake almost the whole night by the barking of dogs—the noise of waggons and waggoners setting off early and lastly the knocking at my door of the accursed houseknecht to tell me the horses were put to the carriage." While traveling, Irving continued to browse in folklore and apparently carried some volumes of stories with him. At night he "read old legends after going to bed,"[79] but left few hints about his reading.

Before the entries of October 21, 1822, when Irving left Salzburg for Vienna, he had recorded the following titles, some of which he may have acquired and was perusing during this journey: *Sagen der Vorzeit* (1782), *Naturwunder des östreich. Kaiserthums* (1807), *Volkssagen und Mährchen der Deutschen* (1820), *Die romantischen Sagen des Erzgebirges* (1822), *Fischergedichte* (1787), *Das Donauweibchen* (1799), and *Märchen und Sagenbuch der Böhmen* (1820). Some of these titles were recorded incompletely, as though Irving had meant to keep them in mind, but had already forgotten the exact title or author. Trent-Hellman failed to transcribe or identify these significant notations and omitted them completely in the printed text of the *Journals*, but they have value. Just such titles reveal what attracted Irving and promised to provide him with the raw material for his next volume. He was also watching for literary associations which the landscape might call to mind. Thus he recorded after passing through Böhmisch-Brod the curious item "vide la petite prophete de Bomische-Brod by Grimm." The reference is not to a fairy tale by the Brothers Grimm, as has been suggested.[80]

After his tedious travels Irving was delighted with the picturesque and romantic approach to Prague. Ruins, the substantial proof of an interesting and ancient past, always thrilled Irving, particularly if a beautiful sunset shed its mellow glow over the scene or a bright moon cast its light over the mysteries of a medieval city:

> Beautiful sunset—little after six we arrive at Prague—approach the town—moonlight on the walls—dry moat and gateway—towers of churches dark—streets spacious. (I like to enter old walled towns in the evening, fine effect of passing under the old gateways—with sentinels loitering about—lanterns, etc.—to hear the re-echoing of the postilion's horn.) . . . beautiful, moonlight night—fine effect of the light on the white spacious buildings of the streets and, the walls and columns of the theatre . . . Fine contrast after travelling thro' sombre, monotonous country of boors and rude villages, to arrive in the evening at a fine town and in half an hour be ushered into a splendid theatre.[81]

Irving was weary of travel and hungry for entertainment. During his brief stay of four days, he heard a performance of his favorite Italian opera, Rossini's *Barber of Seville,* with Henrietta Sontag, who was at the beginning of her great career, in the role of Rosina, and even saw Shakespeare's *King Lear.*[82] He was indulging himself in this favorite form of recreation, as if trying to make up for lost opportunities.

His days were occupied with examining the monuments of Slavic and German culture, the historical relics of one of the most interesting cities of Europe. He saw famous churches with their even more famous tombs of Saint Nepomuk, the patron saint of Bohemia, of ancient kings like Wenceslaus and Ottokar, and of Tycho Brahe, the great astronomer who had been invited to Prague by Emperor Rudolph II. The romance of this city with its battered and deserted palaces particularly appealed to

Irving at a time when he already anticipated a period of literary activity. Innumerable legends filled his mind and every excursion added to his stock. More scrupulously than ever he noted detailed descriptions of many scenes that might later be fitted into his stories, one of a dilapidated palace with

> great portal closed, side door open, grass-grown courts with pigeons and geese feeding in them—long arcades silent and lifeless—great halls and staircases once thronged with servants now desolate—windows broken—patched with paper—old cloths and rags hanging to dry at windows—fountains in hall dry—ruins of statues, dusty, broken—ragged boy driving cackling geese about the courts—poor people burrowing about in the apartments—old woman, washing, drawing water, etc.[83]

But Irving did not need to go in search of weird and grotesque scenes: he found himself in the midst of them in his hotel. Despite having "the two best rooms on first floor" with "window looking upon the place before the theatre," his quarters were unsatisfactory. His hotel, the Stadt Wien, was dirty, expensive, and inhabited by questionable characters, but it was full of atmosphere. Again Irving described the milieu minutely:

> The hotel seems to be a resort of odd characters. In a neighbouring room is exhibited a remarkably fat child eleven years old, and her picture hangs out just below our window—attracts a continual crowd before the door. In the upper floor is an exhibition of wax work. In an adjoining room is an Italian female singer, in another a French *marchande de linge* who importunes us for custom—while in a dark dungeon of a room below stairs, under the *porte-cochère,* there is a party of coachmen, servants, etc., playing cards all day long.[84]

Gladly Irving pushed on through the dreary expanse of prosperous Bohemian agricultural regions, where only now and then a historical battlefield arrested his attention. Two days after leaving the city of Prague and passing through Schlan, Laun, and Teplitz, Irving entered Saxony at Peterswald. Suddenly the roads became better, the weather improved, the landscape grew more interesting, and soon the spires of Dresden beckoned. Thus the weary traveler arrived in the Saxon capital in the evening of November 28, 1822, in a happy and satisfied mood that augured well for his visit. Here he was to remain until the summer of 1823, experiencing one of the gayest periods of his life. His journal entry best expresses the mood that strikes the keynote for a romantic interlude in Dresden:

Beautiful evening and sunset—scenery on the Elbe—distant hills cheerful from evergreen—rosy gleams on the still water, with fishing boats. As the day closes the full moon shines out from among clouds, which gradually draw off and leave her in full splendour in a deep blue sky—fine effect as we approach Dresden—moonshine brings out white buildings—steeples, domes, etc. Enter and drive thro' tall, spacious streets—tho' dark—open into broad, moonlight squares of fine houses—fountains, churches—put up at Hôtel de Saxe.[85]

3

Dresden

Dresden was at the time of Washington Irving's arrival the fashionable and gay capital of the Kingdom of Saxony, but still showed the scars of those tempestuous years of warfare and political misfortune associated with the Napoleonic era. Frederick Augustus had ruled since 1768 as Elector of Saxony and had been raised to the exalted rank of King in 1806, but his devotion to Napoleon proved costly in the end. His country was devastated by invading armies, his capital besieged and sacked, he himself taken prisoner, and when peace was finally made, half of Saxony was absorbed by Prussia. Despite such political calamities the little kingdom overcame all difficulties and bitterness engendered by the partition. It renounced its ambitions for political and economic leadership and was content to focus its attention upon the cultural aspirations of its capital. The venerable and respected figure of the King, who celebrated the fiftieth anniversary of his accession in 1818 and continued to reign for nine more years, gave a certain stability to the regime which, if lacking in leadership and progressive ideas, revealed at least the positive virtues of frugality, conscience, and integrity. Frederick Augustus was not a gifted ruler and had taken over the reins of government at a time when absolutism was the accepted political theory. He neither had practical training in government administration nor was he blessed with brilliant advisers, who might have compensated for his own shortcomings. He watched carefully over the routine affairs of state, guided by an inflexible sense of justice and fairness, which eventually earned him the title "the Just"; he showed real devotion to his people, but he lacked vision as well as understanding of the world and of human nature. In a real sense he never enjoyed great popularity; his stiff, formal manner, his profound piety, and his antiquated sense of royal dignity raised an insurmountable barrier of court etiquette between himself and his people. Tradition directed governmental affairs, and even the basic ideas of the French Revolution had not penetrated into this stronghold of conservatism.[1]

Dresden, beautifully situated on the Elbe River, was a city of about fifty thousand inhabitants when Irving arrived, a small provincial capital, but with a cosmopolitan spirit. Despite its repeated destruction by fire in the seventeenth and eighteenth centuries, Dresden always rose from its ashes, constructing additional churches and palaces and acquiring art treasures which remained monuments to the memory of its art-loving rulers and established its reputation as the German Florence. Life in this capital revolved completely around the court. The humble citizens watched with pride the activities of the nobility and enjoyed vicariously what their poverty and their modest station in life denied them. The nobility, impoverished by the wars, held all important and remunerative positions in the government and were partially compensated for their circumscribed existence by their eligibility to the court circle.[2] Diplomats and courtiers and a few foreigners who enjoyed special privileges were also eligible.

Despite the political and economic ineptitude of the government, Dresden flourished and continued to attract many visitors. Its attractive location—the charming landscape of vineyards and orchards covering gently sloping hills that rise on both sides of the Elbe—and its moderate climate were only incidental factors in Dresden's popularity. The cultural advantages offered by the numerous academies, museums, libraries, theatres, and associations of scientific, artistic, or literary endeavors were loudly proclaimed. Regardless of some exaggeration by its citizens, Dresden could well lay claim to being an important center of art and literature. Among the great figures of contemporary literature, Goethe, Schiller, and Jean Paul had lived here at different times, and Ludwig Tieck had decided to make it his permanent residence.

The Napoleonic Wars had interrupted the orderly processes of everyday life and the period of exhaustion that followed in their wake produced a literature consisting primarily of shallow and trivial romance—far removed from the universality of Schlegel's concept of romanticism—catering to popular taste. The Dresden theatre, however, under the benevolent patronage of the royal family, was unaffected, and was actually one of the best in German lands. The dramas of Shakespeare, Goethe, and Schiller were performed regularly and through Tieck's influence Kleist's dramas, practically unknown at the time, were also presented; along with these, of course, was the standard fare of popular hits. The opera was even more distinguished. Italian music was still supreme, but with Weber as musical director a proper balance was achieved and the first success of *Der Freischütz* soon rivaled the earlier popularity of Rossini's works.

Dresden at this time still showed many aspects of its medieval past. Until 1810 both the old part of the city, generally designated "the residence," being the abode of the royal family, and the so-called "new city," on the right bank of the Elbe River, had been surrounded by walls, moats, and fortifications. The end of the Napoleonic Wars hastened their destruction, and the leveled areas were gradually developed into boulevards encircling the heart of the city. Three city gates still provided possible surveillance of traffic entering Dresden. Beyond these gates lay the Wilsdruffer, See, and Pirnaische Vorstädte, suburbs situated to the west, southwest, and east respectively. The Augustus Bridge, the only span over the Elbe, provided communication with the new part of the city across the river to the north.

The old city was dominated by the royal palaces and nearby government buildings, which housed galleries, archives, and bureaus. The Old and the New Market squares were other focal points of this area. The Kreuzkirche, the Frauenkirche, and the Hofkirche were the most important churches; the latter, situated between the bridge and the palace, was directly accessible to the royal family from their apartments. To the east, facing the river, extended the gardens of Count Brühl, where were situated the academy of arts, the Belvedere palace, and the famous terrace which became one of the best known landmarks of modern Dresden. Along the banks of the Elbe, north and west of the Court Church, was the "Italian Village," a settlement of small houses erected in the middle of the eighteenth century when Augustùs III imported sculptors, painters, and other artists from Italy to build that church. The Zwinger, begun in 1711 and intended as part of a new palace (never completed), included an extended gallery with six pavilions and has remained an outstanding example of rococo architecture.

In the environs, actually the suburbs, the nobility maintained private gardens which, however, were accessible to the public most of the time. Larger and completely public was the Grosse Garten, an immense park in the extreme southeast, somewhat beyond Prince Anton's garden. On the northwestern outskirts was the garden of Prince Max which adjoined the small Ostra Park along the Elbe. It could be reached from town by way of the Ostra, or Zwinger, Boulevard, an impressive thoroughfare lined with stately chestnut trees. The large Ostra Park was a huge meadow lined with lindens, which extended from Friedrichstadt along the entire bend of the Elbe river as far as Übigau.

Into this attractive city Irving and his companion entered,[3] full of enthusiasm and eager to participate in the bustling activities. In many ways Irving's personality, the genial good humor of his own nature, was a fitting counterpart to the simple charm of the Saxon capital. Upon arriving he proceeded at once to the Hôtel de Saxe located on the New Market Place,[4] one of the better hostelries, but surpassed in size and elegance by the Hôtel de Pologne, the Hôtel de Russie, and Zur Stadt Berlin. However, it was centrally located and pleased Irving with its facilities and moderate price:

> The living in fact is wonderfully cheap in many of the finest cities of Germany. In Dresden, for example, I have a very neat, comfortable, and prettily furnished apartment on the first floor of an hotel; it consists of a cabinet, with a bed in it, and a cheerful sitting room that looks on the finest square. I am offered this apartment for the winter at the rate of thirty-six shillings a month. Would to heaven I could get such quarters in London for anything like the money. I shall probably remain here until the spring opens, as this is one of the pleasantest winter residences, and peculiarly favourable for the study of the German language, which is here spoken in its purity.[5]

Irving made no entries in his journals during the first four days in Dresden and left no positive information to shed light on his early social contacts. However, it may be assumed that through his English traveling companion, who surely registered with the British Minister stationed here, Irving met a former friend, John P. Morier, now British Envoy Extraordinary to the Court of Saxony. It was this coincidental reunion that profoundly influenced Irving's visit in Dresden.[6] Morier, who had served as Secretary of the British Legation in Washington in 1812, had been a friend of Irving there, and he now welcomed the author whose fame had since gone far beyond his native shores. In fact Irving's *Sketch Book* and *Bracebridge Hall* were not unknown in Germany, and Dresden was already discussing them. The first selections from his work ("The Voyage" and "Rural Life in England") had appeared in 1819 in the *Morgenblatt für gebildete Stände* (Stuttgart, issues Number 269 f. and 283 f.). This paper later reprinted Jeffrey's praise of *The Sketch Book* from the *Edinburgh Review*[7] and translated "The Stout Gentleman."[8] In the fall of 1822 a translation of five items from *The Sketch Book*, including the three with German influences, had appeared as *Erzählungen von Washington Irving*, translated by W. A. Lindau.[9] Hence Irving was by no means an unknown author in Dresden when he arrived. Literary society—and Dresden boasted of large numbers of intellectuals who prided themselves on their literary interests—was not unaware of Irving as a celebrity, and the newspaper eagerly informed its readers that he would remain in their midst for several months and was tirelessly occupied with the German language which he himself spoke. Later, the *Abendzeitung* even suggested that Irving might be the mysterious author of *Waverley*.[10] Such flattery Irving modestly deprecated, but found satisfying nevertheless. Soon he was to feel as much at home in Dresden as he had a year earlier in London.

Irving's acquaintance with John Morier gave him access at once to the large English colony and to the Diplomatic Corps which was an integral part of the society of Dresden. On December 3, 1822, Irving dined for the first time at the British envoy's home; although this first dinner was in rather small company, he returned barely a week later, when the diplomatic corps was present.[11] Thus began a long series of dinners and parties that continued uninterruptedly until Irving's departure for Prague the following May. At Mr. Morier's Irving met Colonel Barham Livius of Bedford, England, who had arrived in Dresden about a week before Irving. Livius was something of an amateur dramatist and, like Irving, had known Thomas Moore in Paris.[12] Irving and Livius became friends at once and they saw much of each other during the coming year. In fact their associations were resumed later in Paris and even yielded some literary collaboration. But Irving was not forgetting his real purpose in visiting Germany. Almost immediately upon being settled he wrote to his friend Leslie: "I shall now take a master and go to work to study German. If I can get my pen to work, so much the better, but it has been so long idle I fear it will take some time to get it in working mood."[13]

On Sunday, December 22, 1822, at high noon, Washington Irving was presented by Mr. Morier to the royal family, a large and interesting group that came to surprise him as much by its wide interests and unusual talents as by its quaint customs and ceremonials.[14] Irving, the romantic admirer of the historical past, enjoyed such experiences, and wrote the following description of the court to his brother:

> My reception, indeed, at court has been peculiarly flattering, and every branch of the royal family has taken occasion to show me particular attention, whenever I made my appearance. I wish you were here with me to study this little court; it is just the thing that would delight you. It is one of the most formal and ceremonious in Europe,

> keeping up all the old observances that have been laid aside in other courts. The king is an excellent old gentleman, between seventy and eighty, but a staunch stickler for the old school. He has two brothers, Prince Max and Prince Antoine, and the trio are such figures as you see in the prints of Frederick the Great. Prince Max is one of the most amiable old gentlemen I have ever met with; his countenance and manners peculiarly benevolent; he has two sons, Frederick and John (the former will one day inherit the throne), and two daughters, the youngest of whom is the present Queen of Spain. Prince Antoine, the other brother of the king, is a brisk, lively little gentleman; very religious, but withal as great a hunter as Nimrod, and as fond of dancing as King David. He married a sister of the Emperor of Austria, an old lady that is a complete picture of the dames of the old school. Prince Antoine has always shown a great fancy for me, and I believe I owe much of my standing in the old gentleman's favor, from dancing French quadrilles. I have dined with the king, and been at a number of balls and soirées given by the different members of the royal family; as at these balls every one must be in uniform or court dress, they are very showy.
>
> Among the other institutions which the king keeps up, is a grand hunting establishment in the old style. As this is the only place in Europe where anything of the kind is maintained in the ancient manner, I have been very much interested by it. . . . I have followed the king twice to the boar hunt; the last time we had a fine run of upward of two hours. The king was followed by a numerous hunting retinue, all clad in hunting costumes of green. The *chasse* was in a forest, which is traversed by roads, lanes, and paths in every direction; and the noise of the hounds and horns, the sight of huntsmen dashing about through the forest in every direction, and of the old king and his retinue galloping along the alleys of the forest, formed altogether one of the most animating scenes I have ever witnessed. The boar was not overpowered until he had killed one dog and wounded several.[15]

The royal family had literary and artistic interests which gave it stature far greater than that of its politically more important neighbors. Because of the rivalry with Leipzig, the Dresden Court Theatre, which had been a state enterprise, became the Royal Theatre in 1817 and was thenceforth maintained and supported directly by the King. In 1816 the distinguished composer Carl Maria von Weber was made musical director in Dresden, and he brought the century-old dominance of Italian music to an end. Irving discovered that the entire royal family not only patronized music and the drama, but actually participated in private theatricals and musicals, composed music, translated from the Italian, and wrote plays. Much of their leisure time was devoted to music. Weber even gave piano concerts in the Queen's apartments, to which Irving was invited.[16] Like their brother the King, the Princes Anton and Max had studied and written music, so that more than fifty volumes of their compositions, including various cantatas and operas by Prince Max, are preserved in the Royal Music Collection. Dramatic compositions and performances were also encouraged by the King, and the stiff formality of court etiquette, which would not even permit the King to be seen on foot in the streets or allow him to speak with anyone below the rank of a major, was relieved by these simple, unaffected, yet intellectual family interests.[17]

Irving met Queen Marie Amelia, "a very affable old lady," and the Princess Royal a week later;[18] the Princess Amelia, "a little of a Blue Stock'g" who herself was a writer, promptly spoke to Irving about his works. Her brothers, the Princes Frederick and John, and even the King revealed a familiarity with his writings, and "spoke very flatteringly about my works."[19] Irving was welcomed regularly at the court functions, and he found the young princes intelligent admirers of literature. The following entries in his diary are typical of his association with the royal family:

> Dec. 23. Had long conversation with the young princes, Frederick and John—very amiable, pleasing young men, particularly Prince John, who appears to be well informed. Both speak English, but John the best. Made many inquiries about America.
>
> Dec. 29. The *soirée* at Prince Frederick's—all the Royal family there except the King and Queen. Had considerable conversation with Princes Fred[eric]k and John—Prince Jno asked me if it was true that in America we had no servants. I assured him that we had servants as in Europe—the only difference was that we had bad servants.
>
> Jan. 5. Sunday. Went to Court at ¼ past twelve o'clock—Court held at Prince Antoine's apartments and afterwards the King's—at Prince Antoine's I was spoken to by each of the Royal family present—and at the King's by His Majesty—from the King's levee went by invitation to the Queen's apartments, being to dine at the Royal table.
>
> Jan. 29. In the evening went to ball at Prince Antoine's— present, the King, Queen and Royal family—the second and third sons of the King of Prussia—talked with the youngest—a fine young man. I was particularly noticed by the Queen, who complimented me on

my writings of which she was just read'g in the French translation.

Feb. 23. Go in the evening to party at Prince John's—remain there till nine—talk with Princes Max, John, Fred'k, the Princess of Bavaria, etc.

April 27. At six go to ball given by Prince Max in Prince Frederick's apartment—the King and Queen of Bavaria and of Saxony there. Dinner with E. and F. Foster—Queen of Saxony sent Preuss, the Master of Ceremonies, to bring me to her. Said she had not seen me for a century—that she had just read my work from Paris and made many compliments on it. Said she expected I would write something about Dresden, etc., and about the *chasse.*

King of Bavaria told me he knew Franklin in Paris and after Franklin's departure he had bought a horse and cabriolet which belonged to him.

Prince John very weak and pale.

P. Frederick talked with me about the theatre.

July 6. Sunday. Went to Court—held by the Queen and King—Queen very kind and affable—talked a great deal with her and the princess.[20]

Unfortunately for Irving he was not fully aware of the literary and scholarly proclivities of his royal friends. Prince John was particularly interested in Italian literature and was gathering about him poets and scholars who aided and encouraged him in his monumental translation of Dante's *Divina Commedia,* finally published under his pen name Philalethes. Irving, who was studying Italian as well as German at this time, should have found the Prince a stimulating and intellectual influence, but all indications point to another neglected opportunity. A few years later George Ticknor became acquainted with Prince John, subsequently King Johann of Saxony, and maintained an interesting correspondence with him that illuminates their unusual friendship.[21] He praised the Prince as "a man of quiet, studious habits and a good deal of learning,"[22] and participated with him and Förster, Tieck, Carus, and Baudissin in the regular meetings of the so-called Dante Society. But Irving was a dilettante and not a student. He preferred the adulation of admiring friends and the chit-chat of the drawing room. Even the literary talents of Princess Amelia, whose light comedies achieved such popularity that they were reprinted in Boston and New York papers,[23] are barely commented upon by Irving. Prince Frederick even collaborated with Goethe on a botanical study, and Prince John sent some of his poetry to Weimar for criticism.[24] The Court of Saxony was an extraordinary court indeed.

Irving was treated with the respect due a distinguished foreigner and was made to feel welcome in Dresden, but hardly became an intimate friend of the Royal Family. The King and his brothers were old, and official protocol limited their participation in the social life of Dresden. They held court at regular intervals and received their guests with the traditional dignity of their positions.[25] The official Court Calendar contains only two entries of Irving's presence, his presentation on December 22, 1822, at the twenty-second holding of court that year and his invitation to dinner two weeks later.[26] Irving was hardly impressed. The formality of the occasion was apparently not relieved by any animated conversation. Irving listed the names of such guests he could remember and concluded:

> Dinner lasted an hour—not remarkably good—no variety of wines—each man had his little flask of wine and another of water, with an enormous wine glass. Dinner quiet and dull—after dinner adjourned to drawing room—took coffee—talked a little with the Royal family, who then bowed and retired—we did the same.[27]

The younger princes, particularly Prince John whose interest in literature was practically professional, might have become Irving's intimate friends. However, their acquaintance never went beyond an exchange of words demanded by the social amenities. Irving generally preferred to observe and to listen rather than to expound and was not likely to take the initiative in a friendship. Besides, Prince John was absorbed in his own affairs, having been married only a few weeks before Irving's arrival in Dresden. Not until March was Irving invited there.[28]

Through the good offices of the British envoy, Irving met in rapid succession not only the foreign diplomats, who together with the English colony provided almost exclusively the social intercourse and lavish entertainment that made Dresden such a gay city, but also some distinguished Saxon courtiers and the representative figures of the artistic and literary life flourishing at the time. At Mr. Morier's he first met Karl August Böttiger,[29] Director of the Museum of Antiquity, who was perhaps the most influential—though not the most important—figure in the cultural life of Dresden. He had been the Director of the *Gymnasium* at Weimar where he had antagonized Goethe and Schiller through his intrigues and his critical pretensions. But he was a friendly, amiable man with a vast fund of knowledge who established himself, in more mediocre surroundings than Weimar, as the *elegantiae arbiter*. His learning impressed Irving as it did other Americans.[30] His volubility and his ready familiarity with all matters concerning art and literature had their appeal. He was eager to help distinguished foreign visitors and prided himself upon knowing everybody. Tieck, by far the finer critic, was still on friendly terms with him at this time, though he satirized him later in *Der gestiefelte Kater*. Böttiger spoke English, and Irving frequently called upon him for help and advice. The only Irving letter to be traced in German archives is in the form of a brief note to Böttiger thanking him for many kindnesses and asking him to forward a note to a publisher. Among such kindnesses was no doubt the privilege of borrowing from the splendid Royal Library,[31] a privilege of which Irving probably made sparing use because of time-consuming social distractions. About his reading while in Dresden Irving kept a discreet silence, though he jotted down book titles in his notebook. A few years later in Madrid Irving wrote letters of introduction to Böttiger and other Dresden friends for Longfellow.[32] It was at the home of Böttiger that Irving met Karl Christian Vogel von Vogelstein, professor of art and court painter, who invited him to sit for a portrait. Irving recorded two sittings at the end of January, which resulted in the excellent but practically unknown sketch reproduced here as the frontispiece. Signed by Irving and the artist and dated February 1, 1823, this pencil sketch reveals in an unusually realistic manner the regular features, the curly hair, the large expressive eyes, in short, the handsome countenance of the American author who delighted his Dresden friends with the warmth of his genial personality. No portrait was ever painted, but the original sketch has remained in the Vogel von Vogelstein Collection in Dresden.[33]

Wolf Adolph August von Lüttichau,[34] a Saxon nobleman who was at this time in charge of the royal forests, became a close friend to Irving and made it possible for him to study at close range the quaint and archaic customs of the hunt. In England Irving had been fascinated by the picturesque aspects of the chase and had included chapters on horsemanship, falconry, and hawking in *Bracebridge Hall*. But nowhere has Irving become so expansive as in the detailed description of these Dresden hunting expeditions after the wild boar. Lüttichau sent a carriage for him and Irving eagerly observed:

> Here various officers of the *chasse* and forest in uniform of green hunting coat—drab trousers—hunting whip with lash tucked round their waists—hunting sword—horn slung over shoulder . . . pass by kennel and look at hounds—house in which all the hunters, etc., play[in]g on horns singing visit the boar pens . . . hear sound of horn give signal of King approach[in]g—station myself by a large tree of the forest—by roadside—first come one or two horsemen—huntsman with four lancer dogs, who are first put on the track of the boar—then the whippers-in with the pack of hounds. More horsemen arrive—then

> King and Prince Antoine in carriage—horses led out for King and Prince—they mount—the boar turned loose—passes near me—shortly after the four hounds let loose. King and Prince Antoine and suite gallop by—they salute me as they pass—Antoine cries out *Gute[n] Morgen.*
>
> Pack of hounds with huntsmen surround[in]g them blowing low note of horns—Whipper is smacking whips—hounds yelping with impatience and climbing on top of one another. At last a high note of horn gives signal and off they go—making the woods echo to their note.[35] . . . The chase lasts upwards of two hours. Just get in time enough to see the boar overpowered—huntsmen hold him down until King and Prince Antoine come up—P[rince] Antoine despatches him. The latter broke off a branch of a bush and gave me to wear in my hat, as every one does when present at a successful *chasse*—invites us all to his house next week to a dance.[36]

Here was primitive sport and sophisticated country life on the outskirts of a fashionable city that also boasted first-class drama and music! The hunt combined aristocratic traditions of court etiquette and an exhilarating hand-to-hand encounter with ferocious game. It set Irving to thinking wistfully of the changes wrought by time. He speculated upon similar scenes in England:

> Does not the continent continually present pictures of customs and manners such as formerly prevailed in England? The King's chasse at Dresden is quite a picture of ancient hunting in Q[ueen] Elizabeth's reign. The *table d'hôte* at Heidelberg, Munich, Mayence, etc., was the old Host's table in England.[37]

Lüttichau was also deeply interested in music and literature and, though in no sense a scholar, he had sufficient ability and artistic taste to manage quite creditably the Court Theatre when he was appointed its director in 1824. Perhaps it was his highly gifted wife, a daughter of Count von Knobelsdorf (whom Irving regarded particularly highly because he "speaks English well and has been in England"[38]) who really gave their house a reputation as one "where elegance and letters, the first society in rank, and the first in intellectual culture, were always to be found." Ticknor, who characterized Mme Lüttichau's salon thus in 1836, also said of her that she was "not only one of the prettiest ladies in Dresden, but she has more good sense and is more *spirituelle* . . . she speaks French, English, and Italian well, paints in oils beautifully, plays and sings well, [and] talks well upon books . . ."[39] In her home and in that of her father, Irving was most likely to meet important literary figures or to hear about them. Irving recorded hearing one evening at Count Knobelsdorf's about Jean Paul, the German Romanticist who had at times lived in Dresden and whose eccentricities gave rise to innumerable stories.[40] Hellman errs in his biography of Irving when he speaks of an actual meeting of Irving and Jean Paul.[41] The latter had been enthusiastically welcomed in Dresden six months earlier[42] and was, therefore, still the subject of conversation and gossip. Irving heard how Jean Paul refused to visit the Dresden Gallery because an attendant would not permit his pet poodle to accompany him. Irving listened eagerly to such anecdotes, quizzed his language master for further details,[43] read some Jean Paul, and finally bought a set of his works in Prague.[44]

Irving's acquaintance with the Baron Ernst von der Malsburg, the Hessian chargé d'affaires, was doubly important: the Baron was a highly cultivated nobleman and lover of literature who had published some poetry and was preparing, under the influence of Schlegel's enthusiasm for Spanish literature, an excellent translation of Calderón,[45] and he also introduced Irving to Ludwig Tieck, then the most important living figure after Goethe in German letters. Unfortunately, Irving's laconic entry "Go to M. Tieck's at six o'clock in comp[an]y with Baron de Malsburg—conversation, he in German, I in English—his daughters very pleasing girls,"[46] suggests a very limited awareness of Tieck's importance. Though Tieck had not yet achieved the influential position in the Dresden theatre which came with his appointment as *Dramaturg* in 1825, his drama reviews appearing in the *Abendzeitung* had established his reputation as a literary critic. Tieck's own creative writings, which Irving came to know in part, brought him both popularity and distinction. His enthusiasm for the dramatic literature of England, particularly of the Elizabethan age, had taken him to London in 1817, where he began collecting his valuable English library. This library furnished the working basis of the famous Schlegel-Tieck Shakespeare translations in which he, however, only supervised and examined the work done by his daughter Dorothea and Count Baudissin. His brilliant talent as a reader and interpreter of the world's greatest dramas gave his salon an international reputation. Strangers arriving in Dresden sought eagerly to gain admission to these informal meetings at which Tieck would read, preferably Shakespeare, giving to each part its peculiar and fitting interpretation. His salon attained a distinction that rivaled the art galleries and the theatre of Dresden,[47] but Irving made only a brief social call, and nothing indicates that he was aware of Tieck's importance as a writer and critic. From this significant call Irving proceeded directly to the home of the Knobelsdorfs where he heard "pleasant musick from Mad. Lüttichau" in perhaps a more congenial and sociable, if less distinguished, atmosphere.[48] More than ten years later Tieck remembered Irving's visit and spoke to John Lothrop Motley, his guest at tea, "of Irving whom he knew in Dresden, and whom he admired very much."[49] Perhaps Irving's unfamiliarity with spoken German and his reticence to engage in stimulating conversation except among intimate friends explain the trivial comments.

But perhaps, in view of his conventional judgments of literature and his obvious lack of critical perspective, even a greater familiarity with German literature would not have initiated a full understanding of Tieck or his work. To be sure, the handicap of a foreign language was a formidable barrier. Yet it cannot be forgotten that even in England Irving, relishing the animated gossip of the London drawing room, had been utterly unaware of the genius of Wordsworth and Coleridge, and preferred the work of Campbell or Moore to that of the Lake poets.

Only such shortcomings in his own critical faculties explain his enthusiasm for the lesser writers who had joined forces under the name of *Dresdener Liederkreis* and dominated the literary scene in Dresden after 1801. Their special organ, the *Abendzeitung,* was edited beginning in 1817 by Theodor Hell (Hofrat Winkler) and by Friedrich Kind, author of the libretto of Weber's *Freischütz.* Belles–Lettres, as Irving would have designated the regular contributions of Fouqué, Clauren, Houwald, Laun, Castelli, and Van der Velde, gave the paper its prestige and popularity. Böttiger, Breuer, Carl von Miltitz, Baron von der Malsburg, Count Kalckreuth, and Carl Maria von Weber, all of whom Irving came to know, belonged to this literary group which catered to the popular taste of the time and whose work is characterized by triviality, diluted romanticism, and maudlin sentimentality. Their work has been dubbed "pseudo-romanticism" in literary history.[50] Dresden at this time could boast the dubious distinction of harboring more minor literary talent than any other city its size. The nobility encouraged literary work and often served as patrons. Just such a friend of the muses and "a literary man," according to Irving,[51] was Count Friedrich von Kalckreuth, a friend and pupil of Tieck, as was Baron Löwenstein, a Livonian nobleman whose name occurs frequently in Irving's Dresden *Journals* and who often invited Irving to sit in his box at the theatre. At Baron Löwenstein's house he also met C. A. Tiedge,[52] the venerable and highly respected author of *Urania,* a philosophic, didactic poem of God, immortality, and freedom, which had achieved an unbelievable success in 1801. Irving made an effort to record the names of all the interesting people he met in society, but the paucity of his literary background handicapped him. Particularly interested in legendary materials, he listened avidly to the stories of native folklore and sometimes indicated the gist of such stories,[53] but even the most interesting associations produced only a general reference to "literary conversations" or "discussions of the theatre."

The winter in Dresden consisted primarily of a long series of dinners, receptions, social calls, and theatre parties, all of which delighted Irving's gregarious instincts. There was nothing riotous or even Bohemian in the social distractions of Dresden. On the contrary, they had a certain homespun quality and staid propriety that reflected the solid virtues of the court. Irving described the customs of Dresden society to his friends in Paris:

> The mode of living here is somewhat old fashioned as to hours, but still very pleasant. The royal family & the old nobility and people about court dine at *one* oclock the younger part of the nobility, who like more fashionable hours dine at two. The foreign ministers & the English resident here, dine about four—visits of ceremony are sometimes paid at twelve oclock, but more commonly between five and six. At six oclock the fashionable world go to the theatre, where the performance lasts commonly until half past eight or at most nine—after the theatre you pay sociable visits to families with whom you are acquainted, and before eleven you are at home & ready for bed—Such is fashionable life in Dresden. It is true this routine is broken in upon by evening parties, Balls &c—particularly during carnival. You go to Balls and routs about eight oclock—and they rarely last later than twelve—I like the custom of paying visits in the evening particularly —it always puts society upon an easy social footing.[54]

Irving's *Journals* show him spending his time dining at the home of M. Campuzano, the Spanish Minister, or in the evening at a Court Rout, or leaving cards at the homes of various Ministers, visiting Mrs. Williams, dancing at the Hôtel de Pologne, dining at Count Rumigny's, flirting with Mme de Bergh, attending the theatre, the opera, or the Ressource Club—calling, dining, visiting in endless repetition. Yet all such contacts were unimportant and somewhat incidental when compared to his intimate friendship with the Fosters, whose home he soon visited daily.[55] Their cousin Livius, whose enthusiasm for the stage persuaded Irving to try his hand at writing for the theatre, had been one of the first Englishmen whom Irving met in Dresden. In his company he entered their family circle, enjoying once more the simple pleasures of domesticity generally denied to his bachelor's existence, a situation so happily reminiscent of his visits with the Van Warts in Birmingham or the Storrows in Paris. This friendship gradually absorbed Irving's time and thought until it became the pivotal factor in his German experience. He himself, in writing to the Fosters, characterized "the many evenings of homefelt enjoyment I have passed among you . . . the sweetest moments that I have passed in Dresden."[56]

Irving's own notation lists December 19, 1822 as his first visit to the Fosters, where, in the company of only "the family (Mrs. F.—two daughters and two boys), and Col. Livius,"[57] he was a guest for dinner. To fix the exact date when Irving was first introduced to the Fosters is made difficult by inadequate and inaccurate notations. Irving maintained a complete silence upon the time or the occasion of this first meeting. Emily Foster, the attractive eighteen-year-old daughter, noted in her diary without giving any clue as to the date: "At the play tonight Mr. Irving the author of the Sketch book was introduced to us."[58] Forty years later Emily's sister Flora published her own recollections of their friendship with Irving in an unauthorized interpolation to the official biography, and she stated that Washington Irving was "presented to us between the acts of 'La Gazza Ladra' under rather curious circumstances."[59] The circumstances to which Flora referred concerned a letter in which her mother had written with enthusiasm about *The Sketch Book* to her daughter in England. She had even transcribed a favorite passage from it with Irving's name at the end. The letter somehow had become lost and had been opened by the authorities who, finding the name of Washington Irving in it, eventually had it sent to him in Vienna. Delighted with the praise of his work it contained, Irving sought an introduction to the Fosters and aroused their curiosity by revealing bits of family news that had been contained in the letter. Such was the beginning of their friendship. This romantic detail, which in itself could have provided Irving with material for a delightful narrative, is not mentioned by him, but is probably true in its basic essentials. Unfortunately, Irving was prone to suppress all personal experiences or incidents and recorded only the arid details of his daily routine without the leaven of human interest. The long interval of time had, however, tricked Flora Foster's memory of the particular performance that evening, which would otherwise identify their first meeting. The records of the Dresden theatres reveal that Rossini's *La Gazza Ladra* was never performed in the year 1822, having been given often the preceding year. Since it was customary for all theatres to close shortly before the Christmas holidays and since therefore no theatrical performances were given that year after December 14, the meeting must have taken place before that date. Irving did not mention any attendance at the theatre before January 9, 1823, but he was frequently inaccurate or negligent in keeping his records. The only two operatic performances that would have attracted Irving during his first two weeks in Dresden, works of Rossini, his favorite composer, took place on December 4 (*Tancredi*) and December 11 (*L'Italiana in Algeri*). The latter seems the more likely performance to have been the occasion of Irving's introduction to the Fosters, as a week earlier Irving was barely located and had just met the first English residents. Moreover, his acquaintance with the Fosters, sponsored by an incident that put them on a friendly footing at once, would not have lagged two full weeks before his first appearance at their home. It is reasonable to assume that Irving met the Fosters in their opera box on December 11, 1823, during an intermission of Rossini's opera *L'Italiana in Algeri.*

On December 23 Colonel Livius, "who is full of the subject of private theatricals," took Irving to the Fosters and interested them all in his plan for a performance of Tom Thumb. The next evening Irving returned to the Fosters for dinner and spent "a merry Christmas eve—various games—charades—hoodman blind, etc." in the company of the Pigotts, the Willliams', and the Messrs. Livius, Werry, Trotter, Morier, Scott, Airey, Cochrane, Price, Johnson, Butler, and Codrington.[60] The latter were mostly young English army officers and diplomatic officials who, like Irving, had found a hearty welcome at the Fosters. The absence of any Germans is significant; though natural and understandable on this festive celebration, it nevertheless sets the pattern for most occasions. Irving associated primarily with members of the British colony, the diplomatic corps, and a few courtiers and noblemen who spoke English and French, so that he rarely had occasion to use German at social functions. The rehearsals of the private theatricals, which demanded Irving's presence at the Fosters more and more frequently, were obviously all in English. On December 27, Irving recorded his presence there in the morning for breakfast as well as for dinner, and thenceforth hardly a day passed without at least one visit with these English friends.[61] The question naturally arises, Who were the Fosters and what was the source of their fascination for Washington Irving?

Late in the summer of 1820 Mrs. Amelia Morgan Foster with her sixteen- and fourteen-year-old daughters, Emily and Flora, and three small boys had arrived in Dresden, probably to give her children the advantages of continental travel and education.[62] This was the family of the third marriage of John Foster of Brickhill House, Bedford, England, a prominent and wealthy member of that community. The fact that John Foster's older brother was a bishop in the Moravian Church and that three sisters had married Germans—Sarah Foster had married into the von Zezschwitz family of Taubenheim and Deutsch Baselitz in Upper Lusatia, distinguished in Saxon annals—[63]probably explains the Fosters' choice of Dresden as their residence. Unlike Irving, whose reputation as a writer had preceded him and established his social position in the Saxon capital, the Fosters had found no ready-made English society upon their arrival and were quite content with German and Italian friends. The boys' education was entrusted to a German tutor while Mrs. Foster supervised the reading of her daughters. Emily's many notations in French, German, and Italian, despite her numerous mistakes, give ample evidence of a reasonable facility to express herself in these foreign tongues, and reflect a real interest in German literature.

The spirited and discerning entries in Emily Foster's diary give some indication of the charm, vivacity, and merriment that pervaded the household and show how, gradually, the entire family was absorbed in the social whirl. German, Italian, and English cavaliers courted Emily, and her diary entries frequently give amusing pictures of the serious rivalry between the fiery Count Allegri and the good-natured, fun-loving Bavarian, Baron von Gumppenberg, for visible signs of her favor. Of the latter she was genuinely fond, probably she was actually falling in love with him when he was recalled to army service and left Dresden.[64] More than a year had passed after their arrival in Dresden before the Fosters were presented at court by the British Minister,[65] and not until late in 1822 could Emily record, "we have English friends now."[66] And so the Fosters gradually established themselves on friendly footing with Dresden society; above all their hospitality made their home a veritable center for visiting Englishmen. Irving entered the Fosters' drawing room as an American "who is very interesting with his stories about his handsome Indians painting & pluming themselves, & strutting up & down before their cabin doors,"[67] and as a distinguished man of letters who had gained admittance to the literary coteries of Lady Holland and had received from her "the most fascinating smile woman ever wore."[68] At once he became a friend of the entire household. The lack of his own fireside and a congenial family circle was painfully apparent to him on many occasions, and nostalgic longing crept into letters to Brevoort[69] and Paulding who were happily established with wife and child. In the Fosters' home he found the friendship and the simple pleasures of social intercourse which always delighted him. The fashionable routs and assemblies of high society dazzled but exhausted him. Such festivities interested him as an American tourist eager to observe everything that the sophisticated Old World could offer, but for regular fare he preferred small and intimate groups of friends. Only then could Irving overcome his natural shyness and delight his listeners with humorous narrative or amiable conversation.

From the standpoint of the Fosters, Irving's appearance in their set was naturally welcomed. His reputation as a writer had preceded him, and the charm, the good looks, the ingratiating manner of this cultured, well-bred American, had their full effect upon the ladies of the Foster household. Yet he seemed almost an Englishman. His family background, his long residence in England, and his affectionate portrayal of English life had molded him in the conventional pattern of a British gentleman. He was not like a rugged frontiersman of the American republic. In contrast to his contemporary, the caustic and truculent James Fenimore Cooper, who despised Irving as an obsequious flatterer without a social conscience, Irving never espoused a cause or indulged in stubborn controversy. He remained a lover of civilized urbanity whose artistic temperament demanded restraint and dignity. Super-patriots at home, who resented the protracted absence of America's first man of letters, sometimes forgot that Irving, born as victory and peace had come to the Colonies, named for the Father of his country, and even blessed by him, took a fierce pride in his native land and its frontier civilization.

Almost immediately after the first meeting Emily characterized Irving in her *Journal* as "neither tall nor slight, but most interesting, dark, hair of a man of genius waving, silky, & black, grey eyes full of varying feeling, & an amiable smile."[70] Amateur theatricals caught Irving's fancy and soon he "wanted Christmas gambols,"[71] probably for "Twelfth Night" festivities; so Fielding's burlesque, *The Tragedy of Tragedies: or the Life and Death of Tom Thumb,* drastically revised to suit the limited company, was performed.[72] This was but the beginning of a series that absorbed Irving in the following months and brought him into daily contact with the Fosters: Rehearsals for *Maid or Wife: or The Deceiver Deceived,* a musical comedy (first presented at the Drury Lane Theatre in 1821) that Livius[73] had adapted from the French, and for Arthur Murphy's *Three Weeks After Marriage* began almost immediately. Irving who enjoyed these trivial but pleasant distractions gave a full account of such Thespian amusements in a letter to his brother:

> Among the other amusements of the winter, we have had a little attempt at private theatricals. These have been at the house of Mrs. Foster, an English lady of rank, who has been residing here for a couple of years. She has two daughters, most accomplished and charming girls. They occupy part of a palace, and in a large saloon a little theatre was fitted up, the scenery being hired from a small theatre; and the dresses from a masquerade warehouse. It was very prettily arranged, I assure you. We first tried Tom Thumb, which, however, went no further than a dress rehearsal, in which I played the part of King Arthur, to Mrs. Foster's Dollalolla; and the other parts were supported by some of the English who were wintering in Dresden. There was then an attempt to get up a little opera, altered from the

French by Colonel Livius, a cousin of Mrs. Foster, and some such a character as I have described in Master Simon in my last work. The colonel, however, who is a green-room veteran, and has written for the London theatres, was so much of a martinet in his managerial discipline, that the piece absolutely fell through from being too much managed. In the mean time a few of the Colonel's theatrical subjects conspired to play him a trick, and get up a piece without his knowledge. We pitched upon the little comedy of *Three Weeks after Marriage,* which I altered and arranged so as to leave out two or three superfluous characters. I played the part of Sir Charles Rackett; Miss Foster, Lady Rackett; Miss Flora Foster, Dimity; Mrs. Foster, Mrs. Druggett, and a young officer by the name of Corkran, the part of Mr. Druggett. You cannot imagine the amusement this little theatrical plot furnished us. We rehearsed in Mrs. Foster's drawing room, and as the whole was to be kept a profound secret, and as Mrs. Foster's drawing-room is a great place of resort, and as especially our dramatic sovereign, Colonel Livius, was almost an inmate of the family, we were in continued risk of discovery, and had to gather together like a set of conspirators. We, however, carried our plot into execution more successfully than commonly falls to the lot of conspirators. The Colonel had ordered a dress rehearsal of his little opera; the scenery was all prepared, the theatre lighted up, a few amateurs admitted: the Colonel took his seat before the curtain, to direct the rehearsal. The curtain rose, and out walked Mr. and Mrs. Druggett in proper costume. The little colonel was perfectly astonished, and did not recover himself before the first act was finished; it was a perfect explosion to him. We afterwards performed the little comedy before a full audience of the English resident in Dresden, and of several of the nobility that understood English, and it went off with great spirit and success. We are now on the point of playing *The Wonder* which I have altered and shortened to suit the strength of the company, and to prune off objectionable parts. In this, I play the part of Don Felix, to Miss Foster's Violante. She plays charmingly; the part of Colonel Briton I have had to alter into a British captain of a man-of-war, to adapt it to the turn of the actor who is to play it, viz.: Captain Morier of the Navy, brother of the British Minister.[74]

The admiration and praise of "Miss Foster," to whom Irving referred so formally in his correspondence, is further reflected in the growing friendship; youthful Emily showed pleasure in the constant attentions of her latest conquest. Whereas Airey, one of Emily's British beaux, had played opposite her in their first dramatic enterprise, Irving soon managed to replace him in such favored parts. In fact, Emily Foster was sufficiently flattered and absorbed by Irving's attentions to neglect Airey. Her *Journal* begins to deal more intimately with her impressions of Irving. At a ball she had promised Airey the third waltz, but "actually forgot him again, & dance with Irving,"[75] so that her sister reported to her that Airey "had complained of a change towards him."[76] Beginning in January Irving became almost a daily visitor at the Fosters. Dramatics was only one subject that drew Irving there. His eagerness to improve his linguistic skill was not satisfied with German lessons from native tutors; Mrs. Foster gave him lessons in Italian and Emily superintended his French so regularly that he could say, "if I am not acquiring ideas, I am at least acquiring a variety of modes of expressing them when they do come."[77] His own *Journals* are full of entries that give proof of this intimate friendship, and Emily recorded that "Mr. Irving is always with us entertaining & interesting."[78]

But there was another side to Irving's nature, the super-sensitive feelings of an artist lacking confidence in himself and constantly fearful of failure, whose restless and unstable moods plunged him momentarily from carefree gaiety into melancholy fits of depression. He needed praise and encouragement in order to retain what little self-assurance he could muster. And Emily was not long in discovering Irving's weakness.

> "Mr. I—— is in want of constant excitement, & support, interest & admiration of his friends seem the very food he lives on he is easily discouraged & excited I like as I——g says to see a man gather himself up on his pride—pride is the pedestal on which man stands"[79]

Irving's own notations in his *Journals,* always of a factual sort, give no indication of his feelings or moods, but show him completely absorbed by the routine of social distractions in the Saxon capital. Taking the month of February as an example, Irving dined alone only three times—which of course did not prevent social engagements later, as the dinner hour was in the middle of the afternoon. He dined at the Fosters seven times, took tea there twice, and spent eight evenings there; he was a dinner guest of Count Poushkin, Countess Hohenthal, the Pigotts, Mrs. Williams, Mr. Corkran, Baron von Knobelsdorf, Mr. Morier, and Colonel Livius. He attended eight balls or soirées in the diplomatic set and danced until two o'clock in the morning—so that he was indisposed the next day—and found time to attend the theatre and the opera eight times besides. Yet he recorded also "at home all day studying," "at home all day," "at home studying and trying to write," "at home till two o'clock," "at home till one o'clock," "at home all the morn'g writing," "writing all the morn'g," "in my room till one o'clock studying and writing."[80]

Irving tried valiantly to remain true to his purpose despite all distractions. He had intended "going into winter quarters and studying German,"[81] and in a letter written March 7, 1823, he avowed that he was "getting very familiar with the German language";[82] in another letter a week later he characterized his struggle as "fighting my way into the German language."[83] Though Irving made no notation of beginning his German lessons, he must have engaged his tutors promptly. By Christmas he recorded the humorous anecdote told by his language master about Jean Paul's exaggerated affection for his poodle,[84] and the following spring he paid eighty-four dollars for German instruction. Meticulously Irving noted on May 16, "Lesson in morning—paid Schott forty dollars for ninety-six hours of German teaching," and the following day, "pay off Mr. Keysler for five and one half months' German tuition at eight doll. a month. Forty four doll[ar]s."[85] Schott had been professor of English and French at the Royal Cadet Corps and Mr. Kiessler (Irving's spelling was no better in German than in English and phonetic at best) was listed in the *Dresden Adressbuch* as a teacher of English. Such expenditures testify to the seriousness of purpose with which Irving embarked upon his German studies. Eventually his social activities forced him to rise early in order to prepare his lessons and receive his mentor by seven o'clock. In April and May Irving worked feverishly, apparently trying to make up for lost time. His mornings were devoted to his German lesson, further study, and reading. Rising as early as five he began the day with an hour's walk and then returned to meet his language master. His lessons were extended to two hours a morning.[86]

Irving began to put his newly acquired linguistic skill to practical use. Livius, who had been busy with his own dramatic and operatic plans, had succeeded in enlisting Irving's help for translations. In the middle of January they were busy with the songs and music of *Der Freischütz*; on April 20 Irving began to translate the libretto of Weber's *Abu Hassan,* a task that occupied him until his excursion to the Riesengebirge. He had met the composer through Livius and had enjoyed the privilege of attending a concert in the Queen's apartment where "Weber played some of his own music on piano."[87] Irving was also in touch with Dr. Spiker, the Royal Librarian in Berlin, who translated Irving's writings into German, and the mercurial Dr. Montucci, who called "to request permission to publish an edition of 'The Sketch Book' in English," and actually succeeded in this unusual undertaking.[88]

Spring brought further distractions. The parks of the city and the private gardens of the royal princes, open to Irving and the Fosters by invitation, were attractive enough, but the environs of Dresden—Findlater, Pillnitz, Briessnitz, Plauen, Tharandt, and above all the area named Saxon Switzerland for its scenic beauty—beckoned constantly. Drives, picnics, and excursions became the order of the day as warmer weather transformed the barren countryside. Irving, who was deeply sensitive to the beauties of nature, eagerly explored this area and recorded the first "indications of spring in the green twigs—a few buds and the tender leaves of some willows and of lilacs," or "this day heard the cuckoo for the first time this year in the Grosse Garten—lovely sunset and evening," or "beautiful drive up the valley of Plauen—country all in tender leaf larks—fields enamelled with forget-me-nots and heart's ease."[89] To celebrate Irving's fortieth birthday, the Fosters scheduled a drive into the country and gave a small party in the evening at which "the Misses Foster prepare a surprise by getting up tableaux of scenes, in 'The Sketch Book' and 'Bracebridge Hall' and "Knickerbocker' . . . conclude the evening by waltzing."[90]

Yet, despite all outward manifestations of gaiety, an undercurrent of restlessness is apparent in Irving's behavior. There is the cryptic notation of March 31, when Irving, after an evening party at Mrs. Foster's, writes the puzzling unfinished phrase "go home very much. . . ."[91] Two weeks later while laboring over a birthday poem for Emily he unburdens his mind: "endeavour to write poetry, but in vain—write only one verse—determine not to dine today at Mrs. Foster's. Think of leaving Dresden."[92] Despite Mrs. Foster's urgent request Irving remained steadfast and absented himself from dinner, and that evening at Count Palffy's received a scolding from her for not staying. "I [blank] and out of spirits."[93] Yet he could not stay away long. The next day he visited the Fosters, and the following day resumed his dinners with them. Temporarily the crisis had passed. A few days later "Mrs. F. calls on me in carriage and carries me home. Take French lesson—talk with the girls. Emily in good spirits and listens delightfully."[94]

Irving crowded his schedule more than ever. His study periods, his collaborations with Livius in translating *Abu Hassan,* the court functions, the hunting expeditions, the theatre performances, and an endless list of dinner parties gave Irving little time for brooding or melancholy thought. He was determined to be gay and finally managed to record: "Very pleasant evening—returned home in very good spirits—determined to see society and gather myself up."[95] At the end of April he was still struggling with the "verses to E. on birthday"[96] and on May 4, the day of that occasion, he was "early up. Finish lines to Miss F. on birthday—send the lines—

get note of thanks from Mrs. F. . . . Return to Livius and from there to Mrs. F. Emily's birthday—thanks me for the lines—dine there—pleasant dinner."[97] The poem, copied by Emily into her *Journal* and printed by Pierre M. Irving in his biography, consists of sentimental and rather hackneyed phrases about the fair charms of Emily, "frank nature's child," suitable for scrapbooks and memory albums. Irving quite properly expressed "no confidence" in his rhymes, but Emily was obviously pleased and flattered. She, who had previously characterized Irving as "amiable and amusing" now recorded: "that good dear nice Mr. Irving sent me delightful verses the first almost he ever wrote I hope it is not vain to transcribe them I do it more for his sake than for the partial *compliments* (are a cold word) to me."[98] But a note of formality had crept into Irving's poetic effusion. Nothing personal, nothing of deep feeling or emotion, nothing beyond sincere good wishes expressed with almost paternal blessings, found expression. Irving was out of sorts and restless. He needed a change and had determined to leave Dresden for a while. He interrupted the birthday festivities to "drive out in blustering wind to Priessnitz"[99] to look for Cockburn, who was to accompany him on an excursion into Silesia. Another two weeks of routine social intercourse and Emily noted "our last evening with Irving—before his journey—Mama suspects he meant not to return, he said he had thought of it—but that he would he could not help it—We stood on the balcony by moonlight & talked of heaven."[100]

Setting out on May 20, 1823, Irving and his English traveling companion, Lieutenant John Cockburn, traveled to Bautzen, where Napoleon had fought an important battle ten years before, and then proceeded to Herrnhut, where Count Zinzendorf had founded the Protestant sect of Moravian Brethren. Irving had a letter to one of the superintendents of the Brotherhood, Mr. Fabricius, who showed them the settlement. In his diary Irving refrained from passing judgment upon this community, but in a letter to Mrs. Foster he expressed himself unequivocally. His dislike of the gloomy atmosphere of religious asceticism went back to childhood memories of "outward forms and ceremonies of religion." These "dismal associations" remained distasteful to Irving throughout his life and made him impatient and uncomfortable whenever he encountered religious emotionalism or exaggerated fervor publicly exhibited. Hence his blunt condemnation of Moravian Pietism:

> It [Herrnhut] is all very excellent in its way, but I would rather live in a wilderness than there. I have no relish for this *triste* simplicity, that consists in negatives. It seems the study of these worthy people to divest life and nature of everything that Heaven intended should embellish this short existence. . . . Nature is simple herself,

> but then she is varied and beautiful in her simplicity. If the Herrnhuthers were right in their notions, the world would have been laid out in squares and angles and right lines, and everything would have been white, and black, and snuff-color, as they have been clipped by these merciless retrenchers of beauty and enjoyment. . . . May they be blessed here and hereafter! but in the meantime, preserve me from their heaven upon earth. I know nothing more dismal, more quenching to heart and mind, than this sterile, monotonous simplicity.[101]

More appealing to Irving was Wallenstein's castle at Friedland where he was able to indulge himself again in romantic speculations and sentimental hero-worship. For it was not merely the military fame of the great general, but a familiarity with Schiller's drama of that name and the recollection of reading and discussing it at the Fosters that aroused his enthusiasm. He recalled hearing of Emily's visit on an earlier occasion and communicated his reveries to Mrs. Foster:

> We have ransacked the castle of Wallenstein, and I have seen his sword, and a drum with his name on it, and his portrait. . . . I have been to the spot from which I presume Emily took her sketch of the castle. . . . I would have given any thing at the time to have heard her in her own delightful way talk about Schiller's play and the scenes she preferred.[102]

The medieval aspect of old castles and historical reminiscences soon yielded to the magic of the landscape and the general expectation of discovering new treasures of German folklore. In November, 1822, while at Prague Irving had glimpsed "the snowy tops of the *Riesengebirge* or Giant Mountains away to the N.E.—between thirty and forty miles distant,"[103] the home of the Rübezahl legends which he had read in England while preparing *The Sketch Book.* He had not forgotten this attractive region, abounding in goblins and supernatural creatures, which he had been forced to forgo. Irving entered the province of Silesia via Reichenberg and soon reached the gateway to the Riesengebirge. At Hirschberg, where he spent a night, a Whitsuntide celebration gave Irving a glimpse of a typical folk festival with "the sharpshooters bringing home the king" in the manner of the opening scene of Weber's *Freischütz.*[104] It is uncertain whether Irving received the stimulus for this trip from Dresden friends who would naturally find the Silesian mountains an excellent and convenient goal for their summer excursions, or whether he had determined much earlier to visit the home of Rübezahl, if ever a favorable opportunity arose. Quite early in his German travels, while visiting Heidelberg, Irving had "made the acquaintance of a young Silesian prince," who may have directed his attention to this region at a time when Irving was particularly eager to replenish his stock of legends and folk tales. He may also have heard of Silesia even earlier through the writings of his countryman, John Quincy Adams, who had made a three-month tour of this region in the summer of 1800, while serving as Minister to Prussia, and had published his observations in a Philadelphia magazine.[105] Unfortunately, Irving, despite passing "through most beautiful scenery," was somewhat disappointed: "The mountains do not equal my expectations, but that is the case with everything in this world of which we have heard a good deal beforehand."[106] Bad weather and a temporary indisposition, which appears to have been a painful facial neuralgia, prevented any real exploration. Unable to enjoy the mountains because he was deterred "from venturing to the snowy summits, or lingering long among the uncertain valleys" Irving pushed on as quickly as possible.[107] He saw nothing of Silesia and was impressed only by the wretched roads and ancient post horses en route to Prague. From Schmiedeberg via Landeshut to Königgrätz, where Irving thought the landlord resembled the legendary figure of "Rübezahl," and on to Chlumetz and Prague the weary travelers hurried, without much regard for scenery or local customs. They reached the Bohemian capital late at night on May 27.

Tormented by physical discomforts and still trying to regain his equilibrium after suffering "painful vicissitudes of feeling,"[108] Irving found little satisfaction in these travels. Everything was conspiring against him. Hardly had his own health improved when Lieutenant Cockburn was taken seriously ill with scarlet fever, three days after their arrival in Prague, and Irving was forced to remain there about a month in order to nurse him through his illness. The disappointment was all the greater because Cockburn had proved himself an ideal traveling companion. Irving had been delighted not only with his artistic proclivities and his ability to re-create historic scenes or to explain military operations while passing over ancient battlefields,[109] but also with his fun-loving exuberance. At Königgrätz Cockburn had registered Irving with the police as an American Colonel so that military honors were shown them when leaving the city.[110]

Irving utilized this enforced stay at Prague to carry on an extended correspondence with the Fosters, to write or revise his adaptation of *Der Freischütz,* and to attend the daily performance of the theatre, a pastime that always delighted him.[111] A little sight-seeing and the frequent military and religious processions which had to pass below his window in order to assemble opposite the hotel relieved the monotony of his confinement. Vexed and weary after too much society in Dresden, Irving took pleasure in exploring the Bohemian capital and was delighted with its picturesque streets and its martial spirit. He became a little critical of Dresden, a modern and yet "commonplace town," and praised Prague as having "more of a continental look," a city that "still keeps up its warrior look, and swaggers about with its rusty corslet and helm, though both sadly battered,"[112] as he wrote Mrs. Foster.

On June 24, Irving and Cockburn eagerly resumed their journey homeward in company with the Pigotts, an English family of their Dresden circle whom they had accidentally met in Prague. They spent a night at Teplitz, the fashionable watering place where Dresden society regularly sojourned each summer, and where Dr. Montucci awaited Irving to discuss details of the contemplated English edition of *The Sketch Book* to be published in Dresden, and the following evening the travelers arrived home. Irving resumed his residence at the Hôtel de Saxe, but about two weeks later, he left Dresden permanently.

The discovery and publication of *The Journal of Emily Foster* provided significant corroboration of what had previously been only surmised: that Washington Irving tarried much longer in Dresden than he had planned because he fell in love with Emily Foster. To be sure, G. S. Hellman had expressed this opinion and had gone even further. He claimed to have found conclusive evidence of Irving's unsuccessful proposal of marriage to Emily Foster. He bluntly accused Irving's nephew and biographer of suppressing crucial passages in the manuscript notebooks and of "an unwarranted tampering with the text, occasioned by the desire of continuing a romantic tradition" of a life-long devotion to the memory of Matilda Hoffman.[113] Minor inaccuracies and the extravagance of some of his claims weakened his argument, however.[114]

Yet Hellman only revived a controversy that had had a brief moment of publicity sixty years before. Within a few years of Irving's death, his nephew and official biographer, Pierre M. Irving, who was publishing *The Life and Letters of Washington Irving* (1862–1864), was startled and angered by an interpolation in the British edition of his work which gave rise to rumors of Irving's love affair. Emily Foster's sister Flora (Mrs. Dawson) had furnished the English publisher, Richard Bentley, with material drawn from the Fosters' Dresden diaries. This material was inserted at the end of the third volume without the knowledge of the biographer. Pierre Irving's annoyance is all the more understandable because the content of these selections conflicted sharply with his own official version of Irving's friendship with the Fosters. This appended material, never carefully proofread and full of mistakes and typographical errors, was subsequently placed "before the American reader, not as a matter of choice, but of necessity" at the end of the fourth volume.[115] It included extensive extracts from Irving's letters to Mrs. Foster that support the theory of Irving's hopeless love for Emily Foster. It included, besides the general intimations of Irving's devotion and tenderness, some very specific factual details, like Flora Foster Dawson's categorical entry:

> He has written. He has confessed to my mother, as to a true and dear friend, his love for E[mily], and his conviction of its utter hopelessness. He feels himself unable to combat it. He thinks he must try, by absence, to bring more peace to his mind. Yet he cannot bear to give up our friendship—an intercourse become so dear to him, and so necessary to his daily happiness. Poor Irving![116]

Neither Emily Foster Fuller nor Flora Foster Dawson permitted herself to be drawn into any controversy, and they ignored the official biographer's indignant protests. His restrained denials found support in the broader interpretation of the known facts of Irving's deep affection and friendship for the entire Foster family. Privately, Pierre Irving admitted being "exceedingly incensed at their most indelicate, unseemly & impertinent irruption into the English edition" and even accused the ladies of mercenary motives.[117] The absurdity of such a claim reveals the intensity of his bitterness, despite the fact that he had enjoyed their co-operation while collecting Irving's letters in the preparation of the biography. It seems reasonable to assume that Mrs. Dawson and her sister had resented the nephew's deliberate effort to minimize and even to ignore what they considered the most important episode in Irving's Dresden residence and had supplied the English publisher with some factual details from their diaries to balance the picture. The immediate reaction to the somewhat sensational disclosure of Irving's unrequited love for Emily Foster was one of incredulity. The tendency was to ignore these details or to regard them as the vagaries of an elderly matron drawing upon the forty-year-old fancies of a highly impressionable girl!

Later editions of the biography omitted the Foster material. The incident was gradually forgotten and the official version of Irving's life-long devotion to the memory of his beloved Matilda Hoffman became firmly established. Such a romantic legend was cherished in the sentimental decades after Irving's death and seemed characteristic of the shy, sensitive, and tender-hearted writer who epitomized the genteel tradition in American letters. The publication of Irving's *Journals* reopened the question. Their editor, G. S. Hellman, demolished the traditional view, and more recently research has made new material available—even the personal diary of Emily Foster! S. T. Williams in his definitive biography reviewed the entire controversy with scholarly concern and acknowledged the likelihood of Irving's attachment.[118] The importance for our study of such an emotional experience lies primarily in furnishing a reasonable explanation for Irving's inability to work, the complete paralysis of his literary production in the very atmosphere of German romanticism from which he had previously drawn inspiration, and yet his unwillingness to leave Dresden. Emily Foster's diary reveals little new information, but provides an adequate check on her sister's volubility and is in substantial agreement with the factual details recorded by both Irving and Flora Foster. Only the latter was likely to betray what might otherwise have remained a secret. Irving never entrusted to his *Journals* his own emotional experiences or even his personal reflections, and Emily Foster at some later date successfully deleted and obliterated extensive passages that offended her in maturer years. But a reading between the lines in Irving's and Emily's own records, combined with additional testimony of their contemporaries, supports Flora Foster Dawson's contention that Irving was in love with Emily, contemplated marriage, and discussed his hopes with her mother. Obviously it was not a matter of love at first sight, neither was it a violent passion or a momentary infatuation. Washington Irving was almost forty years old when he was introduced to the Fosters in Dresden and had led an independent bachelor's existence. At his age he could not be the impetuous and importunate lover whose affection expressed itself extravagantly like the fiery ardor of Allegri, the exuberant admiration of Gumppenberg, or the flirtatious advances of Airey.

At the outset it was clearly the genial personality of Mrs. Foster, her good-natured charm and gracious hospitality, that attracted Irving. Amelia Morgan Foster was a mature woman with intellectual interests that paralleled his own. She was familiar with his writings, showed genuine interest in his literary plans, had traveled widely in Europe, and was a fine linguist. In time she came to supervise his Italian reading. More important, however, was her sympathetic understanding, her good humor. Almost immediately there sprang up between them a feeling of cordiality and esteem that gave Irving the comfort and solace his sensitive nature constantly sought. Her own experiences as the mother of a large family, including children of her husband's previous marriage, had given her wisdom, tolerance, and a capacity for sincere friendship. She shrewdly recognized Irving's limitations, his appalling feeling of insecurity, his lack of faith in himself, and his hunger for constant praise. Tactfully she encouraged him to unburden himself, to speak freely of his dreams and aspirations, until he gradually forgot himself in the happy atmosphere of their domestic circle. Slowly Irving became aware of a new magnet that drew him toward the Foster household. Emily, the older of the two girls, vivacious, impulsive, and witty as well as beautiful, had begun to fascinate him. He willingly participated in amateur theatricals and eagerly sacrificed his time to play the role of lover or husband opposite her. He forgot the serious purpose that had brought him to Dresden. Perhaps he began to relive a situation of his younger years when his deep affection for Matilda Hoffman grew out of a real friendship with her entire family. With the Hoffmans it had been the two sisters Ann and Matilda, with the Fosters, Emily and Flora (though Emily was the older sister), and in each case the charm and friendly hospitality of the mother had first established the friendship and had momentarily even eclipsed the appeal of the younger generation. Mrs. Hoffman, her husband's second wife, had been almost of an age with Irving. And nearly twenty years later Mrs. Foster was also approximately his own age. Emily was eighteen, a year older than Matilda had been when she died in 1809. Her pathetic death had dashed Irving's youthful hopes and had profoundly affected his sensitive nature; her memory was constantly with him. Tributes to her occur frequently in his writings[119] and the reverence of his feelings gradually apotheosized her.

The frankest confession of emotions hidden deep in his heart, revealing the secret springs and unconscious motivation of his adult life, was made to Mrs. Foster at the end of his Dresden sojourn. This "Manuscript Fragment" of an autobiographical sketch relates not only the sorrows and disappointments of his life, but suggests in its incomplete final paragraph a picture of the restless, unhappy, and despairing lover who is already rationalizing the refusal that seemed inevitable:

> You wonder why I am not married. I have shewn you why I was not long since—when I had sufficiently recovered from that loss [death of Matilda], I became involved in ruin. It was not for a man broken down in the world to drag down any woman to his paltry circumstances, and I was too proud to tolerate the idea of ever mending my circumstances by matrimony. My time has now gone by; and I have growing claims upon my thoughts, and upon my means slender & precarious as they are. I feel as if I had already a family to think & provide for, and such are some of the dark shadows that obtrude themselves upon my brightest moments, haunt me in places where I ought to be full of enjoyment, and suddenly check me in the midst of my vivacity. I am too apt to be absorbed [by] the delights of intimate & social intercourse and to lose all thought and relish for those pursuits on which I depend, and which require complete abstraction & devotion of the mind. And then I am seized with compunction at my selfish indulgence, I reccollect how much good I could & ought to do for others, and that while I am idly amusing myself, the useful purposes of life are neglected. You want to know some of the *fancies*

that distress me; I will mention one as a specimen of many others. I was one evening going to a Ball at the Countess de Hohenthals. I had not slept well the night before & after dressing myself I lay down on the sopha & fell asleep. I dreamt of my poor Brother whom I had lost about eighteen months before, & whom I had not seen for years. We walked & talked together. The dream was most vivid and consistent & affecting. When I went to the Ball I was engaged to dance, I think with both Emily & Flora, I tried to dance but could not; my heart sank at the very sound of the music and I had to give up the attempt & go home. Do you want some of the *real* causes. While at Dresden I had repeated[120]

The missing final page of this manuscript might have given the answer to much of our speculation, but it is irretrievably lost. That Irving permitted the Fosters to share such confessional secrets, however, clearly substantiates his affectionate devotion to these English friends. He, whose reticence about personal matters is everywhere apparent, must have felt a kinship that approached family ties to put into writing what had been locked in his heart. Irving characterized his unusual communication in these words: "I have now talked to you on subjects that I recur to with excessive pain, and on which I am apt to be silent, for there is little gained by the confiding of grievances. It only overclouds other minds without brightening ones own."[121] Flora Foster Dawson observed acutely and correctly when she wrote:

> He has long wished us to know every detail of his first affection, but it has been too painful a theme to him ever to dwell on long. Still the desire was strong within him to communicate all to the friends he loved so well. And though others could hardly have torn from his lips one word on the subject, he felt as if it would be some consolation to past, and perhaps to present sorrows, to lay before us the history of his first love.
>
> It [the manuscript] was left with us under a sacred promise that it should be returned to him; that no copy should be taken; and that no other eyes but ours should ever rest upon it. The promise was faithfully kept, though great was the temptation to keep this history of his early love. Nothing he has ever written was so beautiful, so touching.
>
> There were from sixteen to twenty pages, touching on many incidents of his youth, which led him into that deep and intense attachment which was returned to his heart's desire by that sweet girl. Their

> first, their last interview, all was there; even some faint description of his broken-hearted loneliness when that sweet dream was over.[122]

Checking such recollections of the "Manuscript Fragment" against the document itself attests to the depth of the impression this reading made upon Flora Foster Dawson and further substantiates her claim as a creditable witness. Moreover, Irving's correspondence with Mrs. Foster during his deliberate absence from Dresden supports the theory of his unrequited love for Emily. Here—not in his *Journals*—are the most informative details about his feelings and moods. These letters are a part "of the new matter so unwarrantably obtruded at the end of the third volume of the English edition," against which the nephew expostulated even as he reprinted it at the end of the official biography.[123] Flora Foster Dawson does not exaggerate when she says:

> Some of his letters on this journey are before the public; and in the agitation and eagerness he there described, on receiving and opening letters from us, and the tenderness in his replies—the longing to be once more in the little Pavilion, to which we had moved in the beginning of the summer—the letters (though carefully guarded by the delicacy of her who entrusted them to the editor, and alone retained among many more calculated to lay bare his true feelings), even fragmentary as they are, point out the truth.[124]

Away from Dresden Irving's thoughts were constantly with his friends, reliving past happiness and participating in his imagination in their daily routine. He made known his loneliness in a letter to Mrs. Foster:

> You talk of my coming back—I am ashamed to say it, but I am almost wishing myself back already. I ought to be off like your birds, but I feel I shall not be able to keep clear of the cage. God bless you all! I wish I liked you all only half as much as I do. . . . The evening is now coming on. You are all seated, I suppose, in the little Pavilion. I shall lie down on the sofa, and drive away this pain by picturing you all at your occupations, and recalling the many evenings of home-felt enjoyment I have passed among you. They were the sweetest moments that I have passed in Dresden, though I fear I often trespassed on the patience of others. . . . Still those were sweet moments, for they made me know and prize you all. I would not give up one such evening for all the fashionable parties we were at together. Perhaps there is some selfishness in this. I felt of some consequence in those little domestic scenes; but when we entered the great maze of fashion, I was like the poor duck in the Grossen Garten, and was fain to draw

off to a corner. But I always liked such domestic scenes and full-flowing conversations the best.[125]

During his travels he wrote almost daily and recorded seven letters from Mrs. Foster during his stay at Prague.[126] He reacted more like an impetuous lover than a family friend. "I was so impatient to read it [the letter] that I would not wait till I got to my lodgings which are distant from the post office; yet I would not read it in the bustle and confusion of the street. I tried to get admitted to Wallenstein's garden. It was closed; so I scrambled up to the grassy ramparts and read it in quiet, with old Prague and the Moldau at my feet. I have since read it over half a dozen times; for, whenever I read it, it seems to bring me among you all again."[127] Irving was restless, disgruntled, and unhappy. "I am tired of being among strangers," he wrote to Mrs. Foster; "it seems to me at times as if I am the least fitted being for this wandering life, into which chance and circumstance have thrown me: I have strong domestic feelings and inclinations, and feel sometimes quite dreary and desolate when they get uppermost. The excitement of variety and gay society soon subsides with me and leaves a sad vacancy, and I feel as if I could exclaim in the words of Schiller: 'Das Herz ist gestorben, die Welt ist leer.' "[128] He also had moments in which he berated himself bitterly for his idleness and self-imposed unhappiness: "When I consider how I have trifled with my time, suffered painful vicissitudes of feeling, which for a time damaged both mind and body—when I consider all this, I reproach myself that I did not listen to the first impulse of my mind, and abandon Dresden long since. And yet I think of returning! Why should I come back to Dresden? The very inclination that draws me thither should furnish reasons for my staying away."[129]

In these few sentences Irving betrayed rather definitely the cause of his restlessness: the emotional entanglement that paralyzed his literary activity and yet held him fast. His mind recognized the dilemma, but his heart would not let him go. He needed the calm, kindly advice of Mrs. Foster. His letters, of which we have only extracts in most cases, became daily confessions. He was "quite spiritless and listless," his "mind has been in a restless state of strife and indecision, and has sunk into almost apathy, from its exhaustion."[130] In utter despair he cried out: "I have fifty plans of what I ought to do, and only one of what I should really like to do."[131] The explanation often suggested for his depressed state, that it was a consequence of his inability to write, is untenable in the light of the tortured passages and references cited above. Such an explanation would confuse cause and effect. He was upset and despondent and therefore could not write. To Mrs. Foster he wrote from Prague: "You charge me with tormenting myself almost into a nervous fever, because I cannot write. Do you really think me so anxious about literary reputation, or so nervous about the fleeting popularity of a day? I have not been able to write, it is true, because I have been harassed in mind."[132]

How deeply his feelings were stirred can only be surmised, but his emotional involvement had reached a point that demanded clarification and resolution. Mrs. Foster suggested a brief separation, as with a discerning and solicitous eye, she had recognized the difficulty of the situation (Irving had spoken to her of his love, but Emily felt only admiration and friendship). "My mother counselled him, I believe, for the best, and he left Dresden on an expedition of several weeks," wrote Flora Foster Dawson[133] concerning the excursion into Silesia. Such an absence could serve a double purpose: on the one hand, it was to let Emily evaluate her feelings more accurately and perhaps welcome Irving back with an ardor not previously felt; on the other, it could provide Irving with sufficient time to adjust himself and to accept the Fosters' sincere affection on a permanent basis of loyal friendship. Irving's devotion to Emily had not escaped notice. Gossip about the attractive American author and the vivacious young British girl fascinated Dresden society, but it vexed Emily. Aware of such rumors she had finally noted in her *Journal:* "that report that I am to marry 'certo signor autore'—begins to annoy me—Kleist joking about it . . . I was quite angry."[134] Further proof that this romance was by no means a figment of Flora's sentimental imagination is found in a published article in the literary supplement of the *Abendzeitung* by the ubiquitous Karl August Böttiger. The statement that "later [in Irving's Dresden visit] his feelings and his time were even more taken up by very tender relations"[135] makes it perfectly clear that Irving's friends and acquaintances were fully aware of his affection for Emily. Hence there was talk, but little surprise at Irving's departure. What had seemed to some observers precipitous flight from disappointment in love became an interlude that steadied Irving's feelings and brought him back to Dresden convinced that another episode in his life had ended and that he must proceed to Paris to commence writing. Upon his reappearance at "Court, held by the princes and the King—was very kindly received by them all—they had heard I did not mean to come back to Dresden,"[136] Irving resumed his accustomed routine and gave no indication of any changed status. He recorded how on his return to Dresden on June 26 he arrived at his hotel around eight o'clock in the evening and proceeded at once to "arrange dress and call on Fosters—find Emily alone seated in dusk in salon. The rest of the family came in—pass the ev'g till 12 o'clock."[137] Such a laconic entry is typical for Irving and reveals nothing of the pleasure or embarrassment that such a tête-à-tête may have given him. Emily was much franker and acknowledged both surprise and delight at the unexpected visit, but her pleasure is clearly within the conventional bounds of greeting a welcome friend: "I had just returned from a grey twilight walk, & was sitting in the dusk when some one rushed in, I was delighted before I quite recognised Irving's voice it was him, a pair of handsome moustachios had puzzled me I was so pleased & startled I could not speak only gasp."[138]

Once Irving had returned from the excursion to the Riesengebirge and to Prague nothing further was said. The issue was settled. The final farewell was put off as long as possible, but aside from the natural pangs of parting from loyal and devoted friends, there was a finality in his decision. Thenceforth he had only memories and "a thousand recollections . . . of Emily Foster as I had known her at Dresden, young, and fair, and bright, and beautiful."[139]

Evaluating Emily's attitude toward Irving is not too difficult. She had lived for two years in Dresden and had enjoyed the advantages of travel and foreign culture on the continent. Despite her religious zeal and fervor, unusual in so young and attractive a girl, she eagerly participated in the gaiety and mirth of social distractions. Her beauty and ready wit not only made her popular among the young officers of the English colony, but attracted innumerable foreign beaux as well. Her intellectual interests were broad. She had a working knowledge of French, German, and Italian which she put to practical use while keeping her journal. She was writing a novel, sketched in the art galleries of Dresden, and showed a sincere appreciation of music and literature. She was aware of Irving's literary reputation and was naturally flattered to be singled out by him for special attention. She gained real satisfaction from their friendship, but for her it was less than a love affair. At times she was troubled by her inability "to feel more gratitude for I——g's esteem & regard,"[140] and yet she could never find words more tender than "that good dear nice Mr. Irving."[141] When the happy companionship of those Dresden days was beginning to end, Emily was regretful and reproached herself for her indifference. But beyond the wish, shared by her entire family, for Irving's company on the journey to the port of embarkation she was not really affected by their parting. Although he had further correspondence with the Fosters and visited their Bedford and London homes,[142] the secret of Irving's love was well kept. After the author's death Emily maintained a discreet silence and released only sections of his letters that did not violate "the sacred confidence of a friendship," as he had expressed "so strong a desire that his correspondence should be strictly private." However, she paid a fine tribute to his memory and described eloquently what had made him such a welcome guest in their Dresden home:

> Sought after by all in the best society, and mingling much in the gay life of a foreign city, and a court where the royal family were themselves sufficiently intellectual to appreciate genius; but really intimate with ourselves only, and to such a degree that it gives me a right to judge of some points in his character. He was thoroughly a gentleman, not merely externally in manners and look, but to the innermost fibres and core of his heart. Sweet-tempered, gentle, fastidious, sensitive, and gifted with the warmest affections, the most delightful and invariably interesting companion, gay and full of humor, even in spite of occasional fits of melancholy, which he was however seldom subject to when with those he liked—a gift of conversation that flowed like a full river in sunshine, bright, easy, and abundant.[143]

For Irving, the essence of his German experience, the winter and spring of 1822–1823 in Dresden, is symbolized by his unsuccessful love for Emily Foster. Intent upon learning German and reading widely in its romantic literature, which had impressed him so favorably while still in England, he was deflected from his main purpose by the social life of the gay Saxon capital. He did do some reading and studying, but it became perfunctory; it developed almost into an excuse for further opportunities to visit the Fosters. With them he read German, French, and Italian, as well as some English books, or joined in literary conversations, the telling of ghost stories, or the playing of parlor games. He became resigned that Emily cherished only respect and admiration for him and accepted his fate without protest. Philosophically and tersely he summarized his own plight in the following epigram: "Love cooled down into fr[ie]ndsh[i]p, which is Love retired on half pay."[144] However serious his affection for Emily may have been, the entire family, particularly Mrs. Foster, was dear to his heart. Hence he could return to a solid foundation of friendship with the happy domestic circle. "Perhaps," as S. T. Williams conjectured, "the proposal to Emily was a confused expression of Irving's wish to make enduring the happiness he had known in Mrs. Foster's home."[145]

The two weeks that Irving spent in Dresden after his excursion into Silesia passed quickly and followed the general pattern of his entire visit. Outwardly nothing was changed. He continued to dine with the Fosters or to accompany them on their drives into the scenic surroundings of Dresden; daily they met in society. The time for official farewells was approaching and Irving made numerous calls upon those members of the diplomatic corps who were still in town in midsummer. He had agreed to leave Dresden with the Fosters, who were returning to England, and to accompany them at least part of the way before returning to Paris. This trip completed Irving's travels in Germany and acquainted him with another picturesque region, previously unknown to him, that abounded in historical and legendary lore. Nowhere in his travels has Irving shown greater interest in the folk tales of a region than in the Harz mountains, as his detailed notations concerning German scenes and legends indicate. Perhaps it was the growing familiarity with the country and its people which aroused greater enthusiasm, perhaps it was the stimulus of his charming travel companions, whose knowledge of German stories and anecdotes was surpassed only by their eagerness to share them, or perhaps it was a final and almost desperate effort to fill his notebook with innumerable suggestions for his "German Sketch Book," to make amends for his having frittered away valuable months.

The day before their departure was spent quietly in preparations for travel. Irving packed his trunks, bought a new hat, visited with Cockburn, and finally "took leave of Rumignys and Pigotts and sat some time with the Fosters—Mr. Werry and Livius there—last ev'g in Dresden."[146] The prosaic details, the matter-of-fact entries, the laconic "last ev'g in Dresden" suggest only the bustle of last-minute preparations. After all, the final parting had been put off again. The morning of July 12 another farewell or two were said, and with many a handshake and tearful good-bye from their friends who had gathered to bid them Godspeed, the travelers set out. Colonel Livius and a small escort of friends on horseback made their departure quite impressive.

Irving rode with Mrs. Foster and her two daughters in one carriage, the "three philosophers," as he had dubbed Emily's little brothers and their German tutor, followed in another. "Washington Irving was full of spirits. He sang songs with 'Emily'—a new accomplishment, or an old one new revived, which he had kept back for occasions like the present."[147] The route led along the Elbe to Meissen and then westward to Leipzig where they stopped overnight at the Hotel de Hamburg. In the morning they viewed the city and Irving listened eagerly to the guide's personal anecodotes of Napoleon and viewed with interest the scene of the "Battle of the Nations." With his companions he visited Auerbachs Keller where "Mephistopheles & Faust made wine come out of the table (vide Goethe Faust)," but where Irving ordered lemonade. In the evening they attended the opera and were delighted with the singing of Mme Weissermann in *Die schöne Müllerin*.[148]

The next day they made their way into the Harz, a picturesque region rich in folklore, with which Irving's earliest reading in Musäus and Büsching had made him familiar. Now he refreshed his knowledge of these legends "recorded by Musaeus, whose work in many volumes was our evening study, when stopping for the night. It was in German, but Mr. Irving would get us to translate it to him."[149] He noted that "the Saale is a haunted stream—the hexe or water witches haunt it. As we rode Mrs. Foster read several stories of hexe out of German."[150] Ruined castles and romantic mountain tops along the way stimulated their curiosity and soon the Brocken, famous for its witches' sabbath, appeared in the distance. They passed through Harzgerode, stopped at Alexisbad, and viewed the Rosstrappe, a huge granite rock at Thale, and the Teufelsmauer nearby. Everywhere were visible reminders of the wilful behavior of supernatural creatures, and there was at least one legend for every landmark. A visit to the old castle at Blankenburg, reputedly containing the portrait of the celebrated "White Lady" or *Ahnfrau* haunting the castle, absorbed the travelers and appealed particularly to the Foster girls, whose accounts reveal their delight in romantic legend.[151] Irving, on the other hand, who noted primarily factual details of his travels and put off expanding his notes until the time of literary composition, merely recorded: "Picture of the Weisse Frau who haunts this castle as well as several others of the same family—a good-looking smiling old lady in long waist—white silk gown &c gold watch by her side—little black dog with her—fine view from the castle to Quedlinburgh—in fine weather to Magdeburg—Devils Mauer —Rosstrapp, &c."[152]

And so they traveled through Thuringia, delighted with the scenery and especially interested in the Kyffhäuser Mountain, the legendary abode of the "Sleeping Emperor." Irving, having used the same legend as basis for "Rip Van Winkle," no doubt rejoiced to see for himself this famous mountain that had in a sense contributed to the establishment of his literary reputation. A few days later, after touching Nordhausen, Bleicherode, and Heiligenstadt, the travelers left the Harz and entered the fertile Hessian valleys. At Kassel they stayed an extra day in order to see the picture galleries, the pheasant preserves, and the Wilhelmshöhe, "a beautiful seat of the Electors about a league from town."[153] This red sandstone castle, built at the end of the eighteenth century, with its expansive park full of grottos, temples, imposing statuary, elaborate cascades, and a high fountain, has remained an imposing landmark to the present day. In the evening Irving saw his last theatrical performance in Germany, an excellent presentation of Winter's opera, *Das unterbrochene Opferfest*. Without any further delays the travelers moved on. Time was growing short. Traveling all night, they came to Waldeck, crossed into Westphalia, and stopped only long enough for meals along the way until they reached Düsseldorf on the afternoon of July 26. The following day they were in Holland.

In Kassel, where their common travel route was to end, Irving, having planned to take the trip up the Rhine toward his final goal of Paris, weakened again. Three nights and two days were spent there, "days of delay . . . before parting, and the parting that was no parting" as Flora expressed it cryptically.[154] Once more there were long evenings of intimate companionship and sociability that Irving loved. He recorded in three successive entries: "Interesting evg E. very gentle & amiable," "pass the evening in our appartment chatting," "remained chatting and reading ms. to ladies till near 12 o'clock."[155] And to his brother he wrote, "we remained a couple of days to repose from the fatigues of traveling, and to have a little pleasant time together before we parted, as I had intended making the best of my way for Paris from that place."[156] The wrench which the final separation meant for him was postponed once more and Emily rejoiced that "good Irving has given up the Rhine to go with us to Rotterdam," after she had recorded the previous day: "I suppose Irving goes tomorrow."[157] But it was a short respite. Five days later they were in Rotterdam and the farewells could be postponed no longer. The last evening was a melancholy one. They sorted out the accumulation of "boxes, umbrellas, and all the small paraphernalia" that had collected in the two carriages and "sat around, looking silently upon one another." These comments and the more detailed description of Irving, "like a man expected to be his own executioner,"[158] from Flora's loquacious pen might be treated as girlish exaggeration of a romantic situation if other records were not available. However, in this situation more than anywhere else, Emily Foster betrayed the true state of her feelings in her own *Journal:*

> July 30—Wednesday. After bathing we were hurried pêle mêle into the steam packet—Mr. Irving accompanied us down the river quite into the sea, when he was put down into the boat, as he looked up to us, so pale & melancholy I thought I never felt a more painful moment, such starts of regret, a little self-reproach & feelings too quick to analyse.[159]

When she and her sister published their recollections in the British edition of Pierre M. Irving's biography, Emily altered her comments slightly, and this alteration is significant. After relating in almost identical words how Irving was sent ashore in a little boat, she proceeded: "I shall never, however long I may live, forget his last farewell, as he looked up to us, so pale and melancholy. It was a very painful moment to us all. We have not often felt so grieved at parting with a dear friend."[160] Forty years had passed since that parting and the memories of it had not faded. On the contrary Emily was still profoundly aware of that "painful moment" which had impressed itself indelibly. But her final account has shifted the emphasis from a deep personal awareness of the true situation to a general regret expressed in terms of her family. What were these "starts of regret," these "feelings too quick to analyse"? Emily avoided explanatory details, but the implications are clear. At this moment of the final farewell, as Irving no doubt looked crestfallen and unhappy, she felt "a little self-reproach." Emily was not a shallow, flirtatious coquette who had delighted in a long series of conquests in Dresden, who was flattered and gratified by the attentions of a distinguished man of letters. She was young and gay, perhaps a little capricious, but deeply sincere in her feelings. Away from the distractions of Dresden, alone with her family and Irving, she suddenly felt some misgivings. Perhaps she had encouraged Irving unwittingly, perhaps she was not even fully aware of her own feelings. Of only one thing she was sure: She had caused Irving pain and unhappiness. For that she was sorry, and she felt such an upsurge of emotions, such a confusion of feelings that she suppressed their analysis.

Irving's abridgment of informative details is psychologically even more interesting and revealing. His noncommittal entry, "Wednesday 30 went down to the Brille on steam boat to see Mrs Foster & family off—Breakfast on board—in two hours we arrive at the Brille—go ashore in Custom House officers boat with some other persons & the Agent—Steamboat goes off finely,"[161] is unbelievably naïve. His complete silence speaks eloquently. He forced himself to say absolutely nothing in order not to betray his feelings. To his brother he wrote more frankly, " . . . [I] bade them adieu as if I had been taking leave of my own family; for they had been for nearly eight months past more like relatives than friends to me."[162] After all it had been only the month before that he wrote those anguished letters to Mrs. Foster from Prague. For the rest of his life Dresden remained synonymous with the Fosters, and he sounded the keynote of those memories in his unhappy outcry: "Dresden, Dresden, with what a mixture of pain, pleasure, fondness, and impatience I look back upon it."[163]

Glancing back briefly over Irving's sojourn in Germany and examining his itinerary in retrospect, it becomes increasingly clear that the year spent in travel after leaving England in the summer of 1822 was not an unprofitable one. Irving's ardent desire to familiarize himself with a country whose language and literature had been highly recommended to him by Sir Walter Scott and whose legends had already left their imprint on some of the best parts of *The Sketch Book* was finally realized. He had explored the most colorful as well as the most important sections of Germany and was now intimately acquainted with their history and folklore.

From a tourist's standpoint he could be well satisfied: he had seen the varied landscape the country could offer, he had been received in Dresden as the representative man of American letters, and he had accumulated a vast amount of casual information, such as he might need in his literary workshop. He had watched the vivid scenes of court balls and social distractions, he had partaken of the dramatic and musical activities of Dresden romanticism, and he had heard tantalizing bits of literary gossip across the tea tables or at dancing parties. It was time to assimilate the character and the literature of the German people (a task in which he was to be less successful than in the case of another foreign culture a few years later in Spain). He was ready for a period of creative work and was looking forward to re-establishing residence in his beloved Paris, sheltered from the fatigue of cosmopolitan society, but within easy reach of a few intimate friends of former days.

4

German Studies

BEFORE PROCEEDING TO AN examination of the positive results of Irving's use of German materials, his achievements in the study of the language and literature had best be examined. He had never had great faith in the printed word and preferred personal contacts to literary acquaintance. He welcomed every opportunity to advance personal friendships among those he met abroad. Friends, he felt, gave him greater satisfaction and more accurate impressions than he could gain from mere study. When examining the problem of acquiring a knowledge of the German language and its literature, no greater contrast is possible than to compare Irving's procedure with that of John Quincy Adams. Adams, while United States Minister at the Prussian Court in Berlin between 1798 and 1801, determined to study German and recorded his progress meticulously. His diaries in those years show the serious purpose with which he read and studied, and yet he felt he progressed so slowly that after a year he almost despaired: "I study between two and three hours at least every day and make scarcely any progress."[1] Adams was not easygoing; he made such demands upon himself that he was never fully satisfied with his accomplishments. Depite the fact that he came to know German fluently, writing a keenly analytical study from his travel observations in Silesia, and translating a literary masterpiece—Wieland's popular epic poem *Oberon*—accurately and poetically into English, he summarized his achievements after a year's intensive study pessimistically: "I have learnt in the course of the year something more of the German language, which I can read with tolerable facility and I have sufficiently ascertained that I never shall speak it."[2] What a difference in attitude between this modest claim and Irving's glib estimate of his leisurely attempt to acquire familiarity with the foreign tongue so that he might make his way into German literature! Irving had left England with high hopes and the belief that he could already "read and splutter a little."[3] The following spring he informed his correspondents that he was "fighting his way into the German language,"[4] with which he was "getting very familiar."[5]

Irving had always looked enviously upon those who could speak foreign languages, though he naively supposed their acquisition to be a simple matter. He was interested in languages for their practical value and expressed himself enthusiastically on the subject:

> I am surprised my father has never had me instructed in the modern languages. They are all-important. What is the use of Latin and Greek? No one speaks them; but here, the moment I make my appearance in the world, a little girl slaps Italian in my face. However, thank Heaven, a language is easily learned. The moment I return home I'll set about studying Italian; and to prevent future surprise, I will study Spanish and German at the same time. . . .[6]

Irving lacked the foundation of a classical education which would have given him the basis for language learning. Moreover, he did not pursue his studies too seriously. Despite the aid of the two tutors in Dresden to whom he paid eighty-four dollars for about two hundred hours of drill, he never learned to express himself fluently in German—though he probably understood much more than he could say. He listened to bits of folklore and local gossip from his tutors instead of making himself practice speaking. He was never forced to use the language as the Court, the Fosters, the members of the Diplomatic Corps, in fact practically all the people he met, not only knew some English but were eager to use it. Irving's own notations regarding the good English heard among his Dresden German friends indicate his conversational experiences. His use of spoken German was virtually restricted to the limited needs of a traveler ordering his meals and arranging for his lodging. Flora Foster, whose depiction of Irving's hopeless love for Emily may be tinged with adolescent romanticism, but who is a credible witness on the prosaic subject of his knowledge of German, said in her narrative that Irving was not proficient in German, that he could use only a few words, that he had to have the Fosters copy out for him a simple inscription, "after making an ineffectual attempt to translate into English verse its simple pathos."[7] Allowing for Irving's inability to spell correctly, a fact painfully apparent even in his native tongue, his recorded German generally suggests a limited familiarity with declensional endings and other basic characteristics of the language. Usually his notations in German consist of only single words that he acquired and found useful in specific circumstances. Thus he recorded words like *Trinkgeld* (tip), *Landkutscher* (coachman), *Wald* (forest), *Tiergarten* (park), *Jäger* (hunter), *Wirtshaus* (tavern), *Schlafrock* (dressing gown), *Bürgerschaft* (citizenry), *Pfingsten* (Whitsuntide), *Polizei* (police), *Bauer* (peasant), *Kellner* (waiter), *Hausknecht* (porter), or even the phrase *elegant schöne appartments,* in a variety of spellings. Simple words like *schläfrig* (sleepy), *Weisses Ross* (White horse) have the English translations immediately following, and the routine greeting *Guten Morgen* lacks the proper accusative ending.

A few unusual words, unusual at least for a beginner, are recorded and explained in detail. From his tutor Irving learned that the Saxons disliked the Prussians and called them *Windbeutel* (windbags); somewhere else he heard that a man who busies himself in the petty affairs of the family is called a *Topfgucker*. Perhaps his most ambitious effort in this vein is his correct transcription of the phrase *Bei dem hängt der Himmel voller Geigen* with the accompanying explanation "With him the heaven hangs full of fiddles—German saying of a merry fellow who lives joyously."[8] The most curious selection copied in his notebooks is one from Goethe's *Satyros oder der vergötterte Waldteufel* (a highly personal satire of Herder, written in 1773 but not published until 1817), which Goethe characterized in his old age as "a document of the divine impudence of our youth." Under what circumstances Irving's attention was drawn to this dramatic sketch it is impossible to surmise. Placed on a separate page between statistics of the world's population (copied in French from a newspaper) and some notes on coincidences of the battlefield that might serve as story material, is the following extract:

> Speech of a Satyr in Goethes Satyros
> *Arsinoe.* Von was, o Fremdling, lebst du dann?
> *Satyros.* Vom Leben, wie ein andrer Mann.
> Mein ist die ganze weite Welt,
> Ich wohne wo mir's wohl gefällt.
> Ich herrsch' über's Wild und Vogelheer,
> Frücht' auf der Erden und Fisch' im Meer.
> Auch ist auf'm ganzen Erdenstrich
> Nein Mensch so weis' und klug als ich.
> Ich kenn' die kräuter ohne Zahl,

Der Sterne Namen Allzumal,
Und mein Gesang der dringt in's Blut
Wie Weines Geist und Sonnen Glut.[9]

The significance of this laborious notation in a precise hand—so different from Irving's usual illegible calligraphy—is a practical one. It does not matter that he quoted Goethe, but it is the first connected piece of German that he recorded. It was in the nature of an exercise, learning new words and familiarizing himself with German spelling and print. The fact that he even used the umlaut is out of keeping with his routine practice; he watched his text scrupulously, copied as neatly and precisely as he could, indicated every contraction with a meticulously placed apostrophe, but he forgot to capitalize *Kräuter,* and his mistaking the word *Nein* for *Kein* in the middle of the passage clearly indicates his difficulties with German typography.

At the very end of his German residence, on his way to Paris, the Fosters were still translating the stories of Musäus for Irving.[10] Obviously, his familiarity with spoken German was much more limited than his ability to read, but in both respects his knowledge must have seemed elementary and inadequate to the Fosters who were at home in that language as well as in French and Italian.

In the consideration of Irving's acquaintance with German literature, there are many factors that prevent a complete evaluation of his discursive reading: His diary entries are occasionally too vague to establish the precise titles meant, sometimes it is impossible to discover whether Irving read in German or in translation, and often references to certain books are actually meaningless because the volumes he owned were not read—as their uncut pages so eloquently attest. And since only a small number of books published at the time were sold with uncut pages, the assumption that all the other titles actually were read by Irving is obviously unwarranted. On the contrary, Irving's well-known failings, his good intentions but dilatory tendencies support the assumption that many of his books that he purchased because they appealed to him (as indicated by specific notations) remained unread.

While traveling, especially en route to Dresden and during his excursion into Silesia, Irving had little occasion to do much reading. Travel was strenuous and so induced him to find rest early at night in order to be ready to continue his journey at the break of day; also, the facilities of inns or hotels did not encourage reading at night. Hence his bibliographical notations were primarily of collections of legends, fairy tales, and folklore indigenous to the region through which he was passing. The titles of German, Austrian, and Bohemian folk literature are recorded, and Irving came into possession of a volume of Moravian fairy tales, a collection supplementing the compilations of the Brothers Grimm.

To evaluate Washington Irving's interest in German literature it is necessary to consider the literary scene as it appeared in the early nineteenth century and to conjecture how it would impress Irving, conditioned as he was by his British outlook. The Storm and Stress revolt against the shallow Rationalism of the eighteenth century and its subsequent relationship to German Classicism and Romanticism had little meaning for Irving. He had merely been aware of the early enthusiasm of Scott for Goethe and Schiller, and had interested himself in German Romanticism even before his arrival in Dresden.

The first English contacts with German literature had stressed medievalism and sensationalism. Readers had been fascinated by the lugubrious horrors of "Lenore," the sentimental extravagance of *Werther*, and the violent *hubris* of *Die Räuber*. Although the Gothic romance fed the appetite of the general public, the young generation of English Romanticists became enthralled, momentarily at least, by *Sturm und Drang*. In the 1790's Scott "like the rest of the world was taken in with the bombast of Schiller" as he himself characterized his attitude later.[11] Coleridge wrote a sonnet "To the Author of the Robbers" and expostulated: "My God, Southey, who is this Schiller, this convulser of the heart? . . . Why have we ever called Milton sublime?" Southey, Campbell, and Hazlitt concurred in Coleridge's passionate enthusiasm.[12] Gradually, Schiller's early reputation, so firmly established by the revolutionary excesses of *Die Räuber,* yielded to a fuller appreciation of the poet as a philosophical thinker and high priest of German idealism. Mme de Staël had met Schiller in Weimar in 1803 and had been profoundly impressed by him. In her *De L'Allemagne* (1813) she discussed Schiller's dramatic work in its totality with such enthusiasm and perspicacity that she established a new attitude toward German literature and toward Schiller. Ten years later Carlyle's Calvinistic strain appreciated even more fully the sublimity of moral purpose and the visionary transport of Schiller's transcendentalism and set the pattern for his final triumphant apotheosis.

Washington Irving's own enthusiasm for Schiller clearly reflected the contemporary judgment of his age, as advertised by Mme de Staël and Thomas Carlyle. Irving had nothing of the heroic in his own make-up, but compensated for it by hero-worship. His own easygoing amiability, his tendency to sentimentalize, and his predilection for gracious living did not prevent Irving from esteeming those virtues which he lacked. He and his Dresden friends, the Fosters, looked with warm-hearted admiration and worshipful devotion on the traditional concept of Schiller's moral perfection. He bought a German edition of *Die Räuber* in Liverpool, along with other volumes that have reached the archives of Sunnyside, but the uncut pages suggest some of the unfulfilled hopes of Irving's earliest German studies. Most important of all, however, is the first edition of Schiller's *Sämmtliche Werke* (1812–1815) in twelve volumes, eleven of which have survived at Sunnyside. Here, of course, all of Schiller, with the exception of a few translations and the unfinished dramatic sketches, was included. No other German author was so completely available to Irving or was mentioned so frequently in his notations and letters. In writing to his nephew on the relative merits of various literatures, Irving censured the greater part of Italian belles-lettres as immoral and continued:

> As far as I can judge from my own reading, the literatures the most free from licentiousness in morals are the Spanish and the German. The Spanish, because the greater part was written at a time when romantic notions prevailed in Spain of manly honor and female virtue; and the German, because almost all its *belles-lettres* have been produced within the last fifty years under the restraints of modern decency. I don't know any dramatists who have written so much, and whose writings are so free from anything that would call up a blush on the most sensitive cheek, as old Calderon among the Spaniards and Schiller among the Germans, and I do not know any that have shown a freer scope of imagination and finer sallies of language.[13]

Schiller's *Wallenstein,* the poet's most ambitious drama, accessible in an excellent translation by Coleridge after 1800 and still in Irving's possession in 1825,[14] symbolized for him the acme of poetic achievement. Irving had witnessed performances of this drama in January and in February, 1823, and had apparently read and enjoyed some of its more sentimental scenes with Emily Foster. In his melancholy letters from his excursion into Bohemia and Silesia he remembered an appropriate quotation that revealed his wounded heart. He quoted Thekla's plaintive line, "*Das Herz ist gestorben, die Welt ist leer.*"[15] Even in examining Wallenstein's castle at Friedland, he relived some happy moments spent in the contemplation of Schiller's eloquent verse. "I was all in a glow while looking at these things and thought it was with the recollection of this great man; but it was with the recollection of the glowing poetry in which Schiller has embalmed him," wrote Irving and acknowledged that he would "rather have conceived and written that noble poem than have achieved Wallenstein's greatest victory."[16] Irving's limitations and his romantic approach to life often blurred any distinction between sentiment and sentimentality, between sublimity and bombast. The grim violence and brutish ferocity of

Die Räuber terrified and repelled his sensitive, gentle nature, but the reflective idealism of *Wallenstein,* the unswerving loyalty of Max, the unselfish devotion of Thekla, and their tragic fate as the innocent victims of political intrigue and criminal ambition made a profound impression. Here was a theme of renunciation, sacrifice, and ennobling love which enthralled not only the buoyant nineteen-year-old Emily Foster but this middle-aged American writer as well. Nor was this his first experience with Schiller's emotional appeal. On his visit to Paris in 1821 he had noted the vogue of Schiller's *Maria Stuart* and Shakespeare's *Hamlet* and discussed them together as successes that "may be considered one of the triumphs of what is denominated the romantic school."[17] In Prague Irving saw *Fridolin,* an adaptation of Schiller's poem "Der Gang nach dem Eisenhammer" and a sequel *Der Brautschmuck,* both from the pen of the Viennese theatre poet, Franz Holbein. *Fridolin* in a medieval setting became a typical *Ritterschauspiel.* Some months later en route to Holland, Emily Foster, upon seeing some iron foundries "in a most romantic spot" of the Harz mountains, "thought of poor Fridolin at the Eisenhammer" and no doubt discussed Schiller's poem in her own inimitable way with Washington Irving. No other German poet held Irving's attention so long. For two years after his departure from Germany Irving constantly returned to his reading of Schiller. Aside from general references to his German books and his reading in them, many notations in his *Journals* confirm this. Such general entries as "after breakfast read German (Schiller)," "read in Schiller," are supplemented by special references to "read in Schillers 30 years war," "commence Schillers Don Carlos," "read in Don Carlos," and "lie on sofa all day reading Don Carlos."[18] Though English and French translations existed, Irving probably read the *History of the Thirty-Years' War* in the original German, which was in the sixth volume of the set he owned, but *Don Carlos* he most likely read in the English translation of 1798, which he also owned and brought back to America with him.

Though Schiller lacked the intuitive talent and spontaneity of the true poet, qualities which made Goethe the greater genius, the early decades of the nineteenth century judged differently. The living Goethe had to contend with the growing acceptance of the legendary Schiller, the people's poet, whose fragile body and dauntless spirit rose above physical limitations to expound his doctrine of the dignity of man and of the eternal validity of the ideal. Goethe's artistic objectivity and poetic realism, which the world prizes today, went unrecognized and were often thought limitations in an age that loved romantic idealism. Irving apparently shared this feeling and responded more readily to the noble eloquence of Schiller than to the more restrained, sometimes even austere moods of Goethe. The latter, less talented as a dramatist though the greater poet, was performed less frequently than Schiller, and Irving found during his entire German travels only one of Goethe's minor works on the stage. *Jery und Bätely* was "a beautiful little pastoral piece," a German *Singspiel* with a Swiss setting, written in the manner of the popular French operettas; it delighted Irving so much that he returned the following evening for another performance of it.[19] The simple spoken dialogue, the pretty verses set to appealing melodies by the popular composer Reichardt, and the picturesque costuming made this play a box office success, though it hardly served as an adequate introduction to the work of Goethe.

The acceptance of Goethe in England, primarily through the efforts of De Quincey, Carlyle, and others, came too late to influence Irving, who was at best aware only of Scott's and Byron's personal enthusiasm. The real vogue for Goethe, which drew hundreds of English visitors to Weimar, was just beginning, and Irving's friend Livius visited there shortly after they both had left Dresden.[20] Whether he was received by Goethe cannot be established as Goethe often referred to his English guests as a group without listing all names. That Irving, who was normally eager to hear literary gossip or to meet distinguished authors, missed the opportunity to see Goethe is understandable only in the light of his long and unproductive sojourn at Dresden and of his eagerness to accompany the Fosters to Rotterdam. The real importance of Goethe was only vaguely known to Irving, whose primary source of literary information had been the Fosters' drawing room. There and there alone he participated in animated conversation about *Egmont* in which Emily delighted him with her "excellent observations."[21] The popular pastime of representing scenes from literary works—and Irving's own writings were sometimes portrayed—included a tableau of Egmont and Clärchen at Baron Löwenstein's.[22] Again in the drawing room of the Fosters he listened to "Emily reading Faust, etc.," Goethe's masterpiece, which Irving did not acquire until two years later in Paris, but which found its way to the library at Sunnyside.[23] Apparently certain passages were frequently read and quoted in this intimate family circle because forty years later Flora Foster Dawson could still cite from memory —though somewhat inaccurately—the famous lines: Werd' ich zum Augenblicke sagen: Verweile doch! du bist so schön![24] which she wrote at Irving's request into his scrap book. That she substituted "could" for "should" in the first line reflects her memories of Irving's regret at terminating a friendship that had given him such pleasure. Her simplified second line and her error in ascribing the quotation to their favorite drama, Schiller's *Wallenstein,* are not surprising after so long an interval.[25] Irving's interest in *Faust,* aside from his drawing-room enthusiasm engendered by Emily's effusions, increased after he acquired his own copy.

In the Notebook of 1825 (page 105 of the manuscript copy in The New York Public Library) are two brief extracts from Goethe's "Prologue in the Theatre"[26] which apparently struck a sympathetic chord in Irving's nature. They are concerned with man's restless, hopeless search for contentment and contain the poet's impassioned apostrophe to that blissful state, that early happiness and joy of living, which only youth can bestow. As Irving was prone to look regretfully about him, aware of lost opportunities and fleeting time, he felt the full significance of these lines, particularly at this time when he was struggling vainly to write his "German Sketch Book." His Dresden experience had had a sobering effect upon him; he understood the poet's lament for his lost youth.

Probably in Irving's possession at one time was the eight-volume set of Goethe's works published by Göschen in Leipzig in 1787, but only two volumes have survived at Sunnyside. *Götz von Berlichingen* and *Egmont,* both dramas with which Irving was definitely acquainted, are in these volumes, which, however, were not his source, as their pages have never been cut. In Paris Irving read Scott's early translation of *Götz* while struggling with the composition of *Tales of a Traveller.*[27]

In the Saxon capital Irving found that despite the spirited praise of the universality of Goethe's genius and of the idealism of Schiller, German Classicism had been challenged by the theoretical and critical speculations of the "Romantic School." German Romanticism, systematically organized and firmly grounded in romantic philosophy, developed an arrogant and arbitrary subjectivism that made a work of art only an emanation of the individual genius of the creative artist. Tieck, in *William Lovell,* boldly expressed the notion of the unrestrained freedom of the artist: "I myself am the only law." Nowhere but in the imaginative realm of the fairy tale and in the most subjective field of lyrical poetry could German Romanticism achieve permanent values. An abundance of feeling and fancy without the restraint of formalistic endeavor and sustained poetic craftsmanship proved insufficient for the more demanding art forms like the novel or the drama. Only Tieck, who outlived most of his generation and became the representative figure of German Romanticism, combined keen critical perception with genuine poetic talent.

The disastrous political upheaval of the French Revolution and Napoleonic Wars followed by a reactionary era had emphasized the exaggerated individualism and the flight from reality that characterized Romanticism. In the period of exhaustion that followed these conflicts literature lost some of its dignity and lofty purpose. Reading as an escape, as a source of entertainment for a large section of the rising middle class demanded mass production. The era of almanacs, annuals, and magazine literature was beginning and the theatre flourished. Second- and third-rate writers assumed positions of influence and established their own journals and papers to support their positions. Particularly in Dresden at the time of Irving's arrival such a clique dominated the literary scene. The influence of the *Abendzeitung,* edited by Theodor Hell (pseudonym for Winkler) and Friedrich Kind, was rivaled only by the popularity and prestige of Karl A. Böttiger. These, together with A. von Nordstern, C. M. von Weber, Graf von Kalckreuth, Baron von der Malsburg, Karl Förster, and others, met regularly every two weeks to read their literary wares and to receive the unctuous praise of their fellow poets. They came to be known as the *Dresdener Liederkreis,* a literary society that established its authority far beyond the borders of their city and symbolized the *Zeitgeist* of the first decade after the fall of Napoleon. The return of Ludwig Tieck to Dresden in 1819 hardly curbed the literary pretensions of these pseudo-romanticists. Tieck, a member of the German Romantic School whose prose narratives, prestige as a literary critic, and fame for his readings from Shakespearean and Spanish dramas had made him the most distinguished living writer after Goethe, gradually challenged their uncritical self-appraisals. But Irving, who depended on literary gossip and came to know Böttiger, Kalckreuth, and other members of the *Liederkreis* much better than Tieck, was delighted with the literary society of the Dresden salons.

The booklists Irving made in Dresden are naturally the most extensive and the most significant. Here Irving was in a position to investigate recent German publications and to have the advice and guidance that would make book choices meaningful. The longest book list (at the end of the Notebook of January 20 to May 20, 1823, not in the Trent-Hellman edition but in the manuscript) is full of interesting items. The names of Tieck and Jean Paul dominate. Both authors deserved closer study, but Irving could hardly have found the time to read much of their voluminous and rambling narratives. Sometimes the volumes credited to Tieck and Jean Paul were only edited by them, as in the case of Tieck's publication of Ulrich von Lichtenstein's *Frauendienst* or Jean Paul's edition of Dobeneck's posthumous collection of medieval German folklore; but Irving was reading Jean Paul in Dresden in April, 1823,[28] and a little later bought his work in Prague for eleven Gulden.[29] That none of these volumes were brought home to America suggests Irving's bewilderment in trying to read him. Any casual attempt to browse in Jean Paul was doomed to fail.

A few years later, when Carlyle's fine appreciation[30] had analyzed the singular genius of this German writer, English readers first became aware of his work. Had Irving been able to penetrate the maze of Jean Paul's discursive and philosophical fantasies, expressed grotesquely and extravagantly but never tritely or superficially, he might have found a new approach to humorous tales. The universal and transcendental qualities of Jean Paul's humor were rooted in a deep sensibility and human understanding. Jean Paul with his capricious but sincere manner of writing was perhaps the only foreign author who might have turned Irving out of the beaten paths of literature.

Unfortunately Irving lacked the necessary talents for such a development and preferred to sample the popular books of the day, literary sightseer that he was. Content to browse, he listened to the drawing room conversations, recorded such titles as he heard mentioned, and at times sought to familiarize himself with the books themselves. Böttiger, for example, referred to Irving's favorite authors while in Dresden and mentioned particularly his "reading of Goethe and Schiller, attempting Jean Paul and Van der Velde, besides returning to Milton's "L'Allegro" and "Il Penseroso" and Ben Jonson's *Alchemist*."[31] Carl F. Van der Velde, whose historical novels enjoyed a great vogue and often ran in serial form in the Dresden *Abendzeitung* had a special interest for Irving. He was called the "German Scott," in recognition of his talent for utilizing German historical themes for his prolific production of romanticized narratives. The length of his historical novels may have been something of an obstacle for Irving, but at least one volume, *Die Lichtensteiner*, found its way back to America to the Sunnyside library.

Friends like Böttiger, who loved to serve as mentor to distinguished visitors, familiarized Irving with such recent publications as might provide him with background material. Stories, tales, legends, even the exotic "language of flowers" with its Oriental symbolism were jotted down, but relatively few of these ever influenced Irving directly. The popularity of the Dane, Adam Oehlenschläger, whose *Correggio* was a dramatic sensation throughout Europe, also came to Irving's attention. Nor was Irving's interest in German books confined to his Dresden period. He continued his German reading after he reached Paris in August, 1823. As a matter of fact, the evidence points strongly to the likelihood that much of Irving's reading in German took place after his departure from Dresden while preparing to write his *Tales of a Traveller*. In his *Journals* of 1823–25, kept while working in Paris, are constant references to German books that he was reading assiduously. Even as he was turning his full attention to the Spanish language in anticipation of the visit to Madrid that gave new meaning to his life, he continued to read German and to make notations concerning his reading. Perhaps the end of this period is signaled by an entry of March

21, 1825, revealing that he gave a friend his German dictionary and Italian Grammar.[32] After this his active interest in German and Italian lagged though occasional references to German books continue beyond this year into his actual residence in Spain.

A few additional titles showing Irving's preoccupation with German books should be mentioned. Recurring notations of reading "Travels in Germany" are recorded in August, 1824,[33] but the vagueness of this description permits only a surmise as to volumes meant. An examination of English travel literature of this period makes it likely that Irving had procured Thomas Hodgskin's *Travels in the North of Germany* (1820). Not only does Irving's abbreviated title seem adequate to indicate this volume, but Hodgskin's observations after a residence of some length "with the view of acquiring its language, and of gaining some knowledge of its literature,"[34] suggest a kinship of purpose that must have aroused in Irving a desire to check his own impressions against those of a fellow traveler. Moreover, the first volume opened with a detailed chapter on Dresden and Leipzig, and the discussions of literature in it stressed the great popularity of Grillparzer, Oehlenschläger, and Müllner on the stage.[35] Lengthy quotations from Müllner's *Die Schuld* and *König Yngurd* are reproduced and discussed in detail because these dramas were considered representative. Curiously enough Irving brought home to America both of these dramas and copied some ominous lines from the "fate drama" *Die Schuld* into his notebook.

The theatre, Irving's passion from his youth, not only supplemented but stimulated his German reading. Here he made his first literary contact once he had reached German soil. He felt he needed to hear the language, and attendance at the theatre delighted him besides serving this practical purpose. Dramas and operas that he saw early in his visit aroused his interest later for study and even translation. While traveling through Germany he recorded witnessing over fifty performances. Among them were not only outstanding operas, but an abundance of plays, which included the popular successes of the day, German dramas that have become classics, and a number of Shakespearean performances. Weber's operatic success "*Der Freischütz,*" which he saw first in Darmstadt on September 22, 1822, entranced him. He found in it not only lovely music, but the romantic kind of folklore he delighted in using for his own tales. He saw it five times in less than a year, met its composer, and decided to help Barham Livius translate and adapt the text for the London stage.

Shakespearean performances were a special delight for Irving. Though in German, of course, and often poor translations or inadequate adaptations, they at least provided familiar material. He saw *The Merchant of Venice* once, *King Lear* and *Hamlet* each three times. He commented on the style of acting, the costuming, and made contrasts with performances he had seen in New York and London which reveal his intimate acquaintance with the theatre. He never missed a Shakespearean performance and always discussed the accuracy and adequacy of the translation, even though such judgments depended upon superficial impressions. Neither Irving nor anyone else could have evaluated a translation without a careful textual comparison, but his limited German precluded any such possibility. Here, as in other cases, Irving depended on what he had heard in society, but frequently became confused and erred in his notations. He attributed the Dresden *Hamlet* performances to a translation by Schiller when he must have meant A. W. Schlegel, and credited Iffland with Schröder's translation of *King Lear*. He attributed Iffland's comedy *Der Herbsttag* to Lessing. He saw "a drama called *Kätchen of Heilbronn*,"[36] the romantic drama of Kleist, in a popular adaptation for the stage by the playwright and theatre director Franz von Holbein, but was unaware of its author. Kleist at the time was almost unknown and was unappreciated as a great dramatic talent despite Tieck's edition of his plays, published in 1821. A few months later Irving saw an adaptation of Kleist's *Prinz von Homburg* which he attributed to Humboldt and characterized briefly as "pretty—romantic and extravagant."[37] Such errors, and there were many others, are not surprising. Irving had come with no systematic knowledge of German literature, but had a certain familiarity with the names of poets and dramatists that he heard in the literary conversations of Dresden drawing rooms.

Irving's eclectic taste, the problem of availability, and chance meetings left strange notations in his notebooks. Archenholz' *History of the Seven Years' War* yielded a descriptive passage on the valor and appearance of the "Ulans" and a brief item on the "Siege of Breslau by Laudon."[38] A friend brought him a copy of Klopstock's *Messiah*,[39] probably the English translation, as a Christmas gift in Bordeaux in 1825. Perhaps Irving remembered how much this poet had meant to Thomas Campbell during his German residence. Earlier in the same year Irving rejected indignantly an uncritical judgment of "a French gent[leman] who talked enormously—said Germ[an]s had no esprit—knew nothing of their literature."[40]

Even after his arrival in Spain Irving read German on occasion, though his interests were focused on Spanish history and literature. In Madrid, where Irving had arrived on February 15, 1826, he took an apartment in the house of Obadiah Rich, the American Consul, and soon found himself in congenial surroundings.[41] Alexander Hill Everett, a brother of the famous orator, was in charge of the American Legation; his enthusiasm for literature and history had made him something of an author and student. He had suggested in a letter that Irving might translate the monumental work of Navarrete concerning the voyages of Columbus[42] and arranged that he be attached to the American Embassy at Madrid to facilitate such an undertaking. Once more Irving was quickly established in a foreign city and soon came to know many members of the diplomatic circle. He even found that Mr. Könneritz,[43] the Saxon Minister, was an acquaintance of his Dresden days. In fact there were numerous Germans in Spain and Irving's notebooks name many of them, ranging from casual friends in the diplomatic set to the significant literary friendship with Johann Nikolaus Böhl von Faber and his daughter Cecilia, who later became a popular writer under the pen name of Fernán Caballero.[44]

Very important to Irving were the library facilities available to him in his new residence. Mr. Rich had one of the finest private collections of Hispano-Americana in Europe[45] and like a true bibliophile was happy to find another enthusiastic lover of books. Irving set to work translating the historical documents that were to yield *The Life and Voyages of Christopher Columbus,* but he also sought to familiarize himself with the background and history of Spanish literature and frequently used critical works by German scholars to good advantage. Almost immediately notations of his reading begin to appear in his notebook; the names of Bouterwek, Schlegel, and Sarmiento occur most frequently. Whether Irving read the two German sources in the original is perhaps of little significance, since he had to take what the library of Obadiah Rich offered. Bouterwek's *History of Spanish and Portuguese Literature,* published in London in 1823, about twenty years after its original appearance in Göttingen, was probably available in English.[46] On the other hand, Irving made use of Schlegel's *Lectures on Dramatic Art and Literature* in the original—and here and here alone gave real proof of his ability to use German.[47] An unpublished Notebook of 1825 entitled "Spanish Literature" contains six pages in Irving's writing copied and translated from A. W. Schlegel's *Vorlesungen über dramatische Kunst und Literatur,* a series of fifteen lectures on stage and drama delivered before a distinguished audience in Vienna in the spring of 1808 and published the following year. Examining a small section from the Notebook, with its parallel passages of the original, gives convincing evidence that Irving had acquired an ability to translate and, what was most important for him, had learned to read successfully for content.[48] He had acquired a reasonable proficiency in reading German—but too late for the many plans and projects he had made in England for his German tour.

5

The Aspiring Dramatist

After bidding farewell to the Fosters in Rotterdam Irving proceeded to Paris and on August 4, 1823, took lodgings there at the Hôtel de Yorck on the Boulevard Montmartre. He had only the happiest memories of previous visits to the French capital and was returning assured of finding a large circle of old friends. Thomas Moore, who had been his intimate companion previously, was no longer in Paris, but Irving's good friends the Storrows, in whose family he felt as much at home as at his sister's in Birmingham, and numerous French and British acquaintances of former days, who welcomed his return, were there. Most significantly, Irving soon met John Howard Payne, whom he had known in Paris two years earlier and with whom a friendship had begun in those happy New York days when Irving was establishing his literary reputation with the first numbers of *Salmagundi*. Even then Irving had been fascinated by the stage and was an avid theatre-goer. This enthusiasm increased with time until finally he was no longer satisfied in the role of spectator. In Dresden he had become preoccupied with amateur theatricals and finally with translations and adaptations of German materials. Once settled in Paris, his passion for the stage tempted him to become a full-fledged collaborator of Payne. The thirteen months of travel in Germany, particularly the long period of residence in Dresden, had yielded few literary sketches, but Irving had his "mind tolerably well supplied with German localities, manners, characters, etc."[1]

He was still in no mood for creative work. In fact he was sinking to the level of a literary hack in order to earn a living. He had decided to re-write with Payne French pieces for the London stage. Irving characterized this futile venture vaguely and discreetly in a letter to his brother as being "busy on a slight literary job which I hope will put some money in my pocket without costing much time or trouble, or committing my name. When that is done, and the inventing fit comes over me again, I will strike at something else."[2] What, besides Payne's enthusiastic entreaties, had persuaded Irving to feel "more and more that I have dramatic stuff within me"?[3] Neither the social gaiety of Dresden nor the intimate friendship with the Fosters had allowed Irving to forget completely his purpose in coming to Germany. He reproached himself in his letters for "continual procrastination, and too much distraction and dissipation of mind," realizing that he was drifting aimlessly, but he found some consolation in the knowledge of amassing "a great deal of amusing and characteristic information"[4] for future use. His apparent success in preparing private theatricals encouraged unwarranted hopes that made him an easy prey to Colonel Livius' blandishments that he become an adapter of plays. Naively he informed his friend Leslie, "I had no idea of this fund of dramatic talent lurking within me."[5] Irving was easily persuaded to lay aside the writing of tales and sketches in order to win laurels in a more impressive and perhaps more lucrative genre. In January, 1823, he had become "busy with Colonel Livius about the songs and music of the Freischütz."[6]

Barham John Livius had come to Dresden for the purpose of purchasing from Weber the score of *Der Freischütz* and the right to adapt the opera for the London stage.[7] He was an amateur dramatist and composer who visited the continent in search of literary contacts, encouraged by the moderate success of earlier adaptations. London theatres at this time were crowded, and the managers had difficulty in satisfying the demands of a highly enthusiastic but certainly not discriminating audience. Innumerable hack writers attempted to supply this demand, and Livius was one of them. Originality was not required; on the contrary, "theatre writers sought not for a new way of art, but for that which, being familiar, could hardly fail to make an appeal. . . . They wrote plays, as a cobbler makes shoes, for the purpose of bringing in a few pence or a few pounds, and consequently they sought in Paris, not for what was new and vital, but for what was old and sure to please."[8] In such a manner Livius had written the musical comedy *Maid or Wife: or, The Deceiver Deceived* and had composed the music for some of James R. Planché's adaptations[9] before coming to Dresden. There he was fortunate to find Washington Irving and Carl Maria von Weber, both with established reputations.

Foreign opera, particularly the Italian with its recitative, seemed strange and unnatural to the average Englishman. He preferred musical drama with spoken dialogue. Weber's operas followed the pattern of the German *Singspiel* rather than that of the *opera seria,* and readily appealed to a British audience, especially as their stories resembled the plots of the melodramas so popular in the London theatres. The enormous success of Weber's *Der Freischütz* attracted many impresarios to the continent to secure the rights to such a hit.[10] Livius was aware of the opportunity and had no difficulty in arousing Irving's interest in the projected adaptation of it, as Irving, who had become an enthusiastic admirer of Weber's music, had already seen this opera in Darmstadt and Munich, and was to witness it three more times before fall;[11] one of these performances was in Dresden on May 8, 1823, probably with Weber conducting.[12] The legend of the "Wild Huntsman" was not new to Irving. His eager scrutiny of German folklore had yielded references to this theme which he had used in "The Spectre Bridegroom" of *The Sketch Book* and in "Popular Superstitions" of *Bracebridge Hall.*

Throughout the winter and spring of 1823 Irving's notations in the *Journals* reveal how he first served Livius in an advisory capacity, helping him with the lyrics for *Der Freischütz.* Constant meetings, sometimes at the Hôtel de Saxe, later in the country where Livius had rented an apartment, sometimes with Weber present, brought this project at least to a temporary conclusion by April 12.[13] Almost immediately afterward Irving set to work on a translation of Weber's earlier success, *Abu Hassan,* a *Singspiel* in one act with libretto by Franz Karl Hiemer, based on a tale out of the *Thousand and One Nights.* Between April 20 and May 18, 1823, Irving labored almost daily at this task of translation before he finished the "alterations on 'Ab H' " in time to leave for Prague.[14] But Irving was not content to restrict his dramatic writing to such auxiliary efforts in behalf of Colonel Livius. Once his enthusiasm was aroused it could not be satisfied so easily. In Prague, Irving resumed writing "a little at the Freischütz" and continued these efforts in Paris, first intensively and later sporadically, into October, 1824.[15] He set to work independently and for more than a year devoted himself primarily to dramatic writing.

In his ill-fated attempt to succeed in a literary genre absolutely foreign to his talents, Irving was encouraged not only by Livius but by John Howard Payne. Irving collaborated with Payne as he had done with Livius, perhaps even more seriously despite his amateur standing, in order to produce *Charles II, Richelieu, Azendai, Married and Single,* and *The*

Waggoner.[16] Neither these adaptations nor *Der Freischütz* and *Abu Hassan* are of literary significance.

The lasting success of Weber's *Der Freischütz* rests upon his music, but its immediate popularity depended in no small measure upon the libretto, the story of the wild huntsman and his magic bullets. Though Friedrich Kind, author of the text, one of the members of the *Dresdener Liederkreis* and definitely a third-rate author, later claimed the greater credit for the success of this opera, he did not invent the plot; he merely utilized legendary material. A hundred years earlier the basic story had appeared in a publication that specialized in tales of the supernatural and even then it had been retold in various forms.[17] The story of the struggle of an individual who sells his soul to the devil in exchange for supernatural help, embellished with the legend of the magic bullets, caught the popular fancy. *Der Freischütz,* with its supernatural effects, its romantic music including a rollicking huntsmen's chorus and folk melodies against a background of green forests, and its gruesome incantations in a craggy mountain glen, proved irresistible. The opera had achieved its first success with its original performance in Berlin in 1821, and after taking German theatres by storm continued its popularity abroad. London, Paris, and New York succumbed in turn and witnessed successful performances in 1824 and 1825 despite the violence that translators, impresarios, and actors did to text and music. In London alone at least five adaptations and a few parodies are listed by Allardyce Nicoll,[18] and among them is the co-operative effort of Livius and Irving. This particular text, like all the others merely a trifling piece of translation and adaptation, has actually been credited to three writers: to James Robinson Planché, who in his *Recollections* speaks of it as "my version of that opera, produced at Covent Garden, 14th October, 1824,"[19] to Barham Livius, who published it over his name with appropriate acknowledgments for help received,[20] and to Washington Irving, for whom Hellman claimed it in its entirety.[21]

A comparison of the Irving text of *Der Freischütz,* as printed by Hellman in 1924 from the original manuscript, with that published by Livius exactly a hundred years earlier suggests some practical explanations for the minor differences encountered. How much of the translation and adaptation should be attributed to one or the other of these amateur dramatists is impossible to say. Livius and Irving worked together in Dresden and Paris. They conferred and consulted, they wrote and recast their text frequently, as Irving's notations in his journals indicate. Even after the "Preface" to the London edition was dated "Paris, 10th October, 1824" Irving "call[ed] on Livius—correct[ed] 'Freischütz,' "[22] and continued a procedure that had begun more than a year before. It was a fair partnership and yet an inadequate one. Livius, because of his longer residence in Germany and a probable smattering of German since childhood,[23] was the better-trained translator, but Irving's literary experience promised greater poetic values and stylistic niceties. Livius was more familiar with music, he had written a successful musical comedy and had composed incidental music for some of Planché's adaptations. Neither, however, had much practical knowledge of the theatre or—what was even more essential—had the friendly ear of London managers.

Irving was not willing to risk his reputation as a man of letters by submitting his *Freischütz* under his own name. He first had Livius submit the corrected copy to Kemble and wished Payne in London to inquire "what he feels disposed to do in the matter."[24] Payne had been having enough trouble with his own theatrical pieces, in which Irving was also something of a silent partner, and had met with one rebuff after another in trying to sell *Azendai* and *Richelieu.* Irving, comfortably settled in Paris, tried to bolster Payne's waning spirits with resolute advice: "I don't care which theatre takes Azendai—nor do I care much if either of them takes it—I beg you will let it be understood I ask nothing as a favor, and by no means advise their accepting a piece, as extending a kind of patronage. I feel perfectly independent of the theatre."[25] The success in the spring of 1823 of Payne's operetta *Clari* with its immortal "Home, Sweet Home," which has alone saved his name from oblivion, provided a brief respite in his long and almost uninterrupted struggle to dispose of his plays and to conceal his identity from his creditors.

As long as Livius and Payne negotiated with the theatrical managers Irving was risking nothing and could still hope for sudden fame as a playwright, but by the end of the year the situation had changed. Payne had finally sold *Charles II* and *Richelieu* to the Covent Garden Theatre for two hundred guineas, but what was that sum in comparison to the fifteen hundred guineas that Murray would pay for a volume of tales?[26] Irving began to outline the projected volume of tales, and though in no mood for writing he forced himself to complete the task. He tried to turn his back on playwriting and withdrew from his partnerships with Payne and Livius. To both he continued to give his blessings and advice but also strictest instructions about preserving his anonymity. His letters to Payne speak plainly:

> [Dec. 17, 1823]—do not suffer yourself to be discouraged—and do not on any account suffer yourself to get on ill terms with the managers. Deal with them always cooly & good-humouredly—it is the most dignified, the most advantageous and the most comfortable way. Exert your own discretion as to the disposition of the pieces. I shall

> be satisfied with any bargain you may make; recollect only, that I do not wish my name, on any account, to appear in connexion with them. It would be quite injurious to my present plans. Should Azendai *not be already accepted* and in *train for performance* I wish you to withdraw it definitely. It cannot I fear be represented without my name leaking out as the author. Should it however be in hands & committed beyond recovery, enjoin secrecy on Mr. Kemble in regard to my name. . . .
>
> Do not give yourself any trouble about Abu Hassan & the Freyschütz. You have enough already to occupy you, & it would be only time and trouble thrown away. . . .
>
> [Dec. 29, 1823]—just now I do not on any account wish my name to appear in connexion with any of the pieces. As to Richelieu & Rochester let them appear in your own name and to save your conscience say that they have been revised and occasionally touched up by a literary friend. . . .
>
> [Jan. 31, 1824] I am sorry to say I cannot afford to write any more for the theatres. The experiment has satisfied me that I never should in any wise be compensated for my time and trouble. I speak not with any reference to my talents; but to the market price my productions will command in other departments of literature. If, however, the experiment should produce any material benefit to you I shall feel highly satisfied at having made it. . . .
>
> My long interval of travelling, and the time expended in these dramatic experiments have thrown me quite behindhand, both as to pecuniary and literary affairs: & I am now applying myself to make up for it, but I shall run low in purse before I can get a work ready for publication.[27]

While Payne was trying to place some of Irving's adaptations, Livius was not idle. Before he left Dresden he had prevailed upon Baron Ernst Friedrich von der Malsburg, Hessian chargé d'affaires, a member of Irving's circle of friends and an enthusiastic lover of literature, to translate *Maid or Wife* for the German stage and had actually persuaded Weber to direct it. Though Malsburg, a minor poet who had skillfully translated Calderón and Lope de Vega, achieved a favorable review in the influential Dresden *Abendzeitung*, the play was recognized as trivial, and only two performances were given.[28] Livius continued to ask for other German pieces that Friedrich Kind was preparing and shrewdly used as bait a "*pressing* invitation from the manager of one of the principal London Theatres to look out for & send him *pieces* of this nature."[29] Yet in the same letter he had only moderate encouragement for Weber:

Everything remains *in doubt & uncertainty* respecting the two operas of our honourd & highly gifted friend Weber—it would seem that the London managers are sadly afraid that the music is *too good* for the depraved taste of the frequenters of their houses—& there is really some truth in their notion—for a theatrical audience of the present day in London is far from being composed of people of education & taste— However, as M. Kemble has written to me in the most kind & flattering way respecting the piece which I sent him, founded on the Freyshüts, and expressed *an anxious wish "to venture it"*—I am very much inclind to think that he will prevail on his Colleagues in office to bring it out about Easter next (the time when the best part of the society of London are more in the habit of going to the play). —I understand however from my friend Irving that at *Drury Lane* a piece on the same subject is forthcoming in the shape of a *Melodrama* a la maniere Francaise. "*Abu Hassan*"—not having been deemed "*strong enough*" (to employ the technical term of the Theatre), for one of the *great Houses* and the smaller theatres in London *being very ill mounted for operas*—I have determined to *lay it by* till the *new projected opera house* is established (in which I have embarked myself a considerable property) & where it will be done that justice to which the works of this divine master of Harmony merit.

I pray you my dear & respected Sir, to take an opportunity (at your earliest convenience) to assure M. Weber, of my regrets at not being able yet to give him an account of the *appearance* of his charming operas—and at the same time to reimbourse him for the manuscripts he had the goodness to supply me with—with respect to the *two operas*—I shall consider myself in his debt still further—whenever they appear before the public—[30]

While in England in the summer of 1824 Irving witnessed on July 26, a "wretched translation, badly played" of *Der Freischütz* at the English Opera House.[31] Although Payne had failed to place the opera with Kemble, Livius finally received some assurance from him that their *Freischütz* would be played "early next season,"[32] that is, in the fall of 1824. And so a whole year elapsed before the Livius-Irving version was performed at the Theatre Royal Covent Garden on October 14, 1824. By that time three other adaptations of the opera had been given in London, adaptations that maltreated the libretto as well as the music, until they became travesties of Weber's work. Yet the opera's popularity was so great that even a burlesqued *Freischütz* appeared at the Olympic Theatre,[33] and Kemble agreed to risk this fourth production. He had no cause to regret his decision, as fifty-two performances were given[34] and the published text went into the second edition within a year. The prefatory remarks, offered to the public in the printed version, also "worked over"[35] by Irving, deserve close examination as they shed further light upon this curious collaboration:

> The following Opera was prepared for the English stage during the author's residence in Germany two years since, and was accepted for immediate representation by the manager of Covent Garden Theatre, in the month of February last; had it not, therefore, been for unexpected and unavoidable delays, he would have had the satisfaction of being the first to introduce into England this chef d'oeuvre of musical art.
>
> Various objections having been taken against the German drama, especially with reference to poetical justice, and to the moral, the author of this Opera has been induced to vary considerably from the original.
>
> In justification of the liberties he has taken, it may be observed, without referring to various other defects, that the hero of the German author is represented as of a feeble undecided character; half saint, half sinner; he is easily prevailed on to employ foul means to accomplish his purpose, and is timid only as to the process of procuring those means; he tampers with the devil in a sort of half-and-half manner, as if he would sell half his soul and retain the other half to be saved upon. In the last act, he appears in the light of a condemned culprit; and although by an act of ill-merited grace, he is permitted to hope for the hand of his mistress, after a year's probation, yet the audience are left in doubt whether, though he gain his wife, he has not lost his soul, and they go away quite at a loss to determine whether he be ultimately to be saved or damned; or, indeed, whether he be worthy of either.
>
> Attempt has been made in the present Opera, to obviate this glaring defect, so far at least as was possible, in writing a drama under the trammels of music already composed. It has been endeavoured to describe the hero of the piece inflexible in virtue—firm in resisting temptation, and spurning all base and sinister means of obtaining success; his confidence in Providence remains unshaken, and his steadfastness and constancy meet with their merited reward.
>
> To carry on the supernatural part of the story, another character has been introduced, whose dissolute habits render him a fitter victim of seduction: he is taken in a moment of riot and revelry, and falls an easy dupe to the flattery and artifice of the tempter.

To the character of the hunter, who is in league with the evil spirit, it has been attempted to give somewhat of a more wild and poetic tone of colouring, as better suited to a being who is supposed to hold converse with the invisible world, and who is familiar with supernatural agencies.

A veil of uncertainty has been thrown over the evil power invoked and he appears shrouded in the fanciful and picturesque superstition of '*the Wild Huntsman*', that favourite hero of the forest legends of Germany. This has been thought preferable to making him stalk plain Devil about the stage, as he does in most of the German theatres, prying through doors and windows, and popping his head out of brakes and bushes, like peeping Tom of Coventry.

The author of the following pages is far from flattering himself, that he has succeeded in constructing a good drama out of the meagre materials with which the German opera furnished him; he trusts, however, that he has remedied some of the most glaring defects of the original piece, which appeared to him, a worthless Drama, embalmed in immortal Music.

To preserve entire and uninjured the delicate and beautiful structure of that music, has been the object of the author's chief attention and anxiety. It is the distinguishing characteristic of the composer of the Freyschüts, that he marries sound to sense. Unlike the production of the *modern* school of Italy, the music of this great master is always in beautiful keeping with the general character of the subject to which it is applied: each particular sentiment finds the tones to which it is allied; every particular word its appropriate note. The difficulty of adapting words to music—such music especially under the changes which have been instituted in this piece, may readily be conceived; the Author therefore trusts, that the liberal critic, appreciating the arduous nature of the task, will regard his labours with indulgence.

For whatever of poetic merit this opera may possess, the author is beholden to his friend, Mr. Planché, whose lyric and dramatic labours have so often met their merited meed of public applause, and to whose zealous and well-directed efforts, the stage is indebted for important improvements in the representation of the historical drama. While acknowledging the assistance he has received in preparing this work for the English stage, the author indulges himself in the opportunity of stating the obligation he is under to another friend, whose name, were he permitted, it would be his pride and his pleasure to declare, for various valuable hints and emendations.[36]

Livius' praise of Planché's assistance can only be interpreted as deliberate attempt to flatter an established author and impresario whose influence had already proved invaluable to him. Livius had been dependent upon Planché's good will earlier in his career, and it is not at all unlikely that Kemble made his acceptance of the opera contingent upon Planché's participation in the final revision of the text. Livius' triumph was limited. Only the published text carried his name, whereas the handbills at the theatre attributed the work to Planché and mentioned Livius only as arranging the music. In his *Recollections* Planché took full credit for this work, barely mentioned Livius in a footnote as "an amateur author and composer, who arranged the music of *Der Freischütz* for my version of that opera,"[37] and apparently resented Livius' claim to authorship. He sent him a "very conceited, ungentlemanlike letter . . . about 'Freischütz'," so that Irving deemed it advisable to intercede for Livius with the publisher and "wrote a letter to Miller in his behalf."[38] But no sympathy should be wasted on Livius, who was also guilty of double-dealing. He had failed to transmit Kemble's payments for the *Freischütz* to Weber and had written the unsuspecting composer "an extraordinary, vile, confidential letter."[39] Only Irving's integrity remained untarnished. Fearful that the adaptation might damage his literary reputation, he gladly allowed his dramatic apprenticeship to go without public recognition and relinquished to Livius all credit for their joint efforts.

From a comparison of the published texts it is apparent that Irving and Livius had agreed on changes in the German libretto to make the plot more palatable to British audiences. The differences between Irving's and Livius' versions are no doubt the result of the drastic revision demanded by the theatre and effected by the more experienced, practical dramatist and impresario, Planché. Irving had not been so much concerned with those portions of the opera that were to be sung. Professor Kirby, who noted the insufficiency of the lyrical portion of Irving's libretto, identified the original musical numbers and the interpolations, probably from Livius' pen, that completed the adaptation, and made the logical inference "that Irving was chiefly concerned with the play and only incidentally with the music."[40] But Irving, to whom Livius expressed his obligations in the veiled allusion "to another friend," must share what praise or blame falls upon this version. Operatic plots are generally flimsy, if not absurd, and the *Freischütz* is no exception. Livius and Irving knew the taste of the London public: Strong melodrama, an abundance of action and dialogue marking hero and villain clearly, a denouement compatible with British faith in justice and fair play which makes ultimate reward or punishment inevitable, and melodious music were the necessary ingredients for English operatic success. And so Irving and Livius agreed fully upon definite changes in the plot. By adding and renaming characters in order to free the hero from the reproach of soliciting the help of the devil, the adapters diluted still further the slight action and dramatic conflict of the libretto. This made room for popular high-sounding phrases and self-righteous moralizing. When Albert, the hero, is approached at the end of the first act by Caspar in league with Satan, who is in the guise of the Wild Huntsman, the following dialogue ensues:

Albert (*much moved*): But is this being you speak of good or evil?

Caspar: Pah! Is this a time to stand on squeamish points? The happiness, the life of her who *loves thee,* hangs upon the moment. An earthly paradise—a certainty of present bliss is offered to thee. Seize it and trust not to the uncertain future. So thou art happy, think not of the means. Good spirit or bad, what is it to thee, so that the gift be good? For good is good whether from heaven or hell.

Albert (*starting at the last word*): No gift is good that comes from evil power. Nor can that power be good that walks in darkness. I wake as from a dream. How for a moment have I been beguiled, and laps'd in thought from the strict path of honour! Away! Away! I spurn thy proffered services. All magic means, if such there be, I scorn. On heaven and honest skill I rest my hopes, nor seek by juggling arts to cozen fortune.

Caspar: Poor feeble-hearted wretch! —I thought thou hadst more nerve and spirit. But thou art e'en a canting, virtuous driveller, fit only for the common rabble that I scorn. Henceforth I leave thee to thy fortune. But mark me, Sir (*walks close up to him*)—I've talk'd to you in confidence, because I wished to serve you. I have foolishly opened my soul to you. Betray me, if you have the heart to do so; but recollect you must at the same time have the hand to answer for it.

Albert: Away! Away! Thy offer and thy threats are equally contemptible. To heaven I leave thee—I do naught but scorn and pity thee. (*Exit Caspar.*) Thank heaven, he's gone! The very air seemed tainted by his presence. I blush to think that for a moment I should have listened to his temptings. What were success, gained by unworthy means? Nay, what were Bertha's self, won by base acts? How could I e'er have borne

> her angel look? Her heavenly purity had been a ceaseless torment to me. Now can I clasp her to an honest heart and in her virtuous love find heaven on earth. —But are there powers like this he talks of—that move unseen around us and control our fate? Away with anxious doubts and gloomy fears! If there are powers of darkness to befriend bad men, sure there are spirits of light that guard the virtuous. In such I put my trust to bear me through my trial.[41]

This extended quotation from Irving's manuscript version of *Der Freischütz* is perhaps the worst writing found in any of his pieces. Though Livius is equally responsible, phraseology and stylistic characteristics clearly mark the text as Irving's, even to the mawkish sentimentality and exaggerated moralizing.

Der Freischütz was epoch-making in the historical development of the opera and secured the acceptance of German romantic music after the long domination of Italian operatic style. In England it established the name and fame of Carl Maria von Weber. And Barham Livius attained the high point of his literary career with this adaptation of *Der Freischütz,* which associates his name—as well as Irving's—with Weber's triumph in London. The critic of the London *Times,* who was apparently familiar with the German original, commented upon the technical skill of the presentation, with its weird incantation scene, the effective lightning and thunder, and the awesome dragons and bats with flashing eyes. He also noted the numerous changes and complications wrought in the plot before summarizing his —on the whole, quite favorable—impressions.

> These variations tend to very little, either good or ill, because the drama, in all its shapes, is a dull one. The necessity of having a gentleman for his lover who shall sing, obliges the author to make two heroes where he had business only for one . . . It is the music only, of course, under these circumstances, with the scenery and machinery, that have been the strong objects of attractions; and a great deal in both these features is admirably given as the piece is given at Covent-Garden. . . . Upon the whole, the piece is worth sitting out, almost for the sake of the overture; and besides the overture, there is a great deal worth hearing and seeing, too, to be found in it. . . . In fine, the piece might have been more strongly cast, and probably it would have been, if the manager had possessed stronger performers to put into it; as it is, however, there is a great deal of merit about it; and it was received with applause, by a house thronged from the pit to the very ceiling.[42]

The second of Irving's attempts at translation from the German is *Abu Hassan,* Weber's earlier operatic success, first performed in Munich in 1811. The libretto by Hiemer was based on "The Story of Abu-L-Hasan the Wag, or the Sleeper Awakened," a popular tale of the "Arabian Nights Entertainments";[43] Abu Hassan, who had become the boon companion and favorite of the Caliph, decides to play a trick on his master and to fatten his purse in the process. Impoverished and debt-ridden by his extravagant habits, Abu Hassan and his wife Fatima, who is the favorite of Zobeide, the Caliph's wife, alternately feign death in order to receive financial assistance in their supposed bereavements. There is a secondary plot in which his creditors, under the leadership of one Omar, harass Abu Hassan's domestic tranquillity. Omar's amorous advances are slyly encouraged by Fatima, who hides him in a chest from her returning husband and effects a cancellation of their debts. This operatic trifle, a *Singspiel* in one act, consisting in its final form of an overture and ten musical numbers, naturally appealed to Livius and Irving as suitable for adaptation. Its music was gay, the lines humorous and exuberantly frivolous. All it needed was additional dialogue to fill out a performance.

Irving's manuscript published by Hellman in 1924[44] was the only recorded text of his second collaboration with Livius until Professor Kirby discovered in Paris the loose sheets of a copy of Weber's score purchased by Livius from the composer in 1823.[45] Written into the music are the words of Livius' version, which is by no means identical with Irving's. Professor Kirby concludes that Livius' indebtedness to Irving has been over stressed and "that not only was he capable of turning out a workmanlike translation of his own, but that he was superior to Irving when it came to fitting suitable words to music."[46] This may be correct, but it must be remembered that Irving was not concerned with the music and interested himself only in rendering the German text into English. Yet even so, one must admit that the verses are often awkward and sometimes ludicrous. Such howlers as "And with her purple lip/ Shall first Fatima sip" or "Thou art done over/ Should he thee find," are not at all unusual. Fatima's aria (number 5 in the operatic text) is perhaps a fair example of Irving's translation:

The nightingale ne'er grieves her
When from her cage set free
Once more among the blossoms
She sports from tree to tree.

One glance towards the window
Where her late prison hangs,

Then loud she pours her rapture
And fills the grove with joy.

She flaps her little pinions
And far aloft doth soar
Through heav'n's unclouded regions,
Glad to be free once more.

But, Abu Hassan, without thee
No pleasure have I ever;
Thou dearest, thou inspirest me;
From thee I'd never sever.

I feel myself most blest and free
When in thy gentle power,
And in this tender slavery
I'd spend my latest hour.[47]

Wird Philomele trauern,
Dem Käfig kaum entschlüpft,
Wenn sie im Duft der Rosen
Von Zweig zu Zweigen hüpft?
Scheu blickt sie nach dem Fenster,
Nach dem verhassten Haus,
Und strömt dann ihre Freude
In Dankgesängen aus,
Und hebt die kleinen Flügel,
Und schwimmet nun auf's Neu'
I'm wolkenlosen Aether,
Und jauchzt und fühlt sich frei.

Doch, Abu Hassan, ohne dich
Was wäre mir das Leben!

Du Trauter nur beseligst mich,
Nur du kannst mich erheben.

Ich fühle mich beglückt und frei
In deinen sanften Ketten;
Aus dieser süssen Sklaverei
Soll nur der Tod mich retten.[48]

The fate of *Abu Hassan* was discouraging. Even while Irving was writing to Payne somewhat confidently: "I wish *Abu Hassan* to be offered to Elliston [manager of Drury Lane] by Miller [bookseller who eventually published *Der Freischütz* for Livius], as from Livius,"[49] Payne was already relaying discouraging tidings from London. A new vogue had struck the stage and equestrian feats were all the rage. Planché with his *Cortez, or the Conquest of Mexico* had scored a hit with the novelty of cavalry entering in full gallop.[50] In consternation Payne wrote to Irving: "Nothing answers now but the horses. I could not speak of terms at a first interview . . . and they have no room for Abul Hassan this season, unless, as some one observed, horses could be put in it! ! ! !"[51]

A month later Irving became depressed and felt convinced of the futility of his dramatic writing. He released Payne from the difficult commission of placing his German pieces with a London manager and was content to give a free hand to Livius, who continued to revise their work and even attempted to adapt it for the French theatre.[52] Their version of *Abu Hassan* was never performed, but it was probably the basis of a similar production given at Drury Lane on April 4, 1825, credited to William Dimond.[53] The management of the theatre, requiring a full-length production to fill out an evening and recognizing the inadequacies of the Irving-Livius libretto, called in professional hack writers. William Dimond quickly expanded the text, Tom Cooke incorporated the bulk of Weber's incidental music for *Preciosa,* added a large chorus and a *corps de ballet* for good measure, and within six weeks a new production was written, rehearsed, and performed.[54]

Still Irving could not free himself from the spell of the stage. Because of serious misgivings he had felt concerning his contemplated "German Work," he occupied himself with literary trifles, but even after he had completed his task of writing the *Tales of a Traveller,* he continued to toy with operatic plots, dramatic adaptations, and even original dramas. Hardly more than two weeks after resolutely forswearing further writing for the theatre in a letter to Payne,[55] he received the pamphlet story of Weber's *Euryanthe* from Livius, and upon returning from London, where he had completed his manuscript and had seen his *Tales of a Traveller* through the press, he once more became occupied with operatic adaptations.

With Livius he discussed *The Magic Flute, The Marriage of Figaro,* and *Il Bondicani.*[56] Soon he was helping to write and revise a text for Livius' translation of *Leocadie,* which was performed as *Leocadea* at Drury Lane on December 17, 1825, with its musical arrangement credited to Livius.[57] Irving had witnessed the first performance of this drama by

Scribe and Mélesville with music by Auber at the Opéra Comique and had been greatly impressed.[58] Soon he was helping Payne also[59] and finally struck out for himself with a "plan for dramatic work on story of 'El Embozado'."[60] This story of the dual nature of man came to Irving's attention during his Spanish studies, and he sketched a detailed outline of the contemplated scenes at the end of his diary for 1825.[61] At the same time he was altering *Richelieu* for Payne and listening with apparent pleasure to a suggestion of Charles Kemble's that he "write a play." Though Irving "declined for the present,"[62] it was the sort of siren song he longed to hear. With renewed zeal he busied himself with *Richelieu,* changing or retouching various parts and even completely altering one of the characters before sending it back to Payne in London.[63] He promptly "conceived plan of play 'Cavalier'—noted down a hint or two—sketched a little at the first act—,"[64] but soon experienced the usual difficulties in such a sustained effort. Constantly revising and rewriting, he never reached the second act. He forced himself to write at the play with little satisfaction,[65] until he finally gave it up. It was already December, 1825, when Irving sent Payne for the third and last time a parcel containing *Richelieu.*[66] Two months later he wrote to Payne, "I am on the wing for Madrid!"[67] The beginnings of Irving's Spanish adventure marked the end of his dramatic endeavors.

6

The Tales of a Traveller

I.

While Irving was envisioning stage successes that would make him financially independent and could add to his literary reputation, John Murray, his London publisher, began to inquire about the long expected German volumes. He tactfully wondered what a "publisher may be allowed to expect from you in the course of the winter. I am perfectly ready for you, and the sooner you take the field the better."[1] Murray, shrewd and formidable in dealing with his authors, saw no reason for delaying the publication of this popular American writer whose vogue in England promised an immediate financial success. Whatever misgivings he may have had about Irving's literary future after having published *Bracebridge Hall,* he recognized Irving's popularity and was eager to exploit it. But Irving had been idle too long and found it difficult to concentrate on writing his German sketches. The distractions of Paris—the theatres and the boulevards, the constant invitations of old friends, the visits, dinners, and excursions—encroached upon his time. Moreover, a recurrence of his cutaneous complaints and of the painful swellings in his ankles forced him to resume tedious medication. Such physical indisposition aggravated the fits of depression to which Irving was subject throughout his life, and which were unusually severe at this time. Whether his creative talents were paralyzed by such moods of despair or whether his inability to write engendered the hopeless feelings of despondency must be a matter of opinion.

Modest and sensitive by nature, he recognized the limitations of his talents. He dreaded the spectre of literary failure. As a man of letters whose reputation had spread throughout Europe until his works appeared in French and German translations almost as soon as they were published in England and America, he had much to lose by any ill-starred venture. The assurance and enthusiasm with which Irving had anticipated the exploitation of "the rich mine of German literature"[2] were gone. His journals contain innumerable episodes, folk tales, and legends gleaned from his travels as raw material for later use, but when actual composition was to begin Irving had serious misgivings. In a letter to his brother he said:

> It will take me a little time to get hold of them [the German subjects] properly, as I must read a little and digest the plan and nature of them in my mind. There are such quantities of these legendary and romantic tales now littering from the press both in England and Germany, that one must take care not to fall into the commonplace of the day. Scott's manner must likewise be widely avoided. In short, I must strike out some way of my own, suited to my own way of thinking and writing.[3]

Irving's judgment here was sound. The extravagant and grotesque romances that had ushered in a vogue for German tales now wearied British readers. Literary fashions were changing and Irving was acutely aware of it. He felt, therefore, that he had to write of Germany in his own way, looking romantically at the landscape and recounting humorously yet accurately such details of tradition and folklore as would touch the hearts of his readers without offending their minds. But could he write with enough sincerity and affection of a land that he knew only superficially? Was he not likely to fall into tedious bookishness, so apparent even in the parts of *The Sketch Book* where he had depended upon libraries for his material? Or was there not a danger of slipping into a platitudinous sentimentality that would substitute feeling for thought? Irving was not unaware of his own weaknesses. An indolent and undisciplined routine had become a habit; he was accustomed to await propitious moods for his writing and felt incapable of working under pressure. But readers were eager and his publisher impatient. So, from August, 1823, until the following summer, when *Tales of a Traveller* finally appeared, Irving suffered from periods of intense anxiety and evil forebodings about his literary future. Notations like the following express Irving's despair and bewilderment:

> woke at 4 oclock this morn[in]g—with a strange horror on my mind —a dread of future evil—of failure in future literary attempts—a dismal foreboding that I could not drive off by any effort of reason[4] . . . tried to commence work on Germany but could not do anything—look over papers & try to write on Germany—but the spirit does not move[5]
>
> restless and anxious—full of doubts as to literary prospect— After breakfast tried to summon up ideas to write but in vain—[6]
>
> feel intolerably triste—cannot bring myself to write on my work—tho near 6 weeks have elapsed without writing[7]

He found some consolation in hearing from Captain Medwin that Byron "writes at fits—has intervals when he cannot write sometimes 2 & 3 weeks."[8] In the meantime Irving continued to read at random, often in German and generally about German scenes. Perhaps nothing aroused him so much as the terse message from Murray which made Irving dig out the manuscript of his fragmentary novel of Buckthorne, still called the "History of an Author," which had originally been intended for *Bracebridge Hall,* but was put aside at Leslie's suggestion "as the groundwork of a novel."[9] Irving had carried the manuscript with him in his travels through Germany, had written at it a little in Dresden, and now considered making it the *pièce de résistance* of the projected volume.

Unfortunately, Irving had no clear-cut plan to follow and waited anxiously for ideas. His notebooks show the constant fumbling and uncertain groping that set his nerves on edge. He vacillated between a plan that consisted of descriptive essays of Germany (he began writing a "sketch of Heidelberg Castle"[10] that never reached completion) and a sudden thought of "how to enlarge the Mss. on hand so as to make 2 vols of Sketch Book,"[11] only eventually to dismiss both plans. He wrote laboriously at the Dutch story of "Wolfert Webber," finished some of the "Strange Stories by a Nervous Gentleman," and decided not to complete the "History of an Author" but to break it into parts and to include them in the forthcoming book. Still he needed more stories to fill out the two volumes. Early in February he confessed to his friend Leslie what he kept from his publisher:

> The time that has elapsed without my either publishing or writing, obliges me to make the most of what I have in hand and can soonest turn to account. I have a few other articles sketched out, of minor

> importance. If I could only get myself into a brisk writing mood, I could soon furnish the materials for two volumes, and if these were well received and paid well, I should then have leisure and means to pursue the literary plans I have in view. But I am at this moment in a sad heartless mood, and nothing seems to present to rouse me out of it.[12]

But by March 25, 1824, Irving saw the answer to his dilemma. He changed his plans again and decided to be satisfied with a loosely hung collection of sketches, tales, and miscellaneous narratives, which he offered to Murray for fifteen hundred guineas. Probably as eager to convince himself as his publisher he wrote with emphasis:

> I do not regret having turned aside from my idea of preparing two more volumes of the Sketch Book, as I think I have run into a plan and thrown off writings which will be more novel and attractive. I have the materials for two volumes nearly prepared, but there will yet be a little re-writing and filling up necessary. I hope, however, to lay this work before you in the course of six weeks. I think the title will be Tales of a Traveller, by Geoffrey Crayon, Gent.[13]

Murray did not quibble about the royalties to be paid but "agreed to the terms . . . in the most prompt and handsome manner"[14] and began to advertise the approaching publication of *Tales of a Traveller*. Such advance notice was intended as a spur to Irving's faltering efforts but actually contributed to the anxiety with which the author sought additional material to round out his manuscript. The entire composition of the various sections of the two volumes was a laborious process for Irving; the results of his general complaints of an inability to work and of a restless anxiety concerning his literary sterility are seen in the detailed notations of actual time taken to write many of the individual stories.

When Irving arrived in Paris in the late summer of 1823, he brought with him a very small part of what came to constitute the *Tales of a Traveller*. Aside from a few literary sketches, which were not incorporated in this collection but put aside with other ephemeral material, Irving had only his voluminous notebooks and about half of his "Buckthorne" manuscript. The latter had been a fragment since the summer of 1821 when Thomas Moore had given him the details for the sketch of "A Literary Dinner."[15] This chapter as well as those entitled "Literary Life," "The Club of Queer Fellows," "The Poor Author," and "Notoriety" are sketches of the literary London that Irving had known or heard about and were probably finished before he even reached Germany. While in Dresden Irving recorded only two specific entries of continuing this work. On

December 23, 1822, when his notations had become regular again after getting settled in the Saxon capital, Irving "wrote a little at the 'History of an Author'," and on June 14, 1823, about a month before his departure, he again noted "all day writing on 'Hist[ory] of Author'."[16] During the intervening months there are many entries of "trying to write" or "writing" but no specific mention of this work. In view of the constant references to studying, to acting in or altering dramas for amateur performances, and to his actual work on Weber's *Freischütz* and *Abu Hassan,* little progress was probably made on the Buckthorne manuscript. There is no further reference to it until the entry, writing "a little at Hist of an Author," on December 5, 1823,[17] when Irving actually began to return to this manuscript at fairly regular intervals, sketching many of the shorter stories. Specific notations follow on January 24, 1824, when he "wrote half a page at Author," on March 10 and succeeding days, when he "arrange[d] plan of author" and continued writing and reorganizing his manuscript until the very moment of correcting the proof sheets in London.[18]

In two weeks Irving wrote "Wolfert Webber," but it was exhausting work. Each day he forced himself to write, usually beginning immediately after breakfast, but often being unable "to write above ten or twelve pages tho I keep at it till 3 oclock." He continued to "write a little but very little" until he finished the rough draft of seventy-four pages, followed by days of "touching up and altering" and "retouching and altering."[19]

After a month of such struggle two friends supplied Irving with reports of travel adventures in Italy that stimulated his imagination. On February 15, 1823, Captain Medwin read him extracts from the "journal of a painter while prisoner of the robbers near Rome." That night Irving could not sleep. At breakfast he talked excitedly of these Italian stories and was determined to make use of them. Eagerly he sought out his friend William Foy, the Irish painter, just returned from Italy, who gladly related "an anecdote or two." Now Irving began to write feverishly, and Medwin sat with him beyond midnight like a midwife to help his literary labors.[20] It was uphill work, but Irving wrote before breakfast and after, he wrote "all day at the italian story—finish[ed] the introduction and commence[d] the tale—wr[o]te 28 pages this day—clear & neat writing"; the next day he "scrawl[ed] the Story of the Bold Dragoon," rewrote his previous day's work and added "eight or nine pages."[21]

After working on the Italian stories until March 25, when he offered Murray the *Tales of a Traveller,* Irving wrote with determination. Detailed entries show the laborious efforts expended. Irving knew how much manuscript copy he needed for the promised two volumes and carefully noted the achievements: twenty-three pages one day, fourteen pages another, and twelve pages a third. In such a manner were "The Strange Stories by a Nervous Gentleman" eventually completed.[22] At the same time "The Italian Banditti" stories were furthered by additional anecdotes from Foy and Mills.

Throughout this difficult period of literary composition, Irving also completed such routine tasks as the preparation of an English edition of *Salmagundi,* published by Galignani in 1824. He made an agreement to edit for the same publisher a collection of British literature, of which, however, only the work of Goldsmith appeared. Irving was also invited to become a contributor to the *European Review* at sixteen pounds sterling a sheet, but he remembered his unhappy experiences with the *Analectic Magazine* a decade earlier and steadfastly refused.[23] He was determined to avoid additional hack writing and to concentrate his efforts on the work for Murray.

Irving struggled faithfully and listened eagerly to further conversations about "Italy and the Abruzzi" with Frank Mills, a minor dramatist in his own right, who not only suggested additional stories but read and criticized all the "Robber Tales."[24] Finally in April Irving experienced a "literary fit coming on" and wrote morning after morning on various parts of the "Strange Stories," but a few days later the "fit left" and he struggled uninspired in an effort to complete "Wolfert Webber."[25] In May he rewrote much of the material and added to the last section of American materials before he set out for England with his manuscripts.[26]

In London Irving found old friends like Leslie, Mills, Moore, and Rogers, who welcomed him heartily. Again he succumbed to the temptations of the drawing room, until he had to flee the city and seek seclusion with his sister in Birmingham and with the Fosters at Bedford in order to continue writing and seeing his new book through the press. He faithfully corrected proof sheets as they became available and continued to add to the material still in manuscript; but he was still short of copy to round out the volume. While visiting Moore at Sloperton Cottage Irving received the suggestion for "The Adventure of the German Student," which was written at Birmingham on June 23 and 24 and was forwarded immediately to the publishers, followed by the revised Buckthorne manuscript a few days later.[27] All of July was taken up with the tedious details of correcting, altering, and proofreading in order to meet the objections of Murray and his readers. At the end of the month Irving was still trying "to fill up the volume" and doing "vile Book work" while writing "all the morn[in]g at additions to Buckthorne" only to find "there would be much want[in]g to 2d vol."[28] Doggedly, Irving invented the story of "The Belated Travellers" and attempted to meet the objections of William Gifford,

Murray's editorial adviser, to various passages in his work. Never had Irving worked so hard or so desperately to meet a deadline. Almost daily he was forced to alter and revise, even "marring the story [of Buckthorne] in compliance with critique of Gifford—come to a conclusion per force" in order to complete an unwelcome task.[29]

Irving left London on August 13; he was still correcting proofs not only that morning but the next day at Brighton before he sailed for France. Less than two weeks later—on August 25, 1824—the long heralded German work, the *Tales of a Traveller,* finally appeared in London, one day after the first part (to be followed by the other three in the next seven weeks) was also published in New York. Irving's ordeal was over. Never had he written with more effort and less inspiration. Troubled by doubts and misgivings, fearful of hostile criticism, and exhausted by months of scribbling, revising, expanding, and supplementing, Irving bared his soul to Thomas Moore in a letter written at Brighton while waiting for the boat to return him to his beloved Paris:

> I have dragged myself out of London as a horse drags himself out of the slough or a fly out of a honey pot, almost leaving a limb behind him at every tug. Not that I have been immersed in pleasure and surrounded by sweets, but rather up to the ears in ink and harassed by printers' devils.
>
> I never have had such fagging in altering, adding, and correcting; and I have been detained beyond all patience by the delays of the press. Yesterday I absolutely broke away, without waiting for the last sheets. They are to be sent after me here by mail to be corrected this evening, or else they must take their chance. From the time I first started pen in hand on this work, it has been nothing but hard driving with me.[30]

2.

The genesis of the *Tales of a Traveller* emphasizes its fundamental weakness: a lack of originality and spontaneity. Despite Irving's repeatedly expressed horror of imitating the threadbare and preposterous plots of German romance, he had succeeded only in assembling a heterogeneous group of flimsy stories that lack interest or literary distinction. They show flashes of Irving's wit and bear traces of his stylistic charm, but they disappoint because something more was expected. His travels on the Continent and particularly his lengthy residence in Germany had led everyone to look for a "German Sketch Book." Irving had encouraged such expectations and was sincere in his intentions, but found himself not equal to the task. On the Continent Irving remained a foreigner, amused and puzzled by strange customs. In England he had felt at home and had enjoyed the additional advantage of being the object of curious respect as a literary American who understood and appreciated the British heritage and its hallowed traditions. French, German, and all Continental life was less comprehensible to him and infinitely more bewildering. That he might actually have interpreted German life or written of his travels across the length and breadth of central Europe turned out to be an unrealistic dream. He had never come to know Germany or to feel at home there. At best he was able to transplant his stories into a German milieu, which remained unconvincing or actually appeared counterfeit.

An examination of the individual stories for their origins or sources substantiates what Irving's notebooks have already suggested: they are the result of toil and strain and self-torment during 1823–1824, when he composed his work with the help of friends, books, or whatever other assistance was available. With the vivid background of Rhine romance and Black Forest landscapes, of Rübezahl legends in Silesia, of the Untersberg near Salzburg at his disposal and with the picturesque customs of Saxon Court life to draw on, Irving managed only to fill this long heralded volume with second-rate tales, faintly reminiscent of his German reading and lacking completely in actuality. Even the foreword "To the Reader," purporting to give a precise dating of the composition of these stories during an enforced stay at "Mentz *otherwise called* Mayence," was written largely under pressure in London. The publisher was clamoring for additional material to fill two volumes, so Irving tried "to devise a new story," padded his manuscripts as best he could, and wrote a lengthy introduction that admits the varied sources of his stories.[31] Even where he was able to inject his whimsical humor, it does no more than veil the obvious limitations of his craftsmanship:

> I am an old traveller; I have read somewhat, heard and seen more, and dreamt more than all. My brain is filled, therefore, with all kinds of odds and ends. In travelling, these heterogeneous matters have become shaken up in my mind, as the articles are apt to be in an ill-packed travelling-trunk; so that when I attempt to draw forth a fact, I cannot determine whether I have read, heard, or dreamt it, and I am always at a loss to know how much to believe of my own stories.[32]

Never was an author more ready than Irving to admit his borrowing. That he could not be too specific in most instances resulted from the multiplicity of sources which he blended into his own brand of salmagundi. The German ingredients were barely discernible and the flavor of his earlier work was never matched.

The first section of "Strange Stories by a Nervous Gentleman" links these tales to the narrative of "The Stout Gentleman" in *Bracebridge Hall,* which permits of further persiflage with Sir Walter Scott who, in the "Prefatory Letter" of his *Peveril of the Peak,* had humorously identified the author of *Waverley* as the mysterious stout gentleman. The same nervous gentleman, who had grown even more nervous at the realization of the missed opportunity, of catching full sight of the stout gentleman who was the author of *Waverley,* serves as the actual narrator. Irving again used the setting of an English manor hall in which a fox-hunting old baronet has gathered his cronies around the dinner table. The exigency of the weather prevents any departures for their several homes, the entire company is invited to spend the night, and a long session of storytelling ensues around the banquet table.

This type of *Rahmenerzählung,* or story within a story, so popular in German literature, is by no means a German invention. The Italian *novellas* of Boccaccio and the *Canterbury Tales* of Chaucer are model enough, and Irving also knew the Arabian collection of *Thousand and One Nights.* He may have been influenced by his German reading in his use of the technique of the framed tale, though the good-natured banter of his assembled listeners has nothing of the romantic concept of irony so popular with German romanticists, who delighted in the subtleties of extraneous philosophizing and took the objective detachment of the narrator more seriously than the story itself. Pochmann has suggested that Irving's method of getting the stories told, with realistic interruptions of the narrative by curious listeners and the combats of wit they engage in, points to the framework of Tieck's *Phantasus,* in which a group of men dedicate themselves to the spirit of Fantasy and recount some of Tieck's most popular tales.[33] That Irving knew Tieck personally in Dresden is clear from the record, and that he bought some of his works, noted the titles of others, and heard a good deal about this most influential Romanticist of the time, is also established. A superficial acquaintance with Tieck's shorter narratives, available to Irving also in collections of tales, is a reasonable assumption, supported by his diary notations. The specific reference to an association of roistering university students that young Buckthorne joined, "a special knot of young fellows, of lively parts and ready wit, who had lived occasionally upon town, and become initiated into the *Fancy,*"[34] may be reminiscent of Tieck's story-telling device, but Irving had already used the same technique in his *Bracebridge Hall.*

The first story, "The Adventure of My Uncle," is a ghost story which sets the pattern for the evening's narratives by this company of well-fed hunters, eager for entertainment. The narrator's uncle, while traveling in Normandy, spent a night in the gloomy château of a French marquis. A tall and stately figure all in white swept into his chamber at midnight, warmed herself at the fireside and stared silently at him. The next morning he recognized the features of his nocturnal visitor in the full-length portrait of a distinguished lady adorning the picture gallery. With some embarrassment the host shrugged off the adventure, but spoke of "a strange, mysterious, inexplicable occurrence"[35] that had become a family tradition. The honor of this noble lady had been violated by an ancestor in that very room, and annually on the anniversary of that fateful night her ghost haunted the scene of the crime.

The theme which Irving utilized here is readily recognized as a German legend known to him in several forms. The "white lady" that haunts the vicinity of her former home is common enough in folklore and was included in the collections of German legends acquired by Irving during his travels. In fact he had already referred to "the woman in white that haunted the dark glen at Raven Rock" in creating the atmosphere of supernaturalism in "The Legend of Sleepy Hollow."[36] Büsching,[37] who relates several anecdotes involving the white lady, locates the story in Bohemia, where she appears with a white veil to foreshadow a death, a birth, or a marriage. To indicate a death she wears black gloves instead of white. Gottschalck[38] specifically connects the legend of "Der Burggeist auf Scharzfeld" (which Büsching also includes) with Emperor Henry IV, who violated the wife of one of his subjects. Her ghost continues to haunt the castle. Irving's copy of Grimm's *Deutsche Sagen*,[39] which he acquired in Dresden in 1823 (as shown in his own handwriting on the title page of his copy), treats the legend under the title "Frau Berta oder die weisse Frau."

Aside from such available stories the general theme of the "white lady" who haunts an ancestral castle was the subject of conversations between Irving and the Fosters while traveling through the Harz Mountains. The Foster girls in their recollections of these days speak specifically of their visit to the castle at Blankenburg and the effect it had on Irving: "the 'locale' of the celebrated 'Ahnfrau,' a piece which he had seen acted at Vienna, and which had laid a strong hold upon his imagination."[40] Irving briefly corroborates in his travel diary the more factual details of the "picture of the Weisse Frau who haunts this castle as well as several others of the same family."[41] Flora Foster's reference to the "celebrated Ahnfrau" is, of course, to Grillparzer's stage success about which Irving had probably heard in Vienna, even though he did not witness a performance of it. Grillparzer's is the best-known dramatic treatment of this popular theme, but the ghostly lady appears also in the Danish dramatist Oehlenschläger's *Ludlams Höhle*. This writer not only enjoyed great popularity in Germany at the time of Irving's visit, but had known Tieck intimately at Dresden a few years earlier. Irving apparently jotted down the titles of some of Oehlenchläger's works when he heard the author discussed. Undoubtedly, Irving's interest in the occult, the knowledge of the basic story of the white lady, and the actual experience of visiting a castle where all the trappings of the legend were readily visible, provided sufficient stimulus and background for "The Adventure of My Uncle."

"The Adventure of My Aunt" emphasizes a humorous aspect of ghost-story telling. The mood of supernaturalism is dispelled by the seizure of the quaking culprit, secreted behind the portrait, whose moving eye had aroused apprehension. The intended robbery of the intrepid widow is thwarted by her vigorous and matter-of-fact investigation. Her self-assurance and determination and the acerbity of her character, which had already been too much for a meek and acquiescent husband, make even a ghost tremble. A possible source for the motif of the moving features of a portrait can be found in "The Family Portraits," one of the *Tales of the Dead,*[42] a popular collection of grotesque stories; in it the lips of a picture seem to move and thus frighten the daughter. However, Irving's story gains its effect from the humorous description of a termagant wife who is a match for husband, household, and would-be ghosts.

"The Bold Dragoon," perhaps one of the best stories of this collection, relates with Milesian gusto the adventure of a boisterous Irishman who found lodging in a haunted garret chamber in the old Flemish town of Bruges. This swaggering soldier, who "blarneyed the landlord, kissed the landlord's wife, tickled the landlord's daughter, chucked the bar-maid under the chin," and drank the guests under the table, charmed the entire household and became the center of unrestrained merriment. When he finally sought sleep in his attic chamber, the wine and the feather beds warmed him beyond endurance. He left his room, but upon returning he encountered at his fireside "a pale weazen-faced fellow in a long flannel gown and a tall white night-cap with a tassel to it" playing an instrument resembling a bagpipe. As the musician's performance grew fiercer and fiercer, the claw-footed furniture began to sway until everything in the room was in motion; "all except a great clothes-press, which kept courtesying and courtesying in a corner, like a dowager . . . Like a true Irishman, devoted to the sex, and at all times ready for a frolic, he bounced into the room, calling to the musician to strike up Paddy O'Rafferty, capered up to the clothes-press, and seized upon the two handles to lead her out:—when—whirr! the whole revel was at an end."[43] The Irishman found himself sitting on the floor with the handles of the clothes-press in his hands and its contents scattered around him.

The plot and humor of the story are characteristic of Irving's love for the grotesque and supernatural, which here as always suggests its rational explanation. The only hint of German influence, slight though it be, that may have affected the characterization of the Irishman can be seen in an entry in Irving's diary. It describes a theatrical performance in Prague, in which he saw a blustering, swaggering soldier upon the stage, a "young warrior flushed with wine—fiery—moustaches turn[e]d up—feather thrown back—staggering into house of sturdy bürger. Sitting down, throwing out leg—slapping on thigh, trying to stick arms akimbo, but staggering."[44] Such a soldier might have served as a model for "The Bold Dragoon."

"The Adventure of the German Student," which by its title suggests that here at last Irving drew upon his German sources, has actually no German flavor or background. Only the name of the student, Gottfried Wolfgang, whose terrifying experience is related, is German. Gottfried Wolfgang had fallen in love with a dream vision of feminine beauty. While returning home one stormy night—it was during the French Revolution—he discovered at the foot of the scaffold in the public square where executions were performed a lonely female figure in black in whom he recognized to his astonishment "the very face which had haunted him in his dreams." She yielded to his passionate protestations of love. The next morning his bride's lifeless body was identified by the Parisian police as one of the previous day's victims of the guillotine. They "undid the black collar round the neck of the corpse, and the head rolled on the floor."[45]

The gruesome details create an atmosphere of horror that is unusual for Irving and are in sharp contrast to the farcical mystifications of the preceding ghost stories. Though sometimes likened in spirit to the fantastic romanticism of E. T. A. Hoffmann (whose work Irving apparently did not know) it is a typical *Nachtstück* which reflects the interest in vampires and demonology current at the time. Irving, who never claimed originality when he used sources, frankly observed "that the Adventure of the German Student, or rather the latter part of it, is founded on an anecdote related to me as existing somewhere in French; and, indeed, I have been told, since writing it, that an ingenious tale has been founded on it by an English writer; but I have never met with either the former or the latter in print."[46] It has long been known that Irving, while struggling with the composition of *Tales of a Traveller,* received the suggestion for this story from Thomas Moore, who had noted in his journal on June 17, 1824:

> Told him [Irving] the story which I heard from Horace Smith about the woman with the black collar, and the head falling off; thought it would do well for his ghost stories; but mentioned H. Smith having

told me he meant to make use of it himself; probably *has* done so in the "New Monthly Magazine."[47]

Repeated searching over the years has revealed no such story by Horace Smith in the *New Monthly Magazine* or elsewhere, though a British reviewer of Irving's volume reaffirms that "the story of the Beheaded Lady has not only been told in print ere now, but much better told than it is in Mr. Irving's edition."[48] This may be an exaggeration, but the basic story was available in French in at least three collections.[49] One of these, a volume of supernatural stories published in Paris in 1819, contains an anecdote "Le Revenant succube," which briefly tells how a Parisian gentleman brings a pretty girl, who seeks shelter in a rainstorm, to his room. Her beauty delights him. He prevails upon her to remain. The next morning he leaves while she is still sleeping. When he returns at noon he finds her dead. The police identify her as one hanged on the gallows some months before. It is concluded that a devil assumed this form to ruin the gentleman.[50]

Such stories were commonplace enough and readily available to readers and devotees of the occult, but Horace Smith through Thomas Moore provided Irving the historical setting of the French Revolution and such details as the black band that conceals the mortal wound. Irving, in his desperate efforts to fill the troublesome volumes, expanded the material and provided the tenuous elaboration of the German student and his philosophic vaporings in an attempt to create atmosphere and make the story more plausible. His Knickerbocker flourish at the end, where the narrator vouches for the story's authenticity because he had it directly from the student now confined in a madhouse in Paris, is really Irving's trademark.

The final three stories of the first part are linked together: "The Adventure of the Mysterious Picture" merely provides the motivation for the following stories, "The Mysterious Stranger" and "The Young Italian." In the first of these, an ominous feeling of oppression and impending danger, probably a result of a nightmare engendered by the excesses of the hunting dinner, rouses the narrator from his disturbed slumber. A painting of a face with an expression of agony looks at him from the mantle; it fascinates him and frightens him until he is forced to retreat from its baneful stare and to seek refuge on the sofa in the drawing room. At breakfast time the host offers an explanation by relating his own adventure with "The Mysterious Stranger" who, after a brief acquaintance in Venice years ago, had given him this picture and the manuscript of the story of his unhappy life, as recounted in "The Story of the Young Italian."

It is the story of an unloved son of a Neapolitan nobleman, reared in a monastery. Fleeing from this enforced seclusion, during which he had learned to paint, and unwelcome at home where his father's favoritism to his older brother lacerated his heart, he went to Genoa and became the pupil of a great artist. Eventually he became secretly betrothed to Bianca, the ward of his noble patron. He received news that his brother was dead and that his father wished to restore him to his rights and title. This required his immediate departure for Naples. He confided in his friend Filippo, his patron's son, and entrusted his fiancée to Filippo's care. His father's prolonged illness prevented his return for two years. When he did return, he found Bianca married to Filippo. The latter had intercepted his letters, forged replies, and reported his death at sea in order to win her hand. In a passion he sought out his false friend and stabbed him. Frenzied with rage he mangled his body and fled from the garden "like another Cain,—a hell within my bosom, and a curse upon my head." He could not forget the horrible countenance of his victim which appeared to follow him everywhere. He attempted to free himself of this obsession by carefully painting an exact resemblance of the phantom face, but only doubled his misery. Finally in church he heard a voice that "promised mercy and forgiveness, but demanded . . . full expiation."[51] He gave his story and the picture to the narrator and surrendered himself to justice.

Irving in his introduction to the *Tales of a Traveller* acknowledged that "some of the circumstances in the Adventure of the Mysterious Picture, and in the Story of the Young Italian, are vague recollections of anecdotes related to me some years since; but from what source derived, I do not know."[52] Critics have pointed very specifically to suspiciously similar stories that were readily available. Hartley Coleridge bluntly accused Irving of having appropriated the story of the Phantom Portrait that S. T. Coleridge told at the dinner table in London in May, 1823, which is essentially the story of the "Mysterious Picture" and its subsequent narratives.[53] Some similarities to C. R. Maturin's popular Gothic novel *Fatal Revenge; or, The Family of Montorio* (1807) were noted by S. T. Williams, and a general indebtedness to Schiller's *Die Räuber* was mentioned by Pochmann.[54] Yet there is at least one other source to be considered. While in Dresden Irving noted among books that interested him and which he may have read with the Fosters two volumes of stories by the popular Danish author Adam Oehlenschläger. Among them is the story of "The Portrait," which relates the unhappy quarrel of two friends in love with the same girl. Siegfried, a painter, stabs Ludwig who falls as though dead. Three years later Ludwig, who had recovered and was seeking his old friend, hears in a tavern the story of a picture of a handsome youth with so horrible an expression upon his countenance that no one can bear to look upon it, even sleep is impossible in its presence. Ludwig's curiosity is aroused and he investigates. The custodian of the picture takes Ludwig for a ghost because he identifies him with the picture. The painter, who is living in a nearby monastery, is, of course, Siegfried, atoning for his deed of violence by painting religious pictures. Their reunion makes for a happy ending.

Aside from any possible specific indebtedness for the substance of these stories, "The Young Italian" is charged with the atmosphere of German Storm and Stress. The sensitive, emotional young Italian, unloved by his father, ill treated by his brother, and finally deceived and cheated of his bride by his only friend, seeks redress of these wrongs through lawless violence. Then he becomes an unhappy outcast who finds peace only after giving himself up. Irving's familiarity with Schiller's work is well established. *Die Räuber,* which brought Schiller international fame, gave passionate expression to the *Weltschmerz* of the young generation throughout Europe on the eve of the French Revolution. Irving had known *Die Räuber* since his New York theatre experiences, when he had seen Payne take the role of Karl Moor. Temperamentally, Irving was Schiller's opposite. He lacked intensity of feeling, the fiery indignation of a young iconoclast, but he was familiar with the symptoms. In his depiction of the unhappy Italian painter, he deliberately portrayed the exaggerated emotionalism of *fin-de-siècle* Continental literature.

"Buckthorne and His Friends," the second part of this troublesome volume and longer than any of the others, gently satirizes literary coteries, mercenary publishers, and poor-devil authors. After some slight sketches delineating the "Friends," the tribulations of Buckthorne form the main part of the narrative. Here Pochmann has suggested German influence. He surmised that "the last parts [of Buckthorne] were undoubtedly composed during this period [of Irving's Dresden residence], when he was reading *Faust* with Emily and discussing *Egmont* with her, when he was talking with Baron Lützerode about the English and German theatres. . . ." With only two diary notations indicating work on this story during the entire Dresden residence, however, one must conclude that it was written later in France and England. Pochmann also suggests that "he may well have read *Wilhelm Meisters Lehrjahre* (1796); indeed, with his strong interest in the theatre, it is not easy to see how he could have escaped reading Goethe's story of the apprentice who follows a theatrical calling to prepare himself for life."[55] Whether a knowledge of *Wilhelm Meister* influenced the final development of Irving's story is problematical. That he read this novel of 600 pages of difficult German with endless ramifications of plot without ever noting the fact in his diaries is hard to believe. More likely he heard of it during the many literary conversations in the salons of Dresden, where, it must not be forgotten, Goethe was not a popular figure.

As for the idea for the story, Irving recorded that "Buckthorne was first suggested by seeing a deserted old country place near Birmingham whose owner was nearly such a character as I have made of the old misers."[56] Perhaps what had originally been a mere series of literary portraits for which Irving had drawn on his own knowledge, and what was finally published as a loose collection of episodes in the life of "Buckthorne and his Friends," was hopefully envisaged as a novel of character delineation. Any knowledge of Goethe's work would have encouraged such a plan. The eighteenth century had developed the novel as a literary form, and English, French, as well as German literature could offer representative works that emphasized character studies. Irving knew Fielding's *Tom Jones*. As Irving had neither the ability nor the inclination for serious and sustained writing, "Buckthorne" came to be hastily included in *Tales of a Traveller*.

The intimate story of Buckthorne as "The Young Man of Great Expectations" follows quite logically in the wake of those episodes that introduce Buckthorne and his literary friends. Any specific German influence cannot be detected. The hint for the depiction of the strolling players, if Irving needed such a stimulus, can better be found in one of his favorite authors, Oliver Goldsmith. At the time, when Irving was struggling in Paris to complete the "Buckthorne" story, he included in his literary hack work for the French bookseller Galignani a biographical sketch of Goldsmith[57] that eventually became the nucleus for the full-length biography published in 1849. Irving's indebtedness to Goldsmith has been minimized by Williams as "nebulous" and as "characteristic of the eighteenth-century tradition, which Irving borrowed impartially from the current magazines, from Crabbe, or from Burns, or from such writers as Fielding and Thomson."[58] Even Irving's own "tribute of gratitude to the memory of an author whose writings were the delight of my childhood, and have been a source of enjoyment to me throughout life,"[59] Williams dismisses as hardly more than a general influence that could have shaped only his earliest feelings, perhaps to reappear unconsciously as a stimulus to his imagination.[60] Yet that may have been precisely the stimulus that Irving needed. The general belief of Irving's indebtedness to Goldsmith could be exaggerated, but specific cases of influence in the *Salmagundi* papers or *The Sketch Book* and *Bracebridge Hall* are well established,[61] and the qualities of humor and kindly tolerance of human frailty common to both writers impressed Irving's contemporaries. That Irving was intimately acquainted with Goldsmith's work is certain. He may well have reread some of it while composing the essay to accompany a selection from his works. Certainly, Irving was much more at home in the work of Goldsmith than in that of Goethe. The specific references to the *Vicar of Wakefield* and the tributes to its author in various chapters of "Buckthorne" may be incidental, but are hardly insignificant. Irving's indebtedness to English writers is reflected primarily in the mood and style of his work, aside from any specific borrowing of phrase or incident. Mr. Dribble's residence in Green-arbor Court, where "Goldsmith wrote his 'Vicar of Wakefield',"[62] and the affectionate description of this hallowed spot reveal Irving's devotion to this writer.

In the eighteenth chapter of the *Vicar of Wakefield* the good Dr. Primrose, in search of his unhappy daughter, meets the manager of a strolling company of players driving his cart "carrying their scenes and other theatrical furniture to the next village, where they were to exhibit."[63] The ensuing discussion of the state of the theatre, the low taste of the audiences, and the many tribulations of itinerant actors are not unlike the descriptive details of Irving's "The Poor-Devil Author" and may have been Irving's point of departure for the new development in which Buckthorne recounts the story of his life as a strolling player. Similarities to the story of the theatre apprentice in Goethe's *Wilhelm Meister* are at best so general and superficial that they spring from the basic theme rather than from a knowledge of the novel. To be sure, both Meister and Buckthorne are naive and unworldly youths attracted to the theatre; they have left uncongenial surroundings at home to seek happiness and success and have found solace in sentimental attachments while with an itinerant troupe of actors. Their frequent disappointments and final disillusionment with such a vagabond existence filled with petty jealousies and constant quarrels, and with the sordid character and grasping selfishness of stage folk, contribute to their practical experience in the ways of the world. But the parallels go no deeper. For Goethe the wealth of experience and contacts, despite all pretense and dilettantism, are only the outward manifestations of a higher destiny that guides man—almost despite himself—toward a purposeful goal. Living is an art that can be learned, and the individual passes through various stages of his apprenticeship before he becomes a "Master." Irving, who lacked great analytical powers and preferred short, impressionistic sketches to serious and sustained character delineations, managed to impart to Buckthorne and his quest for literary life something of a grubstreet flavor.

For the third section of *Tales of a Traveller,* "The Italian Banditti" stories, which could easily have been written by the average London literary hack, Irving tapped every possible source to help fill the volume. He compiled the stories from anecdotes and travel yarns of his Paris friends and sketched them against a background provided by a guidebook to Italy.[64] The tavern at Terracina takes the place of the English manor house of the opening section of the volume; instead of ghost stories over their ale after a day's fox hunting, accounts of desperate deeds of the Abruzzi bandits are told by weary travelers partaking of their evening meal while their horses are being readied. One narrative leads to the next and eight robber tales are linked together in a dreary effort to make banditry breath-taking and romantic.

Here, perhaps even more than in the earlier stories of the Italian painter, the influence of Schiller is discernible. The noble bandit, the most popular figure in literature at the end of the eighteenth century, is definitely a German contribution. Karl Moor, the hero of Schiller's *Die Räuber* (1781), was motivated by lofty ideals and driven to crime only by human injustice. As an ardent individualist, disillusioned by deceit and treachery at home, Moor became an outlaw with a conscience, a fictional hero who stirred the imagination of his age no less than the revolutionary cry of "liberty, equality, fraternity." A flood of robber tales appeared in the wake of Schiller's drama, among which Zschokke's *Abällino, der grosse Bandit* (1793) and Vulpius' *Rinaldo Rinaldini, der Räuberhauptmann* (1797) were the most popular. The Italian background became an absolute requisite for such tales of banditry, and Irving unfortunately was still following a trend that had exhausted the limited possibilities of such subliterary fiction. In the rhapsodic outbursts and extravagant emotionalism of the "Bandit Chieftain" and the "Young Robber," Irving gives fullest expression to his concept of the traditional bandit hero wronged by society and mistreated by justice. Yet neither the labored descriptions of violence and bloodshed nor their mock-serious treatment are able to please the reader. Even the faintly humorous account of Alderman Popkins' skirmish with such brigands and "The Adventure of the Englishman," in which the weary travelers who have listened patiently to the various adventures narrated at the inn have their own encounter with bandits, are third-rate writing.

"The Painter's Adventure," along with its sequels, "The Story of the Bandit Chieftain" and "The Story of the Young Robber," is referred to by Irving as the "Lucien story" and was reported in America as "a true account of what befell an artist in the employ of Lucien Buonaparte a few years ago," though no details were known.[65] Curiously enough, Irving's source for these stories was a German account of such an adventure. While he was completely out of spirits because he could not bring himself to write, Captain Medwin had visited him and read him a "journal of a painter while prisoner of the robbers near Rome." Irving studied this account during the next two weeks and finally recorded that he "finished translation of Lucien Story at four o'clock in the morning."[66] "The Painter's Adventure" actually recounts the harrowing experiences of the Swiss artist Friedrich Salathe, kidnapped on June 16, 1819, from the villa of Baron K. F. von Rumohr on the outskirts of Olevano, some thirty miles from Rome, and held prisoner for a high ransom. Because there were many Germans in the artists' colony of Rome, German newspapers widely reported this crime. The following year Heinrich Zschokke, the prolific and popular novelist, published in a Swiss journal edited by him[67] a detailed and somewhat embellished account, "Die Schicksale des Malers Salathe unter den Räuberbanden in den Appenninen, von ihm selbst erzählt." This was the account that came to Irving's attention and gave him new hope of finishing his volume. Making no attempt to hide his indebtedness, but without fully revealing his source, Irving acknowledged in his foreword, "To the Reader," that "The Adventure of the Young Painter among the banditti is taken almost entirely from an authentic narrative in manuscript."[68]

The whole series of robber tales is fundamentally spurious. Irving, who knew the Gothic atmosphere of Mrs. Radcliffe's and Walpole's writings at first hand and recognized its triteness, attempted to make it more palatable through the mocking tone that had helped to establish his reputation. He satirized the romantic Misses Popkins who "were enchanted with the savage scenery around; it was so like what they had read in Mrs. Radcliffe's romances; they should like, of all things, to make sketches."[69] Despite the undertone of ridicule and the obvious burlesquing of Gothic horrors, these stories are tedious, hollow, and absurd.

The fourth part of *Tales of a Traveller,* "The Money Diggers," is taken up with American material reminiscent of Irving's boyhood and purporting to be drawn from the papers of the late Diedrich Knickerbocker. Here too Irving had exhausted his inventive talent and was forced to borrow stories of Captain Kidd and the Spanish Main. Only two tales, "The Devil and Tom Walker" and "Wolfert Webber, or Golden Dreams" suggest any German sources. The first has been called "a sort of comic New England *Faust,* which in the happy blending of the terrifying and the ludicrous, almost rivals 'The Legend of Sleepy Hollow'."[70] Such praise is hardly deserved. The story is primarily an account of a miserly wretch who in his eagerness to reclaim the treasure of Captain Kidd comes to terms with the devil. In the end Tom Walker, after a life of wickedness and avarice, invoked the devil once too often:

> The black man whisked him like a child into the saddle, gave the horse the lash, and away he galloped, with Tom on his back, in the

> midst of the thunder-storm. The clerks stuck their pens behind their ears, and stared after him from the windows. Away went Tom Walker, dashing down the streets; his white cap bobbing up and down; his morning-gown fluttering in the wind, and his steed striking fire out of the pavement at every bound.[71]

Aside from the reference to the wild huntsman of German legend, with which the black woodsman in "Tom Walker" identified himself, only the general theme of a pact with the devil is reminiscent of a German source. The Faust theme, not of Goethe but of the old puppet play, is trivialized and reduced to its simplest formula. More significant is Irving's attempt to recapture his earlier success by delineating humorously against an American background another shrewish wife like Dame Van Winkle and another diabolical night ride like that of Ichabod Crane.

In "Wolfert Webber," another story of buried treasure, Irving repeated the motif of the three-times-recurring dream that establishes the existence of a treasure, a theme utilized in "Dolph Heyliger" and already traced to "The Spectre Barber," a version of Musäus' "Stumme Liebe." In the usual Dutch setting of Irving's Manhattan, the learned High-German Doctor Knipperhausen, who "had passed some years of his youth among the Harz mountains" and had learned "the mode of seeking treasure buried in the earth," participated in this eager search. Eventually, instead of the long sought buried gold, he finds a more likely prosperity in the rising value of his farm land which is subdivided and sold as city building lots.

Here end for all practical purposes the real and discernible German influences in Irving's writings. Whatever else in his later works can be linked to German sources or German influences is slight and inconsequential. Obviously, the broader aspects of German romanticism are reflected in later works in terms of Irving's fondness for wondrous tales and legends. Pochmann[72] has pointed to two stories of *The Alhambra,* the "Legend of the Moor's Legacy" and the "Legend of the Two Discreet Statues," which show slight similarities to the Kyffhäuser legends printed in Otmar's and Büsching's collections of folk tales. But the theme of treasures hidden in hollow mountains is not exclusively German. Even oriental tales like the *Arabian Nights* contain similar stories, and Irving specifically credited Spanish sources. In two stories first appearing in scattered periodicals and published in 1855 under the title *Wolfert's Roost and Other Papers,* Irving did depend on German sources. "Guests from Gibbet Island," published in the October, 1839, issue of *The Knickerbocker,* is another of Irving's attempts to portray against an American background of New York and its earlier Dutch history a legend taken from Grimm.[73] In the Grimm version a drunken innkeeper jocularly invites three men hanged on the gallows, whom he notices on his way home, to sup with him. Arriving at home he finds them awaiting him in his room. He collapses and three days later is dead. Irving expanded this anecdote of less than a page into a routine Knickerbocker story with pirates, hidden booty, a Dutch innkeeper and his shrewish wife, and the gallows guests who cause his death and haunt his house.

The other story, "Don Juan: A Spectral Research," is an account of a libertine nobleman who attempts to scale the walls of a convent in his ardent pursuit of a beautiful young novice. He murders a stranger who intervenes only to discover later that his own funeral is being conducted with all the pomp and solemnity of the Spanish church. In vain does he protest. His name is stricken from the roll of the living. A friar explains this mystery as a miracle intended for his conversion and salvation. He dedicates his wealth to pious uses and becomes one of the most zealous and exemplary of monks. Two stories exist in German that could have provided the skeleton for this story: "Seeburger See" in Grimm's *Sagen* and "Der Wunderfisch" in Gottschalck's collection.[74] In the German stories the crime is consummated and the seducer discovers too late that the victim is actually his own sister. Needless to say, such an incestuous theme would have appealed neither to Irving nor to his readers. This story and "The Gallows Guests" were also available to him in English by the time he used them. They appeared in London in 1826 in a popular collection of German legends and tales published by Thomas Roscoe, son of Irving's famous friend.[75]

Irving's misgivings and doubts during the long period of composition and revision of *Tales of a Traveller* were not unfounded. When he needed the approval of literary critics on both sides of the Atlantic in order to reaffirm his literary position, a position granted him enthusiastically by British and American admirers a few years earlier, he suddenly found himself attacked and censured. Though the book sold well in England and America, and was promptly translated into French and German to satisfy a curiosity about his work, it had only qualified success, and its critical reception was distinctly unfavorable. A general disappointment that he had only repeated himself and had given nothing new was expressed everywhere. Expectations of a series of sketches describing his travel experiences in his own style were not fulfilled, and critics voiced their annoyance openly and often sharply. There were those who saw in the weaknesses of the work new evidence that his reputation had never been merited, and others who became violently abusive in their resentment at being disappointed. All the latent hostility toward Irving at home and abroad suddenly expressed itself vociferously. He was no longer the exemplary American in Europe of whom his countrymen had been proud, a symbol of American democracy and a landmark in world literature. To Americans he had become an expatriate who left his sturdy young country to enjoy the luxury of London drawing rooms, flattering British nobility and mouthing Tory sentiments. Instead of praise as a brilliant stylist, he received cruel taunts as an imitator, plagiarist, and sycophant, and was even berated for coarseness and indecency in his descriptive details. It was a frightening experience for the shy and sensitive Irving with his inherent modesty and courtesy. He, who had dreaded criticism, felt the lash of savage and often unfair attacks upon his work and his character. He felt alone and helpless. His diary notations show him restless, anxious, and sleepless, avoiding his friends and unable to work. In the face of critical attacks he bravely avowed his own satisfaction with his work and attempted a nonchalant air of unconcern, but bitterness and disappointment could not be completely hidden. The following extracts from his correspondence reveal his uneasiness and fear about his future as a writer.

To his sister, September 20, 1824:

> I do not know how it [*Tales of a Traveller*] may please you, as it is written in a different mood from my late works. Much of it was written rapidly. For my own part, I think there are in it some of the best things I have ever written. They may not be so highly finished as some of my former writings, but they are touched off with a freer spirit, and are more true to life; for they are the transcripts of scenes that I have witnessed.[76]

To C. R. Leslie, December 8, 1824:

> Of my own fate I sometimes feel a doubt. I am isolated in English literature, without any of the usual aids and influences by which an author's popularity is maintained and promoted. I have no literary coterie to cry me up; no partial reviewer to pat me on the back: the very review of my publisher is hostile to everything American. I have nothing to depend on but the justice and courtesy of the public; and how long the public may continue to favour the writings of a stranger, or how soon it may be prejudiced by the scribblers of the press, is with me a matter of extreme uncertainty. I have one proud reflection, however, to sustain myself with:—that I have never in any way sought to sue the praises nor deprecate the censures of reviewers, but have left my works to rise or fall by their own deserts.[77]

To Henry Brevoort, December 11, 1824:

> My last work has a good run in England, and has been extremely well spoken of by some of the worthies of literature, though it has

> met with some handling from the press. The fact is I have kept myself so aloof from all clan ship in literature, that I have no allies among the scribblers for the periodical press; and some of them have taken a pique against me for having treated them a little cavalierly in my writings. However, as I do not read criticisms good or bad, I am out of the reach of attack. If my writings are worth any thing they will out live temporary criticism; if not they are not worth caring about. Some parts of my last work were written rather hastily. Yet I am convinced that a great part of it was written in a freer and happier vein than almost any of my former writings. There was more of an artist like touch about it—though this is not a thing to be appreciated by the many. I fancy much of what I value myself upon in writing, escapes the observation of the great mass of my readers: who are intent more upon the story than the way in which it is told. For my part I consider a story merely as a frame on which to stretch my materials. It is the play of thought, and sentiment and language; the weaving in of characters, lightly yet expressively delineated; the familiar and faithful exhibition of scenes in common life; and the half concealed vein of humour that is often playing through the whole—these are among what I aim at, and upon which I felicitate myself in proportion as I think I succeed.[78]

The bitterness and disappointment that Irving felt were really out of proportion to the actual reception of his work by the reading public; but the sharp and caustic utterances of the critics in British and American journals wounded his pride. The criticism leveled at *Tales of a Traveller* not only pointed to specific weaknesses of this work, but raised the more serious question of the basic validity of the earlier enthusiastic appraisals of Irving's writings. The September issue of *Blackwood's Edinburgh Magazine* contained a devastating critique from the pen of Robert Sym under the pseudonym of Timothy Tickler: "Miserably disappointed" in these tales, the reviewer prefaced his detailed denunciations by an oblique attack upon *The Sketch Book* and *Bracebridge Hall:*

> [Irving's] sketches of English life and manners had certainly made no lasting impression on the public mind, . . . on the whole, they were but insipid diet. There was no reality about his Yorkshire halls, squires, parsons, gipsies, and generals; and his pathos was not only very poor, but very affected. [After long delays and much travel] he has produced a book, which, for aught I see, might have been written, not in three years, but in three months, without stirring out of a garret in London, and this not by Mr. Irving alone, but by any one of several dozens of ready penmen about town. [In fact, it was only

> familiar material which had been] much better told than it is in Mr. Irving's edition. . . . There is nothing German here at all, except that the preface is dated Mentz, and that the author has cribbed from the German books he has been dabbling in, some fables which have not the merit either of being originally or characteristically German. . . . It is, indeed, high time that Mr. Irving should begin to ask of himself a serious question,—"What is it that I am to be known by hereafter?" He is now a man towards fifty—nearly twenty years have passed since his first and as yet his best production, "The History of New York," made its appearance. He has most certainly made no progress in any one literary qualification since then. There is far keener and readier wit in that book,—far, far richer humour, far more ingenious satire, than in all that have come after it put together; and however reluctant he may be to hear it said, the style of that book is by miles and miles superior to that in which he now, almost always, writes."[79]

The *Examiner* found only the section dealing with an American background convincing and spirited, but lamented Irving's confirmed "spirit of imitation, being in truth a sort of American mockbird. . . . There is scarcely one of them [the *Tales*] which is not traceable in its elements if not in its concoction. 'The Adventure of my Uncle,' for instance, is in character and locality a loan from the introduction to *Quentin Durward*. 'The German Student' is an avowed piece of borrowing. . . . The *matériel* of the next division, which is entitled 'Buckthorne and His Friends,' is collected, 'sans peur et sans reproche,' from the Essays and Citizen of the World by Oliver Goldsmith; the 'Literary Dinner' borrowing additionally from the similar dinner described by Smollett in Humphry Clinker, as given by himself to his corps of reviewers. . . . [Buckthorne] is hammered out of the Adventure of the Strolling Players in Goldsmith."[80]

The *Westminster Review* recalled that Irving's fame really rested upon the fact that Geoffrey Crayon was "the work of a native American" and "that such a production could have come from such a quarter." Only Irving's flattering eulogies of existing institutions and extravagant praise of British manners and customs had assured him the complete approval of the fashionable Grosvenor Square society. The *Tales of a Traveller* proved what had already been suspected: "Geoffrey is indisputably feeble, unoriginal and timorous; a mere adjective of a man, who has neither the vigour nor courage to stand alone, though it be but for a moment; from the beginning he has looked up for support, not of the strongest and most durable, but of the most conspicuous and prominent kind, and this support he has found in the applause of the Somebodys. . . . We are struck at every step with the poverty of the writer's invention, and the absence of all acuteness in observing manners, and sketching character."[81] A correspondent of *The London Magazine* impatiently bestowed praise upon Irving's general excellence and superiority as the one author of the day, only to condemn sharply this particular work. He "found little in the Tales of a Traveller, but the style, to admire. Here is scarcely a gleam of his playful and Addisonian wit; nothing of his vivid delineation of character. Except in beauty and grace of language they are not a whit superior to an equal number of pages torn from the innumerable garbage-novels which Paternoster pours upon us every publishing day."[82]

But British opinions were by no means entirely derogatory. Numerous journals printed favorable and even enthusiastic comments, tempering their praise only now and then to express disappointment at the tenuous character of the narratives. The *Eclectic Review* saw in the *Tales of a Traveller:*

> "A continuation of the Sketch Book. The same facility of touch, the same elegance, sustained without labour, and polished without art, may be traced in each. . . . Such, however, is the power of our friend Crayon, that we are pleased even while we are disappointed, and follow him with delight through the different avenues of his story; though they 'lead to nothing.' It is, moreover, an undeniable proof of the talent and taste of the writer, that he has conferred upon sketches comparatively so light and unfinished, the full interest of more complete and systematic pictures. In this, the hand of a master is revealed."[83]

The article took exception to some of Irving's humor and protested that "he displays a levity, and sometimes stoops to a vulgarity, which must pain a serious, and disgust a delicate mind."[84] Such criticism only repeated the charge of indecency and obscenity that was made even more violently in America. The *Atlantic Magazine,* which praised the peculiar charm that pervades his stories and appreciated his sprightly humor, objected to the "Adventures of My Aunt" because of "a want of delicacy in the story . . . which offends us, from the pen of a writer who is accustomed to consult, on all occasions, the nicest proprieties of language and allusions"; it objected to the "Bold Dragoon" because of "the admixture of unnecessary indecency. We are by no means fastidious in matters of this sort, and have laughed with the friendliest good will at the story of the Nervous and Stout Gentleman; but we doubt whether even the magic charm of Mr. Irving's inimitable sportiveness can disarm us of the displeasure we feel, when we hear him allude in mirthful and not very ambiguous language to the filthy orgies of a brothel."[85] Others took him to task "for two or three droll indecencies, which everybody, of course, remembers in these *Tales*,"[86] or for "a vein of equivocating ribaldry pervading the whole of these two last volumes" and "the obscenities [which] are most carefully veiled."[87]

Such unfair attacks embittered Irving, especially when coming from America. He, who had succeeded in overcoming the complacent and prejudiced British attitude toward American letters and who was accepted in London literary circles as an equal, resented such ingratitude at home. Anonymous letters and bitter attacks in the press almost persuaded him that he was cast off by his own countrymen.[88] A caustic review in the *Philadelphia Columbian Observer* was promptly reprinted in *The New York Mirror* after an introductory paragraph of fulsome praise:

> This is a mere shadow of the previous works of the same writer, without their spirit, humour, or interest; being a dull imitation of himself, by a writer who was never remarkable for originality of genius, richness of invention, or vivacity of fancy. No man in the republic of Letters has been more overrated than Mr. Washington Irving. With very moderate powers of *description*, he has been *puffed* to an artificial magnitude, which he cannot realize by his productions. Take away his *Dutchman with his pipe*, his *old mansion with his ghosts*, his *Uncle Trim*, and his *Aunt Tabitha*—and perhaps a clown of an *Old Bachelor*, and Mr. Irving is like the lion with his claws drawn out—he has nothing left either formidable, or pleasing; nothing to excite a smile, (for although he affects the humourist, he never can raise a laugh,) or to inspire admiration. In fine, Mr. Irving's powers are limited to the telling of a story, and it must be a ghost story, and even then he is a dull and prosing narrator.[89]

The Quarterly Review, John Murray's own publication, which naturally looked upon Irving's work with a benevolent eye, was also critical. Examining the newly published *Tales* (in the March, 1825, issue after a flood of hostile comments had already appeared) as a part of the totality of Irving's publications, the reviewer prefaced his discussion with an account of Irving's rise to literary fame with *Salmagundi, Knickerbocker History of New York,* and *Bracebridge Hall,* and suggested that Irving "has shared, perhaps to an undeserved degree, the fate of public favourites, and has experienced that there is an ebb, as well as a tide, in the affairs of men, more particularly literary men." The first section of the new volume, recounted by the same "Nervous Gentleman" of *Bracebridge Hall,* "is indeed a most amusing specimen of that piquant cookery which makes something out of nothing," but "The Money-Diggers," the Knickerbocker division of the *Tales,* "is a puny degenerate bantling: and apparently made up, like Frankenstein's unruly puppet, of the parings and shreds of its brethren. . . . The Italian Banditti . . . which Mr. Irving honestly confesses to be the sweepings of his scrapbook [include] the story of the Young Robber, [a story that] ought not to have been written—it ought not to be read—the feelings which it excites are not tragic horror or pity, but pure unmingled disgust: it is simply shocking to the feelings of our nature . . . and if the book should ever reach a second edition, we trust Mr. Irving will expunge it." In contrast to most critical utterances, nothing but praise is bestowed upon "Buckthorne," a tale which makes it seem probable that Irving "might as a novelist prove no contemptible rival to Goldsmith, whose turn of mind he very much inherits and of whose style he particularly reminds us in the life of Dribble. . . . Too much praise, indeed, cannot be bestowed on the strictly moral tendency of Buckthorne. Throughout the whole of the ludicrous incidents with which the tale abounds, Mr. Irving has never once abused the latitude which the subject afforded him, and of which Goëthe [*sic*] has made such filthy use in Wilhelm Meister." But despite such approbation of moral rectitude, the reviewer uttered the stern warning that Irving "must in future be true to his own reputation throughout, and correct the habits of indolence which so considerable a part of the 'Tales of the Traveller' evince. The indulgence which he so fairly deserved at his outset, as an ingenious stranger, intuitively proficient in the style and ideas of the mother-country must now cease, and he must be considered in future as not only admitted to the full freedom and privileges of the English guild of authorship, but amenable also at the same time, as an experienced craftsman, to its most rigorous statutes."[90]

In retrospect some of these exaggerated criticisms sound absurd, even where Irving's fundamental weaknesses are laid bare. Public taste in literature had become surfeited with the sentimental trifles of gift books and annuals. The *Tales of a Traveller* was too much of a mixture, too clearly a conglomeration. Haunted castles were no longer the fashion and ghost stories palled. And Irving had not succeeded, as in *The Sketch Book,* in transplanting German legends into American settings where the native landscape could reflect the spirit of the tale. Here were no flesh and blood characters like Rip Van Winkle or Ichabod Crane or Herman Von Starkenfaust, shrewdly drawn, whose human behavior transcended all supernatural fancies.

It was a rude awakening for Irving and a cruel blow to his hopes for the future. He had reached an impasse and he determined to turn from belles-lettres to the more prosaic work of historical investigations. Perhaps this hostile criticism was the inevitable reaction to the overenthusiastic recognition of his limited powers only a few years before. As an anonymous critic expressed it:

> Irving has been foolishly praised; cruelly, wickedly abused. He went up too high: he has fallen too low. They made an idol of him; they could see no fault or blemish in him; they crowned him; set him above other men; offered up his fellows to him—in spite of his continual, sincere expostulation.
>
> Now—mark the change—*now,* in the freak of the hour, as if they could never forgive *him,* for their own folly—*now,* in the first paroxysm of returning reason—they have torn off his crown; tumbled him into the dirt, with brutal derision, cries; and would, if they had power, grind him to dust; casting the precious metal, that *is* within him, with all that he has of common earth, upon the waters, or the winds. They anointed him wickedly: they are now dishonouring him, far more wickedly. It is high time for us to interpose.[91]

The high hopes with which Irving had set out upon his German adventure were not realized. Though his notebooks were filled with all sorts of anecdotes and legends gleaned from many collections of German folklore and though he had faithfully recorded his travel observations, he had been unable to use these German experiences either to stimulate his own creative talents or to influence his literary style. German Romanticism with all its philosophical implications had never really touched him, nor had German Classicism with its humanistic tradition. His unsuccessful love for Emily Foster became the central experience of these years and symbolizes his failure.

But on the Continent and particularly in Germany, Irving had not failed. His fame was still in the ascendancy. No harsh criticisms were heard, and the reception in Germany of the *Tales of a Traveller* was happily different from that in England and America.[92] Together with his earlier works it helped to establish Irving's fame there and to make the delicate, polished prose style of his sketches a pronounced influence on German nineteenth-century narrative writers.[93] And so Irving, the first American literary ambassador to the Old World, did not merely borrow from German sources, but himself inspired younger writers in Germany. Such literary interrelations were a new development, and in this cultural exchange Irving gave at least as much as he received.

Notes

1

[1] *Washington Irving and the Storrows. Letters from England and the Continent 1821–1828*, ed. S. T. Williams (Cambridge, Mass., 1933), p. 15.

[2] C. R. Leslie, *Autobiographical Recollections* (Boston, 1860), p. 230.

[3] *Letters of Washington Irving to Henry Brevoort*, ed. G. S. Hellman (New York, 1918), pp. 385f.

[4] P. M. Irving, *The Life and Letters of Washington Irving* (New York, 1863), II, 79. (Cited as *Life and Letters.*)

[5] *Ibid.*, p. 90.

[6] E. g., this frank statement in a letter to Brevoort (*op. cit.*, p. 356): "I have, by patient & persevering labour of my most uncertain pen, & by catching the gleams of sunshine in my cloudy mind, managed to open to myself an avenue to some degree of profit & reputation. I value it the more highly because it is entirely independent and self created; and I must use my best endeavours to turn it to account."

[7] See the various sketches in O. W. Long, *Literary Pioneers* (Cambridge, Mass., 1935).

[8] A full realization of his shortcomings was clearly indicated by his urgent plea to Bancroft in Paris in 1821 "to lay aside all cares, and only be bent on laying a stock of knowledge for future application . . . scramble to it; get at it as you can; but be sure to get at it . . . The time will soon come, when it will be too late for these things." M. A. De Wolfe Howe, *The Life and Letters of George Bancroft* (New York, 1908), I, 107.

[9] S. T. Williams, *The Life of Washington Irving* (New York, 1935), I, 15. (Cited as *The Life.*)

[10] *Ibid.*, p. 37.

[11] F. H. Wilkens, *Early Influence of German Literature in America* (Philadelphia, 1900), pp. 12–31.

[12] See S. H. Goodnight, "German Literature in American Magazines prior to 1846," *Bulletin of the University of Wisconsin, Philology and Literature Series,* IV (1908), 115–23.

[13] *The Life,* I, 136.

[14] *Ibid.,* p. 138.

[15] *Analectic Magazine,* II (Nov., 1813), 419.

[16] V. A. Stockley, *German Literature as Known in England 1750–1830* (London, 1929), p. 77.

[17] Wilkens, *op. cit.,* pp. 92–93.

[18] Irving's Notebook of 1818 (unpubl.; in New York Public Library).

[19] *Analectic Magazine,* III (Apr., 1814), 297ff. Among the many names and titles mentioned are the following: Hagedorn, Weiss, Gellert, Bodmer, Klopstock, Wieland, Lessing, Werner, Gerstenberg, Illinger [Klinger], Tieck, Oechlenschläger [*sic*], J. P. Richter, William and Frederic Schlegel, Goethe, Schiller; *Robbers, Leonora, Oberon, Wallenstein, Nathan, Iphigenia in Tauris, Goetz of Berlichenzen* [*sic*], *Niebelungen, Mary Stuart, Joan of Arc, William Tell, Torquato Tasso,* and *Faust.*

[20] The English ed. of three volumes (London: J. Murray, 1813) was followed by an American one: *Germany* by the Baroness Staël-Holstein. Translated from the French. (New York: Eastburn, Kirk & Co., 1814).

[21] *Notes and Journal of Travel in Europe 1804–1805,* ed. W. P. Trent (New York, 1921), III, 38, 59, 65, 68.

[22] See *Journal of Washington Irving (1823–1824),* ed. S. T. Williams (Cambridge, Mass., 1931), pp. 63, 163; and *The Journals of Washington Irving* (from July, 1815, to July, 1842), eds. W. P. Trent and G. S. Hellman (Boston, 1919), II, 145, 150.

[23] *Life and Letters,* IV, 285.

[24] *Ibid.,* I, 136–37.

[25] See letter of Washington Irving to Harper and Brothers:

"My acquaintance with Campbell commenced in, I think, 1810, through his brother, Archibald, a most amiable, modest, and intelligent man, but more of a mathematician than a poet. He resided at that time in New York, and had received from his brother a manuscript copy of 'O'Connor's Child; or, The Flower of Love Lies Bleeding,' for which he was desirous of finding a purchaser among the American publishers. I negotiated the matter for him with a publishing house in Philadelphia, which offered a certain sum for the poem, provided I would write a biographical sketch of the author to be prefixed to a volume containing all his poetical works. To secure a good price for the poet, I wrote the sketch, being furnished with facts by his brother; it was done, however, in great haste, when I was 'not in the vein' and, of course, was very slight and imperfect. It served, however, to put me at once on a friendly footing with Campbell, so that, when I met him for the first time a few years subsequently in England, he received me as an old friend." In William Beattie, *Life and Letters of Thomas Campbell* (New York, 1855), I, xi–xii. Reprinted at the end of "Thomas Campbell" in *The Works of Washington Irving,* Hudson ed. (New York, 1882), XVII, 166–67. (Cited as *Works.*)

[26] *The Poetical Works of Thomas Campbell* (Baltimore, 1810), pp. xix–xxii. When Irving revised this biographical sketch into the essay "Thomas Campbell" and

printed it in the *Analectic Magazine* two years later, he eliminated these naive, absurdly uncritical comments on German philosophy and restricted himself to a brief noncommittal reference to Campbell's German contacts. See *Analectic Magazine,* V (Mar., 1815), 234–50. The essay was reprinted first with other biographical sketches in *Spanish Papers* (New York, 1866). Also see *Works,* XVII, 141–65. The reference to German philosophy in Campbell's letter was printed later by his biographer (See Beattie, *op. cit.,* I, 283).

[27] Beattie, *op. cit.,* I, 233. See also D. B. Shumway, "Thomas Campbell and Germany," in *Schelling Anniversary Papers* (New York, 1923), pp. 233–61.

[28] *Life and Letters,* I, 240.

[29] Irving to his brother Peter. *Ibid.,* p. 381.

[30] James Skene, *Memories of Sir Walter Scott,* ed. Basil Thomson (London, 1909), p. 3: ". . . in his quest for a supply to feed the craving for German romance that seized him, Sir Walter learned that I had recently returned from a several years' residence at school in Germany, and that I had brought a collection of the best authors along with me, which he, of course, became desirous to obtain access to . . . However, the objects of his research were there before him in a goodly range of German volumes, comprehending the works of most of the German authors then in repute."

[31] F. W. Stokoe, *German Influence in the English Romantic Period, 1788–1818, with Special Reference to Scott, Coleridge, Shelley and Byron* (Cambridge, Eng., 1926), pp. 48, 65. For a comprehensive survey of Scott's literary and personal relations with Germany see John Koch, "Sir Walter Scotts Beziehungen zu Deutschland," *Germanisch-Romanische Monatsschrift,* XV (1927), 36–46, 117–41.

[32] *Two Ballads, from the German of Gottfried Augustus Bürger.* (Edinburgh, 1796). The second ed. of 1807 gave Scott's name.

[33] See [R. P. Gillies], "Recollections of Sir Walter Scott," *Fraser's Magazine,* XII (Sept., 1835), 265: ". . . *Goetz of Berlichingen* had more influence in disposing his mind for the course which he afterwards pursued than any other production, either foreign or domestic, which fell his way."

[34] Scott acknowledged his source in his preface (*The Poetical Works of Sir Walter Scott, Bart.,* XII (1834), p. 117): "The story of the Ghostly Barber is told in many countries; but the best narrative founded on the passage, is the tale called Stummé Liebé [*sic*], among the legends of Musaeus."

[35] Irving in his essay "Abbotsford," *Works,* VIII, 281.

[36] See *Catalogue of the Library at Abbotsford* (Edinburgh, 1838), particularly pp. 38–55.

[37] See Catalogue of Washington Irving's German books at Sunnyside, Appendix, pp. 199–202.

[38] *The Life,* I, 162.

[39] P. M. Irving in *Life and Letters,* I, 395f.

[40] Manuscript fragment at Yale University, printed in *The Life,* II, 260.

[41] Notebook of 1818.

[42] *The Life,* I, 168.

[43] Notebook of 1818. The German phrases sound like designations of inns that he recorded while reading.

[44] J. K. Riesbeck, *Travels through Germany,* tr. P. H. Maty (London, 1787), II, 208f.: "Wieland, is, without a doubt, the first of all the German writers. No writer, Lessing alone excepted, unites so much study with so much genius as he does. He has

not only formed and fixed his taste on a thorough acquaintance with the beauties of the ancient writers, but possesses also all the literature of France, Italy, and England. His works are not like the rhapsodies of the modern German poetasters, but have the true smack of art. Even the most fugitive trifles that fall from his playful and humorous pen, bespeak a workman who is thorough master of his business, and has a manner of his own. . . . None of the German writers know so well how to please the public as Wieland does. He is most fruitful in the invention of trifles, in order to make his journal, which is as good as any other we have, sell."

[45] Notebook of 1818. Quoted from Riesbeck, *op. cit.*, I, 140–42; 160f. The legend of the sleeping monarch or *Kaisersage,* here referring to Charlemagne, is generally related to Frederick Barbarossa, Frederick II, Otto I, or Otto II, and at times even to Charles V.

[46] Ferdinand Künzig, *Washington Irving und seine Beziehungen zur englischen Literatur des 18. Jahrhunderts* (Heidelberg, 1911), pp. 10–12.

[47] *The Life,* I, 179.

[48] Stockley, *op. cit.*, pp. 324–28.

[49] *Chambers's Cyclopaedia of English Literature,* quoted in *Life and Letters,* I, 418.

[50] Francis Jeffrey, in *Edinburgh Review,* XXXIV (Aug., 1820), 160, a sixteen-page review that reprinted almost half of "Rip Van Winkle."

[51] Legends of enchanted sleep are common enough in all European literatures and are found even in Oriental lore. The Japanese version of Rip Van Winkle is of Chinese origin and tells of Lu-wen, a pious woodcutter who lost his way and watched two lovely ladies play checkers. Returning to his village as a wrinkled old man, he finds only his descendants in the seventh generation. A stranger in their midst, he returns to the mountain to find solace in the company of those spirits. In W. E. Griffis, *The Mikado's Empire* (New York, 1895), 8th ed., pp. 502f.

[52] *Blackwood's Edinburgh Magazine,* IX (May, 1821), 225.

[53] "Abbotsford," *Works,* VIII, 298.

[54] Printed in the London ed. (1822), II, 230, from which it was translated for the German ed., Washington Irving's *Sämmtliche Werke* (Frankfurt, 1826–37), XVII, 94–95. This note is missing in the first American edition of 1822, but a revised edition of the same year (in New York Public Library) prints the note in Vol. II, p. 187.

[55] *Works,* XIX, 74. The spellings Kypphäuser or Kipphäuser occur around 1800 as variants of the usual Kyffhäuser.

[56] "Peter Klaus. The Legend of the Goatherd. Rip Van Winkle," *Port Folio, and New York Monthly Magazine,* XIV (Aug., 1822), 144–47.

[57] B. Taylor, "By-Ways of Europe,"*Atlantic Monthly,* XXI (May, 1868), 623; J. B. Thompson, "The Genesis of the Rip Van Winkle Legend, *Harper's New Monthly Magazine,* LXVII (Sept., 1883), 617–22.

[58] R. Sprenger, "Über die Quelle von W. Irvings Rip Van Winkle," *Programm des mit Realabteilungen in Tertia und Sekunda verbundenen Progymnasiums zu Northeim, Nr. 344* (Northeim, 1901), 3–14.

[59] [J. C. C. Nachtigal] *Volcks-Sagen nacherzählt von Otmar* (Bremen, 1800), pp. 153–58.

[60] F. L. Pattee in *The Development of the American Short Story* (New York, 1923), p. 11, n. 1, speaks of "Grimm's tale 'Peter Klaus, the Goatherd'," but is definitely in error.

In the foreword to *Deutsche Sagen* (Berlin, 1818), pp. xviif, the Brothers Grimm paid tribute to Otmar: "In Absicht auf Treue und Frische verdient Otmar's Sagen [Sammlung] der Harzsagen so viel Lob, dass dieses den Tadel der hin und wieder aufgesetzen unnöthigen Bräme und Stielverzierung zudeckt. Viele sind aber auch selbst den Worten nach untadelhaft und man darf ihnen trauen." Proof of their recognition of Otmar's importance as a collector of folklore is found in the credit line of their legends, numbered (Vol. I) 153–56, 190, 201, 215, 228, 304, 305, 311, 312, 320, 326, 328, 355; (Vol. II) 575 and 583.

61 H. A. Pochmann, "Irving's German Sources in *The Sketch Book,*" *Studies in Philology,* XXVII (1930), 477–507.

62 *Ibid.,* p. 496.

63 J. G. Büsching, *Volks-Sagen, Märchen und Legenden* (Leipzig, 1812), pp. 327–31.

64 Unpublished MS which was in the possession of the late Dr. Roderick Terry. See *The Life,* I, 183, n. 93.

65 William Roscoe, *The German Novelists* (London, 1826), II, 55–60.

66 *Letters of Irving to Brevoort,* pp. 286f.

67 E. Burritt, "Birthplace of Rip Van Winkle," *Packard's Monthly,* n. s., I (Nov., 1869), 333.

68 *Life and Letters,* I, 448.

69 O. S. Coad, "The Gothic Element in American Literature," *Journal of English and Germanic Philology,* XXIV (1925), 84.

70 J. K. A. Musäus, *Volksmährchen der Deutschen* (Gotha, 1782–87); a new edition stylistically revised by C. M. Wieland (Gotha, 1804–5) became very popular. Recently E. L. Brooks has also called attention to the Beckford translation. See "A Note on Irving's Sources," American Literature, XXV (May, 1953), 229f.

71 [William Coleman] *The Gnome-King; or, the Giant Mountains,* a dramatic legend in two acts (London, 1819).

72 Scott wrote to his friend Daniel Terry (Jan. 9, 1823) in reply to a query from a bookseller: "Unquestionably I know many interesting works of the kind he mentions, which might be translated from the German:—almost all those of Musaeus, of which Beddoes made two volumes, and which are admirably written; many of La Motte Fouqué; several from the collection bearing the assumed name of Beit [*sic*] Weber." In J. G. Lockhart, *Memoirs of Sir Walter Scott* (London, 1900), IV, 78.

Dr. Thomas Beddoes, father of the poet, "was master of the French, Italian, Spanish and German languages; with the polite and the scientific authors in the last, in particular, he was equally conversant, and his library contained a rich collection of works of both descriptions." J. E. Stock, *Memoirs of the Life of Thomas Beddoes, M.D. with an analytical account of his writings* (London, 1811), p. 409. No reference to such a translation is made by Stock. Professor H. W. Donner, whose authoritative works on Thomas Beddoes, the poet, have utilized all manuscript materials available, has kindly checked this matter for me and found no evidence of such a translation.

As Beckford's work was published anonymously and as Dr. Beddoes was known to be keenly interested in foreign literature, he may have been looked upon as the possible translator, unless Scott, writing thirty years after the appearance of these volumes, simply confused the somewhat similar names.

73 The following parallel passages from Musäus and then Irving reveal the actual borrowing:

"All the stories of Number-Nip, which he had formerly devoured with such eager attention, came rushing at once into his mind, now he was traversing the stage where these adventures had happened, and he could have wished with all his soul never to have heard a syllable about the matter. . . . From time to time he cast a timid look on every side: often sweeping, with his half closed eyes, the two-and-thirty points of the compass in less than a minute's time. When he espied any suspicious appearance, a cold shudder ran down his back, and his hair grew stiff like bristles.

"Peeping up cautiously he saw, to his utter confusion, stalking on about a stone's throw before the coach, a jet-black figure, of a size exceeding that of man, crowned with a broad Spanish tippet; but what was the most suspicious circumstance in its whole appearance, was its being without an head. If the coach halted, the figure also halted; and when the postilion drove on, it proceeded also . . . It was now plain to be seen that John's eye had taken a false measure—the man on foot had an head as well as other people, only he did not wear it, according to the usual fashion, between his shoulders, but carried it under his arm, just as if it had been a lap-dog. . . . John . . . began, in the anguish of his heart, the salutation appointed to be addressed to all good spirits, *Angels and Ministers* . . . but, before he could speak it out, the monster took his head from under his arm, and hurled it at John: it struck him right on the forehead, and the blow was so severe that he tumbled headlong from the box over the forewheel, and at the same time the postilion was stretched in the dust by a severe stroke with a club." *Popular Tales of the Germans* (London, 1791), II, 143–51.

"All the stories of ghosts and goblins that he had heard in the afternoon, now came crowding upon his recollection. The night grew darker and darker; the stars seemed to sink deeper in the sky, and driving clouds occasionally hid them from his sight. He had never felt so lonely and dismal. He was, moreover, approaching the very place where many of the scenes of the ghost stories had been laid . . . As Ichabod approached this fearful tree, he began to whistle. . . . Suddenly he heard a groan—his teeth chattered and his knees smote against the saddle . . . he beheld something huge, misshapen, black and towering. It stirred not, but seemed gathered up in the gloom, like some gigantic monster ready to spring upon the traveller.

"The hair of the affrighted pedagogue rose upon his head with terror . . .

"He appeared to be a horseman of large dimensions, and mounted on a black horse of powerful frame. . . . Ichabod, who had no relish for this strange midnight companion, and bethought himself of the adventure of Brom Bones with the Galloping Hessian, now quickened his steed, in hopes of leaving him behind. The stranger, however, quickened his horse to an equal pace. Ichabod pulled up, and fell into a walk, thinking to lag behind—the other did the same. . . . On mounting a rising ground, which brought the figure of his fellow-traveller in relief against the sky, gigantic in height, and muffled in a cloak, Ichabod was horror-struck, on perceiving that he was headless!—but his horror was still more increased, on observing that the head, which should have rested on his shoulders, was carried before him on the pommel of the saddle: his terror rose to desperation. . . . Just then he saw the goblin rising in his stirrups, and in the very act of hurling his head at him. Ichabod endeavored to dodge the horrible missile, but too late. It encountered his cranium with a tremendous crash—he was tumbled headlong into the dust, and Gunpowder, the black steed, and the goblin rider, passed by like a whirlwind." *Works,* XIX, 510–16.

[74] *Popular Tales of the Germans,* II, 165.

[75] "The Author's Account of Himself," *Works,* XIX, 17.

[76] *Ibid.,* pp. 230–31.

[77] *Ibid.*, p. 237.

[78] *Ibid.*, p. 229.

[79] For a full treatment, see A. Brandl, "Lenore in England," in Erich Schmidt, *Charakteristiken* (Berlin, 1886), pp. 244–48.

[80] B. Q. Morgan, *A Critical Bibliography of German Literature in English Translation 1481–1927* (Stanford University, 1938).

[81] *Popular Tales and Romances of the Northern Nations.* (London, 1823), p. xi.

[82] "Preface to the Revised Edition," *The Sketch Book, Works,* XIX, 6.

[83] *Ibid.*, pp. 11ff.

[84] *Memoirs, Journal and Correspondence of Thomas Moore,* ed. Lord John Russell (London, 1853), III, 252f.

[85] *Ibid.*, p. 211.

[86] *Bracebridge Hall, Works,* IV, 19.

[87] *Ibid.*, p. 410.

[88] *Ibid.*, p. 468.

[89] *Ibid.*, p. 480.

[90] *Life and Letters,* IV, 369.

[91] *Tales of the Dead.* Principally translated from the French [by Mrs. Sarah Utterson] (London, 1813).

[92] *Ibid.*, p. ii.

[93] *Ibid.*, pp. vif.

[94] *Fantasmagoriana, ou recueil d'histoires d'apparitions de spectres, revenans, fantômes etc.; traduit de l'Allemand, par un amateur* [J. B. B. Eyriès] (Paris, 1812), 2 vols.

[95] Edward Dowden, *The Life of Percy Bysshe Shelley* (London, 1886), II, 33: "During a few days of uncongenial weather, which confined them to the house, some volumes of ghost stories, *Fantasmagoriana* . . . a collection translated into French from the German—fell into their hands, and its perusal probably excited and overstrained Shelley's imagination."

[96] Mrs. Julian Marshall, *The Life and Letters of Mary Wollstonecraft Shelley* (London, 1889), I, 139f.

[97] *Blackwood's Edinburgh Magazine,* XI (June, 1822), 689.

[98] *Gentleman's Magazine,* LXXXXII (July, 1822), 54.

[99] *London Magazine,* VI (Nov., 1822), 438.

[100] *Eclectic Review,* XIX (Mar., 1823), 236.

[101] *Edinburgh Review,* XXXVII (Nov., 1822), 338.

[102] *Bracebridge Hall, Works,* IV, 10ff.

2

[1] "The Spectre Bridegroom," *The Works of Washington Irving,* Hudson ed. (New York, 1882), XIX, 219. (Cited as *Works.*)

[2] Letter to his brother Ebenezer, in P. M. Irving, *The Life and Letters of Washington Irving* (New York, 1863), I, 346. (Cited as *Life and Letters.*)

[3] *Washington Irving and the Storrows. Letters from England and the Continent 1821–1828,* ed. S. T. Williams (Cambridge, Mass., 1933), p. 17. (Cited as *Washington Irving and the Storrows.*)

[4] *Physiognomical Travels,* preceded by a physiognomical journal. Tr. from the German of J. C. A. Musaeus by Anne Plumptre. To which is prefixed a short sketch of the life and character of the author by his pupil Kotzebue (London, 1800), pp. xixf.

[5] Factual data from official records still available giving exact information on arrivals and departures on the first part of this trip are revealed in Eduard Arens' essay, "Washington Irving im Rheinland (1822)," *Eichendorff-Kalender* 1927–28 (Aichach, 1927), pp. 93–120.

[6] *Life and Letters,* II, 92.

[7] *Ibid.,* pp. 91ff.

[8] *Ibid.,* pp. 83f.

[9] In a letter to T. W. Storrow, dated Aug. 21, 1822, Irving wrote: "I was very much confined to my room and very lonely & dispirited; when luckily an English gentleman, an old acquaintance arrived there; and I was induced, lame as I was, to accept a seat in his carriage & come on to Wisbaden to try the waters here." *Washington Irving and the Storrows,* p. 19.

[10] See *The Journals of Washington Irving* (from July, 1815, to July, 1842), eds. W. P. Trent and G. S. Hellman (Boston, 1919), I, 51ff. The details of Irving's impressions on this trip are recorded here and in his correspondence. (Cited as *Journals.*)

[11] *Ibid.,* pp. 55f. The brief list of wines, given in the manuscript notebooks available in the Irving Collection of the New York Public Library, is omitted in the Trent-Hellman edition. Whenever inaccuracies are cited in the printed text of these journals, the source for the correction is the original notebook.

[12] *Life and Letters,* II, 94.

[13] *Journals,* I, 54. Probably through an error of omission rather than as an incognito Irving was merely listed as "Washington aus London" in the roster of guests. See Arens, *op. cit.,* p. 99.

[14] *Life and Letters,* II, 94f.

[15] *Washington Irving and the Storrows,* pp. 20f.

[16] *Life and Letters,* II, 98.

[17] *Ibid.,* pp. 95f. However, after the novelty of seeing German scenes and German people wore off and personal problems influenced his mood, Irving became more impatient. Cf. his letter to Mrs. Foster (*Life and Letters,* IV, 402): " . . . and how intolerable are those tedious Germans with their post horses and post offices, that letters, when they are written, are so slow in coming to hand! Really I grow heartily weary of this *langsam* country."

[18] *Ibid.,* p. 99.

[19] *Ibid.,* p. 101.

[20] *Journals,* I, 57f.

[21] See "To the Reader," introduction to *Tales of a Traveller,* in *Works,* XXI, 11–15.

[22] *Life and Letters,* II, 99.

[23] *Ibid.,* p. 102.

[24] *Ibid.,* p. 103.

[25] *Ibid.,* pp. 104ff.

[26] Moore had written Irving: "I want you very much here, and often express my wants aloud . . ." *Ibid.,* p. 107.

[27] *Ibid.,* pp. 102ff, 109f. Irving's letters make this assumption reasonable, but his own notations(*Journals,* I, 59f. and 65f.) give contradictory information. Possibly Irving returned to Darmstadt a second time. The only performance of *Der Freischütz* took place Sept. 22 according to theatre records. His reference to being in Hirschhorn

"on Tuesday, Sept. 25, on our way from Darmstadt to Heidelberg" is erroneous because Sept. 25 was a Wednesday. Irving sometimes neglected his diaries and, in filling the gaps later, made mistakes in dates and sequence of towns visited.

[28] *Ibid.*, p. 110.

[29] This and other travel information in the original journal are omitted in the Trent-Hellman edition.

[30] See *Journals,* I, 59f.

[31] *Life and Letters,* II, 111f.

[32] Arens (*op. cit.*, p. 115) acknowledges the extraordinary underground passages and vaults of this castle built in 1479, but doubts their employment for purposes other than routine incarceration.

[33] *Life and Letters,* II, 110f.

[34] *Ibid.*, p. 113.

[35] *Journals,* I, 68.

[36] *Life and Letters,* II, 114.

[37] Of Thomas Campbell on this clash between Bavarians and Frenchmen, Irving wrote (*Biographies and Miscellanies, Works,* XVII, 149f.): "This awful spectacle he has described with all the poet's fire, in his 'Battle of Hohenlinden'; a poem which perhaps contains more grandeur and martial sublimity than is to be found anywhere else, in the same compass of English poetry."

[38] Irving's notation (*Journals,* I, 78) that he arrived on Tuesday, Oct. 10, is definitely erroneous. Oct. 8 was a Tuesday and is the correct date for the theatrical performance he recorded.

[39] *Journals,* I, 80.

[40] *Works,* VIII, 298.

[41] *Life and Letters,* II, 116. The three theatres referred to were the Königliches Hof- und Nationaltheater, the Königliches Hoftheater am Isarthor, and the Residenztheater.

[42] *Journals,* I, 91.

[43] *Life and Letters,* II, 119.

[44] *Washington Irving and the Storrows,* pp. 23f.

[45] *Journals,* I, 91–95.

[46] Entries in *Journals* that precede the period covering Oct. 21–Nov. 15, 1822, are omitted in the Trent-Hellman edition. See German titles listed in Appendix, pp. 202–6.

[47] They are not found in a collection of hundred legends of the Untersberg published by Dr. Franz Ziller in *Mittheilungen der Gesellschaft für Salzburger Landeskunde,* 1860–61, I, 81–138. Another scholar emphasizes the abundance of such stories still living among the people in 1831, but imparted to strangers more and more unwillingly. Cf. "Vorwort", *Bayrische Sagen mitgetheilt und geschichtlich beleuchtet von H. F. Massmann,* (Munich, 1831).

[48] This is supported by Irving's notation that "the *valet de place* told me he knew the woman" involved in one of the legends recorded. *Journals,* I, 95.

[49] From an unpublished letter of Oct. 10, 1822, in the possession of the Pennsylvania Historical Society.

[50] *Washington Irving and the Storrows,* p. 28.

[51] *Life and Letters,* II, 124.

[52] *Journals,* I, 106.

[53] Omitted in the Trent-Hellman edition. The Hotel Stadt London was opened

in 1820 as one of the finest hostelries in the city and still stands, though its name has been changed to Hotel Post because of its proximity to the main post office.

[54] *Journals,* I, 100; and *Life and Letters,* II, 121.

[55] *Journals,* I, 101.

[56] *Ibid.,* p. 111, where, however, Trent-Hellman transcribed the text inaccurately.

[57] *Life and Letters,* II, 122f.

[58] Letter to Susan Storrow. *Washington Irving and the Storrows,* p. 23.

[59] *Journals,* I, 109–10.

[60] *Life and Letters,* II, 120, 124.

[61] P. E. Turnbull, *Austria* (London, 1840), I, 213. Additional information about Vienna in 1822 is taken from the introductory chapter of Otto Forst de Battaglia's *Johann Nestroy* (Leipzig, 1932), pp. 9–20.

[62] Baroness Staël-Holstein, *Germany* (London, 1813), I, 81.

[63] Unpublished Notebook of 1825, which was in the possession of Dr. Terry.

[64] S. T. Williams, Chapter X, "Geoffrey Crayon in London and Paris," *The Life of Washington Irving* (New York, 1935), I, 192–214.

[65] See Schreyvogels *Tagebücher,* 1810–1823, ed. Karl Glossy (Berlin, 1903), I, lxx.

[66] See Josef Nadler, "Goethe und Grillparzer," *Corona,* 1933, p. 494.

[67] See Karl Glossy, introduction to "Zur Geschichte der Theater Wiens, II (1821 bis 1830)," *Jahrbuch der Grillparzer-Gesellschaft,* XXVI (Vienna, 1920), pp. vii–xxiii.

[68] See W. v. Wurzbach, "Das spanische Drama am Wiener Hofburgtheater zur Zeit Grillparzers," *Ibid.,* VIII (1898), 108–31.

[69] See August Sauer, "Zur Geschichte des Burgtheaters," *Gesammelte Reden und Aufsätze zur Geschichte der Literatur in Österreich und Deutschland* (Vienna, 1903), pp. 81–101.

[70] See Caroline Pichler, *Denkwürdigkeiten aus meinem Leben,* ed. E. K. Blümml (Munich, 1914), 2 vols.; especially the informative introduction.

[71] *Ibid.,* II, 68–71, 450–53.

[72] See H. A. Lier, "Karl August Böttigers Reise nach Wien im Herbst 1811," *Jahrbuch der Grillparzer-Gesellschaft,* XIII (1903), 123–50.

[73] *Life and Letters,* II, 124.

[74] *Journals,* I, 177, where Irving actually wrote Briar [not Brün as Trent-Hellman reads] to represent the pronunciation of Breuer; or *The Journal of Emily Foster,* eds. S. T. Williams and L. B. Beach (New York, 1938), p. 20, where Emily wrote "Crassie" for "Grassi," or pp. 53, 72, 107 where "Blauen" is always written for "Plauen."

[75] See *Neues Gemählde von Dresden* (Dresden, 1817), pp. 168f.; and the anonymous publication, *Dresden wie es ist, und wie es seyn sollte* (1805), quoted in E. Haenel and E. Kalkschmidt, *Das alte Dresden* (Leipzig, 1934), p. 113: "Es ist eigentlich eine jämmerliche Sprache, welche die Dresdner im gemeinen Leben führen, und man verwechselt hier das Reine mit der schlechteren Mundart selbst in den angesehensten Familien und Gesellschaften. . . . Auch das B und P, D und T, G und K wird hier gar nicht unterschieden und ganz einerlei ausgesprochen, daher denn auch oft bei einigen Leuten, von denen man es nicht erwarten sollte, die ungeheure Menge Schreibefehler . . . kurz es ist eine verdorbene Sprache."

[76] J. G. Lockhart, *Memoirs of the Life of Sir Walter Scott* (Boston, n. d.), I, 238.

[77] *Letters of Washington Irving to Henry Brevoort,* ed. C. S. Hellman (New York, 1918), pp. 154, 304.

[78] "Extract of a letter from a young American Clergyman abroad, to his friend in Philadelphia," *Analectic Magazine,* XII (July, 1818), 84. In the September, 1818, issue (pp. 258f) is another "Extract of a letter from a Gentleman in Dresden."

[79] *Journals,* I, 114f.

[80] *Ibid.,* p. 120. Trent-Hellman went completely astray in assuming a reference to a fairy tale of the Brothers Grimm. The exact title *Le petit Prophète de Boehmischbroda* has nothing to do with legends or fairy lore, but is a witty satire on French music and French society written by Friedrich Melchior von Grimm, the friend of Diderot and the Encyclopaedists, who did much for the cultural relations between France and Germany in the eighteenth century. Grimm favored the musical innovations of Rameau and wrote his satirical defense of the new Italian style in music and comic opera which eventually triumphed over the classical compositions of Lulli. Where Irving had become familiar with the issues of this dispute cannot be ascertained, but his strong predilection for Italian opera and particularly the music of Rossini may explain his interest. That this unusual title was fixed in his mind is another proof of his wide and somewhat unorthodox reading.

Grimm's tract appeared in Paris in 1753 and went through three printings within a month. It is reprinted and most easily accessible in Maurice Tourneux, ed., *Correspondance littéraire, philosophique et critique par Grimm, Diderot, Raynal, Meister,* . . . (Paris, 1882), XVI, 313–36.

[81] *Ibid.,* pp. 121f.

[82] *Ibid.,* p. 123. See performances witnessed as listed in Appendix A, pp. 193–98.

[83] *Ibid.,* p. 122.

[84] *Ibid.,* p. 129.

[85] *Ibid.,* p. 134.

3

[1] See C. W. Böttiger and Th. Flathe, *Geschichte des Kurstaates und Königreiches Sachsen* (Gotha, 1870), II, 558ff.

[2] Irving recognized the situation and recorded: "Saxon nobility—poor—live in lodgings—do not entertain nor receive anybody. Primitive houses of Saxon *beau monde.*" In *The Journals of Washington Irving (from July, 1815, to July, 1842),* eds. W. P. Trent and G. S. Hellman (Boston, 1919), I, 139, where Trent-Hellman transcribed the text inaccurately. (Cited as *Journals.*)

[3] The *Dresdner Anzeiger* of Dec. 2, 1822 (p. 1930), recorded their arrival as of Nov. 28: "Mr. Droing [Irving] aus Amerika, Mr. Montagu aus England von Prag, im Hôtel de Saxe."

[4] The hotel was torn down in 1888. It had stood on the corner of the New Market Square, identified as Neumarkt 9 and Moritzstrasse 1.

[5] Letter of Dec. 2, 1822, in C. R. Leslie, *Autobiographical Recollections* (Boston, 1860), pp. 248f.

[6] See Irving's letter to Mr. Storrow, written Dec. 22, 1822: "I came here without any letters, but Mr. Morier the English Ambassador has been uncommonly attentive to me. He has made his house almost like a home to me; has introduced me to all the foreign ministers who form the gayest & most agreeable circle here, has made me

acquainted with some of the first characters of the place and this day he is to introduce me to court." *Washington Irving and the Storrows. Letters from England and the Continent 1821–1828,* ed. S. T. Williams (Cambridge, Mass., 1933), p. 30. (Cited as *Washington Irving and the Storrows.*)

[7] See supplement *Literaturblatt,* 1821, No. 5, p. 20.

[8] "Ein Reiseabenteuer." Aus dem eben erschienenen neuen Werke des Amerikaners anonimous Geoffrey Crayon, in zwei Bänden . . . und Bracabridge [*sic*] Hall betitelt ist. *Ibid.,* June 26–28, 1822, No. 152–54.

[9] Published in Sept., 1822, by the Arnoldische Buchhandlung, Dresden. The Dresden *Abendzeitung* of Oct. 23, p. 338 carried an announcement of it. Irving wrote of his popularity to Mr. Storrow: " . . . there are German translations of my works just appearing, and my writings & myself are topicks in the little literary papers which abound in Germany. This has made me an object of blue stocking curiosity and instead of quietly taking a part of observer in society I have to talk—and to fight my way through tough conversations with the aid of bad french and worse german." *Washington Irving and the Storrows,* p. 31.

[10] Dresden *Abendzeitung,* Jan. 22, 1823, and Feb. 7, 1824.

[11] *Journals,* I, 139.

[12] *Memoirs, Journals and Correspondence of Thomas Moore,* ed. Lord John Russell (London, 1853), III, 113.

[13] C. R. Leslie, *Autobiographical Recollections,* p. 248.

[14] Contrasting with the stiff ceremonials of court etiquette was the curious custom of having a sort of "open house" at the summer palace at Pillnitz, where the populace was admitted and eagerly watched the royal family at dinner. This established custom was observed by Irving. See *Journals,* I, 218.

[15] P. M. Irving, *The Life and Letters of Washington Irving* (New York, 1863), II, 138f. (Cited as *Life and Letters.*)

[16] *Journals,* I, 182.

[17] Robert Prölss, *Geschichte des Hoftheaters zu Dresden* (Dresden, 1878), pp. 370f:

"Gleich ihrem königlichen Bruder gaben sich auch die Prinzen Anton und Max in ihren Mussestunden mit Eifer und Talent dem Studium und der Ausübung der Musik hin. So besitzt die königl. Musikaliensammlung (wie Fürstenau: 'Die musikalischen Beschäftigungen der Prinzessin Amalie' mittheilt) mehr als 50 Bände Compositionen vom Prinzen Anton, und auch vom Prinzen Max finden sich dort verschiedene musikalische Werke vor (Cantaten und Opern), die wohl mehrenteils im engen Familienkreise aufgeführt wurden. König Johann erinnerte sich z. B. noch mit Vergnügen der Darstellung einer solchen Oper: 'La famiglia felice, opera buffa in due atti,' welche sein Vater 1812 von seiner Familie aufführen liess. Dieser lieferte auch meist zu den Compositionen seines Bruders Anton die (italienischen) Texte. Beide waren, wie ihre jüngste Schwester Maria Anna, im Clavierspiel und auch im Gesange geschickt. Musikalische Unterhaltungen und Aufführungen schmückten fast alle ihre Feste und machten ihr Familienleben zu einem überaus genussreichen. Die Kinder des Prinzen Max, die Prinzen Friedrich August, Clemens, Johann und die Prinzessin Amalia, wurden, heranblühend, mehr und mehr, an denselben betheiligt. Sie erhielten Gesangsunterricht von Rastrelli und Micksch, und Joseph Schuster unterrichtete die Prinzessin Amalia, Kammermusikus Schmiedel die Prinzen im Clavierspiel. Auch pflegte Prinz Max seinen Kindern öfter Gelegenheit zu verschaffen, sich in dramatischen Spielen zu üben. Schon seit 1808 wurden von ihnen Opern, Ballete, und französische

Lustspiele zur Aufführung gebracht. So gemessen, förmlich und ceremoniell sich Alles in der unmittelbaren Nähe des Königs, besonders in den Beziehungen nach Aussen, bewegte, so heiter, ungezwungen, anspruchslos und geistig angeregt war das Familienleben der Prinzen."

[18] *Journals,* I, 146f.

[19] *Ibid.,* pp. 142f.

[20] *Ibid.,* pp. 143, 147, 150f., 163, 185, 219. Further entries (148, 158, 165, 186f.) give additional testimony to Irving's hearty welcome at court.

[21] *Briefwechsel König Johanns von Sachsen mit George Ticknor,* eds. Johann Georg, Duke of Saxony, and E. Daenell (Leipzig, 1920).

[22] *Life, Letters, and Journals of George Ticknor* (Boston, 1877), I, 462, n.

[23] Johann Georg, ed., *op. cit.* Letter from Ticknor, March 15, 1842, p. 14: "The one [newspaper] printed at New York, contains Mr. Jamieson's translation of the Princess Amelies Oheim—the one printed in Boston contains an original translation of the Verlobung. Of each of these papers, eight or ten thousand copies were printed. Please to give those I send you, with my best respects, to the Princess. It will amuse her to see how popular she is in the New-World."

[24] *Flora Marienbadensis oder Pflanzen und Gebirgsarten, gesammelt und beschrieben von dem Prinzen F. A. Mitregenten von Sachsen und von J. W. von Goethe,* [ed., C. J. Heidler] (Prague, 1837).

On May 24, 1829, Prince John ordered a selection of his verse sent to Goethe's daughter-in-law Ottilie after the poet had promised to read them. Goethe's judgment is not known, but the poems and the accompanying letter are still in the Goethe-Schiller-Archiv. *Goethe Jahrbuch,* XXI (1900), 192.

[25] Traditional dignity, however, did at times give way to the King's humor. The following anecdote about the King's indulgence in practical jokes was related to me by the King's grandnephew, Prince Johann Georg, Duke of Saxony: At the royal hunting lodge at Moritzburg was a "great *pokal* or drinking horn made of the horn of a stag —that cannot be set down" (*Journals,* I, 186). The King delighted in presenting this goblet to an unsuspecting guest and watching his behavior. Aside from its size which in itself was formidable, the goblet continually spilled some of its contents (in the manner of a dribble-cup). The King later recorded in a special guest book how the victim had reacted and acquitted himself. Though Irving describes the drinking-horn, he was exempted from the ordeal as his name does not occur in the King's notation. Apparently, Irving's dignity and prestige deterred such levity.

[26] Information received through courtesy of Dr. E. Hensler of the Saxon Archives. The entry concerning the dinner in the *Hofkalender* reads: "5. Januar. Den. 5. Cour bey Sr. Maj. dem Könige u. Prinz Anton Kgl. Hoh. . . . Mittagstafel zu 20 Couverts, Gäste: Fürst Mentschicoff; Herr Scott u H. Buttler, Englische Capitains; H. Graf Zandowsky; H. Graf. v. Blome-Salzau, dänischer Kammerherr; H. Price; H. Brochocki; H. Washington Irving; H. Unterstaatssekretair v. Minckwitz; H. Kammerherr v. Globig."

[27] *Journals,* I, 151.

[28] Irving's notations show a lacuna (*Journals,* I, 171), but the unpublished Tagebuch der Prinzessin Amalie (Schlossbibliothek Moritzburg bei Dresden), II, 21 (March 9, 1823) shows: "Soirée bey Johannes mit dem Corps Diplomatique und Familien Loss und Friesen, und W. Irving."

[29] *Journals,* I, 139. Irving at first spelled the name Bötticar, which approximates the pronunciation given the name in Dresden.

[30] Ticknor respected Böttiger's great learning and mourned his death in 1835, saying he left "no man in Germany who can fill his place." *Life, Letters, and Journals of George Ticknor,* I, 457.

[31] Emily Foster recorded: "Old Böttiger called to give us permission to have books from the royal library—after endless compliments he turned round to me with a solemn bow, entreating me to explain my wishes—it was like 'Mlle parlez de la religion, de la morale de la politique, & ensuite nous parlerons d'autre chose' I was so embarrassed I could not say a word so he sent me heaps of rubbishy almanacks & stories—He has sent me Heeren on the middle ages—& Xenophon's retreat." *The Journal of Emily Foster,* eds. S. T. Williams and L. B. Beach (New York, 1938), pp. 43f. (Cited as *Journal of Emily Foster.*)

[32] Samuel Longfellow, *Life of H. W. Longfellow* (Boston, 1886), I, 117: "On the 30th of August, [1827] he [Irving] notes that he had written 'letters of introduction for Mr. Longfellow, to Rumigny, Böttiger, Löwenstein, Sir Walter Scott and Sotheby'."

[33] The only reproductions—and very poor ones—that I have been able to discover of this unusual sketch are in R. P. Halleck's *History of American Literature* (New York, 1911), p. 114, and in *Der grosse Brockhaus* (Leipzig, 1931), IX, 222.

[34] Trent-Hellman transcribed Irving's uncertain spelling of this name as Lutichan.

[35] *Journals,* I, 154.

[36] *Ibid.,* p. 160.

[37] *Ibid.,* p. 162 where, however, Trent-Hellman made the passage meaningless by transcribing "chasse" as "chapel."

[38] *Ibid.,* p. 143.

[39] *Life, Letters, and Journals of George Ticknor,* I, 491, 476.

[40] *Journals,* I, 145.

[41] G. S. Hellman, *Washington Irving Esquire* (New York, 1925), p. 140.

[42] See Paul Nerrlich, *Jean Paul und seine Zeitgenossen* (Berlin, 1876), p. 103, where his departure from Dresden is given as of June 12, 1822.

[43] The Trent-Hellman transcription omits the identification of the language master as the source of such information, as shown in Irving's manuscript.

[44] *Journals,* I, 187, 198. Irving also noted book titles by Jean Paul at end of his notebook covering Jan. 20–May 20, 1823, an entry not included by Hellman.

[45] *Schauspiele von Don Pedro Calderón de la Barca* (Leipzig, 1819–25), 6 vols.

[46] *Journals,* I, 155. Professor E. H. Zeydel first called attention to Irving's meeting with Tieck (*PMLA,* XLVI, 946f.), a notation which the Trent-Hellman transcription mangled almost beyond recognition.

[47] See Rudolf Köpke, *Ludwig Tieck* (Leipzig, 1855), II, 67: "Ihr Ruf ging weit über Dresden hinaus, und Tieck's Meisterschaft im dramatischen Lesen trug vielleicht ebenso viel dazu bei, ihn zur öffentlichen Person zu machen, als sein dichterischer Ruhm. Seine Vorlesungen wurden zu Dresdens Merkwürdigkeiten gezählt. Bisweilen fragten sogar die Lohnbedienten der Gasthöfe im Namen angekommener Fremden an, ob heute Abend Vorlesung sein werde. Man sprach von ihnen, wie von der Gemäldegalerie, von der Kapelle der katholischen Kirche, oder dem Theater. Wer nach Dresden kam, musste Tieck besucht, irgendeine seiner Vorlesungen gehört haben, das war unerlässlich. Sie vollendeten den künstlerischen Charakter der Stadt. Wie Goethe zu Weimar, gehörte Tieck zu Dresden."

[48] *Journals,* I, 155.

[49] *The Correspondence of John Lothrop Motley,* ed. G. W. Curtis (New York, 1889), I, 36.

[50] The fullest treatment of this group, with detailed analyses of their membership, is in H. A. Krüger, *Pseudoromantik. Friedrich Kind und der dresdener Liederkreis* (Leipzig, 1904).

[51] *Journals,* I, 151.

[52] *Ibid.,* p. 179. Irving's faulty spelling of the name was probably influenced by the peculiarities of the Dresden pronunciation.

[53] *Ibid.,* pp. 165, 173.

[54] *Washington Irving and the Storrows,* pp. 31f.

[55] *Journals,* I, 143ff.

[56] *Life and Letters,* II, 159.

[57] *Journals,* I, 141.

[58] *Journal of Emily Foster,* pp. 108f.

[59] *Life and Letters,* IV, 339.

[60] *Journals,* I, 143f.

[61] *Ibid.,* pp. 146ff.

[62] *Journal of Emily Foster.* Entries on pp. 151 and 169f. make this assumption reasonable.

[63] See J. B. Burke, *Landed Gentry* (London, 1939), p. 816.

[64] W. A. Reichart, "Baron von Gumppenberg, Emily Foster, and Washington Irving," *Modern Language Notes,* LX (May, 1945), 333–35.

[65] *Journal of Emily Foster,* p. 49.

[66] *Ibid.,* p. 100.

[67] *Ibid.,* pp. 110f.

[68] *Ibid.,* p. 114.

[69] *Letters of Washington Irving to Henry Brevoort,* ed. G. S. Hellman (New York, 1918), pp. 269, 289, 293.

[70] *Journal of Emily Foster,* p. 111.

[71] *Ibid.*

[72] *Journals,* I, 152.

[73] See W. A. Reichart, "Washington Irving's Friend and Collaborator: Barham John Livius, Esq.," *PMLA,* LVI (June, 1941), 517–21; also P. R. Kirby, "Washington Irving, Barham Livius and Weber," *Music and Letters,* XXXI (1950), 133–47.

[74] Letter of March 10, 1823, to Peter Irving, *Life and Letters,* II, 140–42. *The Wonder; a Woman Keeps a Secret* by Mrs. Susanna Centlivre (1714) was performed privately in the Foster salon on April 2 and repeated before their guests two days later.

[75] *Journal of Emily Foster,* p. 115.

[76] *Ibid.,* p. 117.

[77] Letter of March 7, 1823, to his sister, *Life and Letters,* II, 137.

[78] *Journal of Emily Foster,* p. 116.

[79] *Ibid.,* p. 118.

[80] *Journals,* I, 163–70.

[81] *Washington Irving and the Storrows,* p. 28.

[82] Letter to Mrs. Van Wart, *Life and Letters,* II, 137.

[83] C. R. Leslie, *Autobiographical Recollections,* p. 252.

[84] *Journals,* I, 145.

[85] *Ibid.,* pp. 194f.

[86] *Ibid.,* pp. 179–94.

[87] *Ibid.,* p. 182.

88 *Ibid.*, p. 177. Trent-Hellman assumed a slip of the pen and suggested that a German edition was meant, but such an English edition actually appeared in 1823. See S. T. Williams and M. A. Edge, *A Bibliography of the Writings of Washington Irving* (New York, 1936), p. 103.

89 *Ibid.*, pp. 174f., 191, 194.

90 *Ibid.*, p. 175. Also detailed account in *Journal of Emily Foster*, pp. 122f.

91 *Ibid.*, p. 174.

92 *Ibid.*, p. 179. Trent-Hellman omitted the important last phrase in the printed version of the *Journals.*

93 *Ibid.*

94 *Ibid.*, p. 181.

95 *Ibid.*, p. 188.

96 *Ibid.*, p. 185.

97 *Ibid.*, p. 189.

98 *Journal of Emily Foster*, pp. 126, 130ff; also *Life and Letters*, II, 152f.

99 *Journals*, I, 189.

100 *Journal of Emily Foster*, pp. 138f.

101 *Life and Letters*, IV, 390–91. See also S. T. Williams, "Washington Irving's Religion," *Yale Review*, XV (1926), 414–16, which includes a letter from Irving to Emily Foster that emphasizes his suspicions of "the external forms of religion."

102 *Ibid.*, II, 155.

103 *Journals*, I, 126.

104 *Ibid.*, p. 204; and *Life and Letters*, IV, 391.

105 John Quincy Adams, "Journal of a Tour through Silesia," *Port Folio* (Philadelphia, 1801) I, Nos. 1–45. Published in 44 letters, one appearing on first page of each issue. Unauthorized publications in book form as *Letters on Silesia* (London, 1804), *Briefe über Schlesien* (Breslau, 1805), and *Lettres sur Silésie* (Paris, 1807) reflect the general interest. See S. D. Stirk, "John Quincy Adams' *Letters on Silesia*," *New England Quarterly*, IX (1936), 485–99.

In writing to a friend Adams characterized his impressions of this remote region in these words: "There is not, I believe, in all Europe, a province so little visited by foreign travelers as Silesia; yet there are very few, if any, which contain such a multiplicity of objects calculated to afford both amusement and instruction; certainly none where a soul susceptible of enjoyment from the contemplation of the beauties of nature, or a mind curious to investigate the world of human industry, can find greater and more varied satisfaction." *Writings of John Quincy Adams*, ed. W. C. Ford (New York, 1913), II, 469.

106 *Life and Letters*, IV, 391f.

107 *Ibid.*, p. 394.

108 *Ibid.*, p. 389.

109 *Ibid.*, p. 399.

110 *Journals*, I, 207.

111 See the letters reproduced in *Life and Letters*, II, 155–60, IV, 392–403; and the numerous entries in *Journals*, I, 208–13.

112 *Life and Letters*, IV, 397.

113 See *Journals*, I, 173f., 179n.

114 In his biography, *Washington Irving Esquire*, Hellman stated categorically: "Emily refused the offer of marriage from the delightful American who was, after all, so much her senior" (p. 143). The new evidence submitted as conclusive proof

that Irving was the rejected suitor consists primarily of Hellman's conjectures regarding certain barely decipherable and partially deleted lines in the original journals. Most of his surmises seem plausible except the transcription "Early part day triste—Emily delightful," which formed the basis for his deduction "that the rest of the deleted portion referred to Irving's determination to put his fortune to the test, and that on March 31 (which entry shows another deletion—this time probably of the word 'depressed') Irving asked Emily to become his wife, but without success" (*Journals,* I, facsimile of a page of the diary, following p. 173). S. T. Williams pointed out that the reading "Early part day triste—Evening delightful" is not only a more accurate transcription but a more logical entry (cf. S. T. Williams, "Washington Irving, Matilda Hoffman, and Emily Foster," *Modern Language Notes,* XLVIII, 182–86). Irving was describing, as he often did in his *Journals,* weather conditions and noted the pleasant evening following a disagreeable morning. The use of the word "triste" occurs frequently in his notations and refers to climatic aspects as well as to human moods.

Overlooked so far has been a separate notation on the next to the last page of the second Dresden Journal, where aside from the titles of Weber's operas *Der Freischütz* and *Abu Hassan* (with the translations of which Irving occupied himself) stands a clear and unmistakable entry: "March 27 Early part of day triste. Emily delightful" (unpublished; in New York Public Library). Why these phrases should be inscribed without any context, quite remote from the narrative itself and preceded only by blank pages containing stray notations, addresses, and book titles, is puzzling indeed. That Irving was not likely to bare his soul in any sort of personal confession is in keeping with his tendency to chronicle only factual details of his travels, details that he would otherwise have forgotten. Hence his constant and often inadequate efforts to record place names of towns visited or of personages met in society. Any personal reactions beyond general observations or reflections never found their way into the *Journals.* Emotional experiences that might touch his sensitive nature required no recording. The phrase "Emily delightful" would be an unnatural and inadequate description of the moment of elation that preceded Irving's momentous decision to put his fortune to the test. The simplest and therefore the likeliest interpretation of this entry, requiring no key, doing no violence to our knowledge of Irving's habits, and yet fitting into the context of the March notations, is to accept its literal meaning. Emily Foster may have been feeling poorly (see Irving's April entries, "Emily very unwell," "Emily unwell with headache," "Emily somewhat better—very pale," "Emily still with headache," *Journals,* I, 177ff.), she had shown "capricious coldness fits" which she recorded (*Journal of Emily Foster,* p. 126), so that Irving naturally welcomed a return of the happy, carefree mood that usually prevailed at the Fosters and which had so often cheered or encouraged him when subject to periods of dejection. A number of such happier moods are also recorded: "Emily in good spirits and listens delightfully," "Emily looking much better—in good spirits," "Emily much better" (*Journals,* I, 181f.).

[115] *Life and Letters,* IV, 337–408.

[116] *Ibid.,* p. 358.

[117] See P. M. Irving's letter to an unknown correspondent, published by F. P. Smith in "Washington Irving, the Fosters, and some Poetry," *American Literature,* IX (1937), 228–32.

[118] S. T. Williams, *The Life of Washington Irving* (New York, 1935), I, 236–54. (Cited as *The Life.*)

[119] See *Ibid.*, pp. 406f., n. 183; also Irving's poignant words: "She died in the flower of her youth & of mine but she has lived for me ever since in all woman kind. I see her in their eyes—and it is the remembrance of her that has given a tender interest in my eyes to every thing that bears the name of woman." *Journal of Washington Irving (1823–1824)*, ed. S. T. Williams (Cambridge, Mass., 1931), p. 117, n. 2. (Cited as *Journal of 1823–1824.*)

[120] *The Life,* II, 255–62.

[121] *Ibid.*, pp. 260f.

[122] *Life and Letters,* IV, 361.

[123] *Ibid.*, pp. 220, 337–408.

[124] *Ibid.*, pp. 362f.

[125] *Ibid.*, pp. 388f.

[126] *Journals,* I, 208ff, where Irving mentions the receipt of letters on May 28, 31, June 8, 15, 17 (which Trent-Hellman omitted), 18, 19.

[127] *Life and Letters,* IV, 396.

[128] *Ibid.*, II, 157f.

[129] *Ibid.*, IV, 389.

[130] *Ibid.*, p. 394.

[131] *Ibid.*, p. 395.

[132] *Ibid.*, p. 398.

[133] *Ibid.*, p. 362.

[134] *Journal of Emily Foster,* pp. 128f.

[135] "Späterhin wurde sein Gefühl und seine Zeit durch sehr zarte Verhältnisse noch mehr in Anspruch genommen" . . . *Wegweiser im Gebiete der Künste und Wissenschaften.* (Literary supplement to the *Abendzeitung*), Feb. 11, 1824.

[136] *Journals,* I, 216.

[137] *Ibid.*, pp. 215f. Trent-Hellman transcribed "fine ev'g alone seated in dusk" instead of "find Emily alone seated in dusk," which, of course, misses the whole point of this passage.

[138] *Journal of Emily Foster,* p. 147.

[139] *Life and Letters,* IV, 218.

[140] *Journal of Emily Foster,* p. 158.

[141] *Ibid.*, p. 130.

[142] W. A. Reichart, "Washington Irving, the Fosters, and the Forsters," *Modern Language Notes,* L (Jan., 1935), 35–39.

[143] *Life and Letters,* II, 128.

[144] *Journals,* I, 221.

[145] *The Life,* I, 253.

[146] *Journals,* I, 221.

[147] Flora Foster Dawson in *Life and Letters,* IV, 366.

[148] *Journal of 1823–1824,* pp. 4f.

[149] Flora Foster Dawson in *Life and Letters,* IV, 369.

[150] *Journal of 1823–1824,* p. 6. Emily recorded similarly: "We are reading the country legends full of water nymphs—& geniuses, no wonder this is the fairy land of Germany it deserves to be." *Journal of Emily Foster,* p. 154.

[151] Flora Foster Dawson erroneously identified the local legend with Grillparzer's *Die Ahnfrau,* locates here "the very real and true site of the drama," and gives a dramatic and highly colored account. She also refers to Irving's attendance at a performance of Grillparzer's drama in Vienna, which cannot be substantiated. See *Life and Letters,* IV, 369f., 382f.; and *Journal of Emily Foster,* pp. 158f.

[152] *Journal of 1823–1824,* pp. 12f. It is curious that in the most important detail, the significant color of the dog in the picture, there is complete disagreement in the accounts; Emily and Flora Foster both emphasize the good omen of the *white* dog but Irving speaks of the "little black dog."

[153] *Ibid.,* p. 16.

[154] *Life and Letters,* IV, 375.

[155] *Journal of 1823–1824,* pp. 16f.

[156] *Life and Letters,* II, 162.

[157] *Journal of Emily Foster,* p. 163.

[158] *Life and Letters,* IV, 376f.

[159] *Journal of Emily Foster,* pp. 167f.

[160] *Life and Letters,* IV, 386.

[161] *Journal of 1823–1824,* p. 20.

[162] *Life and Letters,* II, 162.

[163] *Ibid.,* p. 160.

4

[1] From the unpublished diaries of John Quincy Adams as quoted in A.B. Faust's edition of Adams' translation of Wieland's *Oberon* (New York, 1940), p. lv.

[2] *Ibid.,* p. lxii.

[3] *Letters of Washington Irving to Henry Brevoort,* ed. G. S. Hellman (New York, 1918), pp. 286f.

[4] C. R. Leslie, *Autobiographical Recollections* (Boston, 1860), p. 252.

[5] P. M. Irving, *The Life and Letters of Washington Irving* (New York, 1863), II, 137. (Cited as *Life and Letters.*)

[6] "Mountjoy," *The Works of Washington Irving*, Hudson ed. (New York, 1882), XXVII, 105. (Cited as *Works.*) A faintly autobiographical essay, first published in *The Knickerbocker*, Nov.–Dec. 1839, was already partly written in London in 1818—see S. T. Williams, *The Life of Washington Irving* (New York, 1935), II, 218. (Cited as *The Life.*) The quoted passage on language learning is virtually identical with one written for "The Story of Rosalie." See *Tour in Scotland 1817 and Other Manuscript Notes*, ed. S. T. Williams (New Haven, 1927), p. 100.

[7] *Life and Letters,* IV, 358f, 369, 373.

[8] *The Journals of Washington Irving (from July, 1815, to July, 1842)*, eds. W. P. Trent and G. S. Hellman (Boston, 1919), I. 97. The other words and phrases listed are sprinkled throughout volume I.

[9] *Ibid.,* pp. 73f. Trent-Hellman reproduced Irving's copy somewhat inaccurately, giving neither the correct Goethean text nor the precise deviations in Irving's manuscript.

[10] *Life and Letters,* IV, 369. He also recorded: "As we rode Mrs. Foster read several stories of hexe out of German," *Journal of Washington Irving (1823–1824)*, ed. S. T. Williams (Cambridge, Mass., 1931) p. 6. (Cited as *Journal of 1823–1824.*) Surely, if the reading had been done *in* German he would have expressed himself somewhat differently.

[11] Written to Lady Abercorn. *The Letters of Sir Walter Scott 1808–1811,* ed. H. J. C. Grierson (London, 1932), p. 495.

[12] F. Ewen, *The Prestige of Schiller in England 1788–1859* (New York, 1932), pp. 59, 81–82.

[13] Letter to Pierre Paris Irving in 1825. *Life and Letters,* II, 236f.

[14] *Journals,* II, 86.

[15] *Life and Letters,* II, 158. Taken from Thekla's melancholy song, Act III, Scene vii, l. 2869. *Die Piccolomini. Schillers Werke,* ed. Ludwig Bellermann (Leipzig, n.d.)

[16] *Ibid.,* p. 155.

[17] "Conversations with Talma," *Works,* XVII, 189.

[18] *Journal of 1823–1824,* pp. 72ff., 107, 108, 110, 243; also *Journals,* II, 77, 83, 86.

[19] *Journals,* I, 165.

[20] Irving recorded "rec'd letter from Livius dated Weimar" on Oct. 15, 1823. *Journal of 1823–1824,* p. 55.

[21] *Journals,* I, 180.

[22] *Ibid.,* p. 172. Trent-Hellman transcribed "Martha" instead of "Clärchen." The reference in the same entry to "Tasso and Leonora" may also refer to Goethe's *Tasso* drama.

[23] *Ibid.,* p. 173. Irving recorded on Sept. 17, 1825: "Bo[ugh]t Goethe's 'Faust' for six fr[ancs] twelve sous." *Ibid.,* II, 156.

[24] Georg Witkowski, ed., Goethe's *Faust* (Leiden, 1949), I, lines 1699–1700.

[25] *Life and Letters,* IV, 357, where the quotation reads:

"Könnt ich dem Augenblicke sagen
O Bleibe doch, du bist so schön," &c.

[26] Was plagt ihr armen Thoren viel
Zu solchem Zweck, die holden Musen?
Ich sag' euch, gebt nur mehr, und immer, immer mehr,
So könnt ihr euch vom Ziele nie verirren,
Sucht nur die Menschen zu verwirren,
Sie zu befriedigen ist schwer—

(*Faust,* I, ll. 127–132)

So gib mir auch die Zeiten wieder,
Da ich noch selbst im Werden war,
Da sich ein Quell gedrängter Lieder
Ununterbrochen neu gebar,
Da Nebel mir die Welt verhüllten
Die Knospe Wunder noch versprach,
Da ich die tausend Blumen brach
Die alle Thäler reichlich füllten.
Ich hatte nichts und doch genug,
Den Drang nach Wahrheit und die Lust am Trug.
Gib ungebändigt jene Triebe,
Das tiefe, schmerzenvolle Glück,
Des Hasses Kraft, die Macht der Liebe,
Gib meine Jugend mir zurück!

(*Faust,* I, ll. 184–197)

[27] *Journal of 1823–1824,* pp. 78, 88.

[28] *Journals,* I, 187.

[29] *Ibid.,* p. 198.

[30] In *Edinburgh Review,* XLVI (June, 1827), pp. 176–95.

[31] *Wegweiser im Gebiete der Künste und Wissenschaften,* Literary supplement of the Dresden *Abendzeitung,* Feb. 11, 1824).

[32] *Journals,* II, 105.

[33] *Ibid.*, pp. 9, 11, 19.

[34] Thomas Hodgskin, *Travels in the North of Germany* (Edinburgh, 1820), I, v.

[35] *Ibid.*, II, 346.

[36] *Journals,* I, 163.

[37] *Ibid.*, p. 185.

[38] Johann W. von Archenholz, *Geschichte des siebenjährigen Krieges in Deutschland von 1756 bis 1763* (Berlin, 1793), II, 55f, 64.

[39] *Journals,* III, 190.

[40] *Ibid.*, p. 102.

[41] *Ibid.*, pp. 6f.

[42] *Ibid.*, II, 197.

[43] *Ibid.*, III, 8.

[44] *Ibid.*, pp. 8ff; and *The Life,* I, 348–54.

[45] *The Life,* I, 304.

[46] In the Notebook of 1825 dealing with Spanish Literature is a reference to Bouterwek I, 242, concerning the five-year-long incarceration of Louis (Ponce) de Leon, the lyric poet. This reference is in the German edition of Bouterwek, *Geschichte der Künste und Wissenschaften,* on p. 241 but in volume three!

[47] *Journals,* III, 11–13.

[48] Irving's Notebook of 1825 (in New York Public Library) and A. W. Schlegel's *Vorlesungen über dramatische Kunst und Literatur,* ed. G. V. Amoretti (Bonn & Leipzig, 1923), II, 269f.

Schlegel: Says Cervantes had a right to consider himself one of the founders of the Spanish stage, for before writing Don Quixote he had, as he negligently says, written twenty or thirty pieces, which were represented with applause. He made no higher pretensions from them, but, after they had attained their momentary purpose, he printed some of them, and it is but lately that two of them have been published. One—El trato de Argel, in overcharging of the narration, in meagerness & in the want of bringing out the characters & situations gives signs of the infancy of the art. The other, the Destruction of Numantia, rises on the elevation of the tragic cothurnus and is through unconscious and unsought approach to ancient greatness & purity a remarkable appearance in the history of this new poetry.

Er war berechtigt, sich als einen der Stifter dieser Kunst anzusehen, denn ehe er durch seinen Don Quixote unsterblichen Ruhm erwarb, hatte er fleissig für die Bühne gearbeitet, und zwanzig bis dreissig Stücke von ihm, so nachlässig redet er davon, waren mit Beyfall aufgeführt worden. Er machte damit keine höheren Ansprüche, liess, nachdem sie ihre augenblickliche Bestimmung erreicht hatten, nichts davon drucken, und erst vor kurzem sind zwey dieser älteren Arbeiten herausgegeben worden. Das eine von diesen Schauspielen, vermuthlich das Früheste des Cervantes, *die Lebensart in Algier,* (el trato de Argel) trägt im Uebergewicht der Erzählung, in der Magerkeit des Ganzen und in der mangelnden Hervorhebung der Figuren und Situationen noch Spuren von der damaligen Kindheit der Kunst an sich. Das andre aber, *die Zerstörung von Numantia,* steht ganz auf der Höhe des tragischen Kothurns, und ist durch die bewusstlose und ungesuchte Annäherung an die antike Grösse und Reinheit eine merkwürdige Erscheinung in der Geschichte der neueren Poesie.

Lope de Vega arose & eclipsed Cervantes—The latter however would not entirely give up his earlier claims but before his death in 1615 had 8 plays & as many interludes printed, which he had not brought upon the stage—They are indifferently spoken of by Bouterwek. Schiller says they are flimsy and extravagant. Though Bouterwek shows no enthusiasm for these dramas he does not cite Schiller. [Where Irving gained the impression that Schiller calls them "flimsy and extravagant" cannot be determined.] That Cervantes evidently complied, in writing them with the taste of the times for Stage trick[s], wonderful situation[s] &c— He thought it an indispensable quality in a popular piece to be superficial. In none of his first works are there just negligence & frivolities.

Lope de Vega erschien, und bemeisterte sich bald der Alleinherrschaft auf der Bühne, so dass sich Cervantes nicht neben ihm behaupten konnte. Doch wollte er seine auf früheren Beyfall gegründeten Ansprüche nicht ganz zurück nehmen, und liess kurz vor seinem Tode, im J. 1615, acht Schauspiele und eben so viel kleinere Zwischenspiele drucken, weil er sie nicht nach Wunsch auf die Bühne hatte bringen können. Man hat sie allgemein tief unter seinen sonstigen prosaischen und poetischen Arbeiten gefunden; ihr neuerer Herausgeber meynt sogar, sie seyen Parodien und Satiren auf den verderbten Zeitgeschmack: aber man darf sie nur unbefangen lesen, um diese Hypothese abgeschmackt zu finden. Unter dieser Voraussetzung wären sie das Verfehlteste, was sich denken lässt. Einen solchen Zweck würde Cervantes ganz anders durch ein einziges Stück, aber dann auf eine durchaus nicht misverständliche und sehr belustigende Art zu erreichen gewusst haben. Nein, es sollen Stücke in der Manier des Lope seyn; gegen seine Ueberzeugung suchte sich Cervantes dem Hange seiner Zeitgenossen durch buntere Mannichfaltigkeit, wunderbare Anlagen und Theaterstreiche zu fügen. Allein es scheint, er sähe die Oberflächlichkeit der Composition für die Hauptbedingung des Beyfalls an; wenigstens ist sie meistens so locker und lose, dass in seinen prosaischen Werken von einem ähnlichen Leichtsinn nirgends ein Beyspiel ist.

If the Spanish theatre had ended with Lope—Guillen de Castro, Montalban, Molina, Matos-Fragoso &c it would only have deserved praise for the great sketching out & promising design instead of the fulfilment [sic]—But Calderon appeared—as fertile a brain & as industrious a writer as Lope & quite another kind of poet—he was a poet, if ever any one deserved the name—

Wenn es bey dem bisherigen, nämlich den Werken des Lope und seiner vorzüglicheren Zeitgenossen, eines *Guillen de Castro, Montalban, Molina, Matos-Fragoso u.a.*, ein Bewenden gehabt hätte, so müsste man an dem spanischen Theater mehr den grossen Entwurf und die versprechenden Anlagen, als die reife Vollendung loben. Aber nun trat *Don Pedro Calderon de la Barca* auf, ein eben so fruchtbarer Kopf, eben so fleissiger Schriftsteller als Lope, und ein ganz andrer Dichter, ein Dichter, wenn je einer den Namen verdient hat.

Notwithstanding the quantity of Calderon's pieces none seems done at random. They were worked out in a masterly manner, on certain principles. This cannot be denied, even if Calderon's high & pure style of Romantic theatricals should be mistaken for manner, and his bold flight of poetry to the utmost verge of the imaginary, should be held as error.

Unter diesem fast unübersehbaren Ueberfluss von Werken findet sich nichts aufs Gerathewohl hingeworfne, alles ist nach sichern consequenten Grundsätzen mit den tiefsten künstlerischen Absichten in vollkommner Meisterschaft ausgearbeitet. Diess lässt sich nicht läugnen, wenn man auch Calderons reinen und hohen Styl des Romantisch-Theatralischen als Manier verkennt, und diese kühnen Flüge der Poesie bis an die äusserste Gränze des Ersinnlichen für Verirrungen hält.

5

[1] P. M. Irving, *The Life and Letters of Washington Irving* (New York, 1863), II, 166. (Cited as *Life and Letters.*)

[2] *Ibid*, pp. 166f.

[3] "Correspondence of Washington Irving and John Howard Payne," ed. Thatcher T. P. Luquer, *Scribner's Magazine,* XLVIII (1910), 475.

[4] *Life and Letters,* II, 138.

[5] C. R. Leslie, *Autobiographical Recollections* (Boston, 1860), p. 252.

[6] *The Journals of Washington Irving (from July, 1815, to July, 1842)* eds. W. P. Trent and G. S. Hellman (Boston, 1919), I, 156. (Cited as *Journals.*)

[7] P. R. Kirby, "Weber's Operas in London, 1824–1826," *Musical Quarterly,* XXXII (1946), 334.

[8] Allardyce Nicoll, *A History of Early Nineteenth Century Drama 1800–1850* (Cambridge, 1930), I, 80f.

[9] W. A. Reichart, "Washington Irving's Friend and Collaborator: Barham John Livius, Esq.," *PMLA,* LVI (1941), 517ff.

[10] Kirby, *op. cit.*, p. 333.

[11] See Appendix, pp. 193–98.

[12] *Journals,* I, 191. Irving does not give the title of this performance, though the Dresden theatre records show it to be *Der Freischütz.* This explains Professor Kirby's insistence that Irving did not see this opera in Dresden. See P. R. Kirby, "Washington Irving, Barham Livius and Weber," *Music and Letters,* XXXI (1950), 135f.

[13] *Journals,* I, 156ff., 162f., 166f., 174, 178.

[14] *Ibid,* pp. 195f.

[15] *Ibid.*, pp. 208f, 219; *Journal of Washington Irving (1823–1824)*, ed. S. T. Williams (Cambridge, Mass., 1931), pp. 57, 60; and *Journals,* II, 33.

[16] S. T. Williams, *The Life of Washington Irving* (New York, 1935), I, 270. (Cited as *The Life.*)

[17] See Felix Hasselberg, *Der Freischütz. Friedrich Kinds Operndichtung und ihre Quellen* (Berlin, 1921), pp. 7–11, 15–44, 49–112.

[18] See "Handlist of plays produced between 1800–1850" in Nicoll, *op. cit.,* II.

[19] *The Recollections and Reflections of J. R. Planché* (London, 1872), I, 79.

[20] *The Freyschütz; /or, the/ Wild Huntsman of Bohemia. A Romantic Opera, /in three Acts,/altered from the German by/ Barham Livius, Esq. The music composed by the Chevalier Carl Maria de Weber/ maître de Chapelle to the King of Saxony, and Director of/ the Opera of Dresden. /First Performed/ at the / Theatre Royal Covent Garden/ Thursday, October 14, 1824. /London:/ Printed for John Miller, New Bridge Street, /Blackfriars/ 1824. (Two Shillings and Six-pence.)*

[21] *The Wild Huntsman by Washington Irving with an Introduction by George S. Hellman* (The Bibliophile Society, Boston, 1924). At the end of the introduction (pp. 17f.), Hellman says: "What happened to Livius's manuscript, if it was ever written is not known."

[22] *Journals,* II, 32f.

[23] "Washington Irving, Barham Livius and Weber," p. 141.

[24] Luquer, *op. cit.*, p. 472.

[25] *Ibid.*, p. 475.

[26] *Journal of 1823–1824*, p. 154.

[27] Luquer, *op. cit.*, pp. 478–80.

[28] Reichart, *op. cit.*, p. 521.

[29] *Ibid.*, p. 523.

[30] *Ibid.*, pp. 523f.

[31] *Journal of 1823–1824*, p. 239.

[32] *Ibid.*, p. 187.

[33] "Weber's Operas in London, 1824–1826," pp. 336–41.

[34] J. Genest, *Some Account of the English Stage from the Restoration in 1660 to 1830* (Bath, 1832), IX, 299. The vogue of this opera is described in these words: "An Opera, called Der Freischütz, had been brought out in Germany with great success—Weber's music was considered as particularly good—these circumstances excited a rage for adapting the German piece to the English stage—6 alterations were made of it."

[35] *Journals*, II, 32.

[36] *The Freyschütz; . . . by Barham Livius, Esq.* (London, 1824), pp. v–viii.

[37] Planché, *loc. cit.*

[38] *Journals*, II, 46.

[39] "Weber's Operas in London, 1824–1826," pp. 349f.

[40] "Washington Irving, Barham Livius and Weber," pp. 142f.

[41] *The Wild Huntsman*, pp. 71–74.

[42] London *Times*, Oct. 15, 1824.

[43] Though not in the manuscript of the *Thousand and One Nights* from which Galland translated, but included in his version, it is found in Richard F. Burton's *Supplemental Nights* (privately printed, n.d.), I, 1–35 and in E. W. Lane's *The Thousand and One Nights* (London, 1883), II, 313–34.

[44] *Abu Hassan by Washington Irving with an Introduction by George S. Hellman* (Boston: The Bibliophile Society, 1924).

[45] "Weber's Opera in London, 1824–1826," p. 344.

I am grateful to Professor P. R. Kirby of the University of the Witwatersrand, Johannesburg, South Africa, for a copy of his detailed comparison between Irving's and Livius' versions of the *Abu Hassan* texts, which he placed at my disposal.

[46] "Washington Irving, Barham Livius and Weber," p. 147. See also G. R. Price, "Washington Irving's Librettos," *Music and Letters*, XXIX (1948), 348–55.

[47] *Abu Hassan*, pp. 50–51.

[48] F. K. Hiemer, *Abu Hassan* (Leipzig, n.d.), pp. 9–10.

[49] Luquer, *op. cit.*, p. 472.

[50] J. Genest, *op. cit.*, IX, 248–49. Genest says: "This historical drama in 3 acts, was written by Planché—much praise cannot be given to a piece, written for horses and abounding in songs, it must however be acknowledged, that Planché's play is far from a bad one."

[51] *Life and Letters*, II, 171.

[52] *Journals*, II, 12.

[53] Nicoll, *op. cit.*, II, 297

[54] "Weber's Operas in London, 1824–1826," pp. 344f.

[55] See quotation from letter of January 31, 1824, on p. 126.

[56] *Journals*, II, 55.

[57] *Ibid.*, pp. 62ff; Nicoll, *op. cit.*, II, 481.

[58] *Journals*, II, 54.

[59] *Ibid.*, pp. 81ff.
[60] *Ibid.*, pp. 107f.
[61] *Ibid.*, pp. 171ff.
[62] *Ibid.*, p. 154.
[63] *Ibid.*, pp. 153ff., 162.
[64] *Ibid.*, p. 169.
[65] *Ibid.*, pp. 169f.
[66] *Ibid.*, p. 184.
[67] Luquer, *op. cit.*, p. 608.

6

[1] P. M. Irving, *The Life and Letters of Washington Irving* (New York, 1863), II, 177. (Cited as *Life and Letters.*)

[2] *Letters of Washington Irving to Henry Brevoort,* ed. G. S. Hellman (New York, 1918), p. 287. (Cited as *Letters of Irving to Brevoort.*)

[3] *Life and Letters,* II, 166.

[4] *Journal of Washington Irving (1823–1824),* ed. S. T. Williams (Cambridge, Mass., 1931), p. 30. (Cited as *Journal of 1823–1824.*)

[5] *Ibid.*, pp. 83–84.
[6] *Ibid.*, pp. 86f.
[7] *Ibid.*, pp. 126f.
[8] *Ibid.*, p. 117.
[9] *Life and Letters,* II, 55.
[10] *Journal of 1823–1824,* p. 85.
[11] *Ibid.*, p. 89.
[12] C. R. Leslie, *Autobiographical Recollections* (Boston, 1860), p. 260.
[13] *Life and Letters,* II, 191.

[14] *Washington Irving and the Storrows. Letters from England and the Continent, 1821–1828,* ed. S. T. Williams (Cambridge, Mass., 1933), p. 36.

[15] *Memoirs, Journal and Correspondence of Thomas Moore,* ed. Lord John Russell (London, 1853), III, 252f.

[16] *The Journals of Washington Irving (from July, 1815, to July, 1842),* eds. W. P. Trent and G. S. Hellman (Boston, 1919) I, 143, 211. (Cited as *Journals.*)

[17] *Journal of 1823–1824,* p. 82.
[18] *Ibid.*, pp. 113, 146ff, 239.
[19] *Ibid.*, pp. 93–97.
[20] *Ibid.*, pp. 128f.
[21] *Ibid.*, pp. 130f.
[22] *Ibid.*, pp. 132–213.
[23] *Ibid.*, p. 128.
[24] *Ibid.*, pp. 141, 165, 184.
[25] *Ibid.*, pp. 169–74.
[26] *Ibid.*, pp. 176–87.
[27] *Ibid.*, pp. 213f.
[28] *Ibid.*, pp. 239f.
[29] *Ibid.*, pp. 240ff.

[30] *Life and Letters,* II, 206f.

[31] *Journal of 1823–1824,* pp. 240ff.

[32] *The Works of Washington Irving,* Hudson ed. (New York, 1882), XXI, 14. (Cited as *Works.*)

[33] H. A. Pochmann, "Irving's German Tour and its Influence in his Tales," *PMLA,* XLV (1930), 1170.

[34] *Works,* XXI, 246.

[35] *Ibid.,* p. 43.

[36] *Ibid.,* XIX, 506.

[37] Johann Büsching, *Volks-Sagen, Mährchen und Legenden* (Leipzig, 1812), pp. 143–58, 341–43.

[38] Friedrich Gottschalck, *Die Sagen und Volksmährchen der Deutschen* (Halle, 1814), pp. 220–24.

[39] Jakob Grimm, *Deutsche Sagen* (Berlin, 1818), I, 314f.

[40] *Life and Letters,* IV, 369ff, 382f.

[41] *Journal of 1823–1824,* p. 12.

[42] *Tales of the Dead.* Principally translated from the French [by Mrs. Sarah Utterson] (London, 1813).

[43] *Works,* XXI, 57ff.

[44] *Journals,* I, 135.

[45] *Works,* XXI, 66ff.

[46] *Ibid.,* pp. 13f.

[47] *Memoirs, Journals and Correspondence of Thomas Moore,* ed. Lord John Russell (London, 1853), IV, 208.

[48] *Blackwood's Edinburgh Magazine,* XVI (1824), 294.

[49] F. P. Smith, "Un Conte Fantastique chez Irving, Borel et Dumas Père," *Revue de littérature comparée,* XVIII (1938), 344ff.

[50] Mme. Gabrielle de P[aban], *Histoire des fantômes et des démons qui se sont montrés parmi les hommes, ou choix d'anecdotes et de contes . . .* (Paris, 1819), p. 151f.

[51] *Works,* XXI, 136ff.

[52] *Ibid.,* p. 14.

[53] Hartley Coleridge, *The Table Talk and Omniana of Samuel Taylor Coleridge* (London, 1917), pp. 53f.

[54] S. T. Williams, *The Life of Washington Irving* (New York, 1935), II, 288f. (Cited as *The Life.*) The results of H. A. Pochmann's investigation are also summarized in this discussion.

[55] Pochmann, *op. cit.,* p. 1166.

[56] Quoted by Williams from Irving's unpublished Autobiographical Notes in *The Life,* II, 290.

[57] *Ibid.,* p. 218. Actually, within two days of the notation: "Looked over Buckthorne Mss: Idea struck me of work called Buckthorne and his times," Irving mentioned writing "the introductory remarks to Goldsmith's life" (*Journal of 1823–1824,* pp. 167f.). Having been busy with these projects at the same time, is it unlikely that the solution to his difficulties of composition may be linked to Goldsmith's work?

[58] *Ibid.,* p. 221.

[59] *Works,* IX, 8.

[60] *The Life,* II, 221.

[61] *Ibid.,* pp. 219f.

[62] *Works,* XXI, 157.

[63] *Works of Oliver Goldsmith,* ed. Peter Cunningham (New York, 1908), III, 131.

[64] *Journal of 1823–1824,* pp. 129–65.

[65] See S. T. Williams, "Supplementary Studies," *The Life,* II, 293; and the *United States Literary Gazette,* Nov. 15, 1824.

[66] *Journal of 1823–1824,* pp. 128, 139.

[67] *Ueberlieferungen zur Geschichte unsrer Zeit. Gesammelt von Heinrich Zschokke* (Aarau, 1820), pp. 176–89. See also *Allgemeine Zeitung* (Augsburg), No. 190, 1819; *Morgenblatt* (Stuttgart), No. 176, 1819; *Wiener Zeitschrift,* No. 88, July 24, 1819.

In 1905 a copy of a letter of Salathe's describing his experiences was published by Daniel Burckhardt-Werthemann in an article ("Das Abenteuer eines Basler Malers," *Basler Jahrbuch,* 1905, pp. 175–96) in which he emphasized that the imitative tales of banditry, so popular in the nineteenth century, have their source in Zschokke's, i.e. in Salathe's, narrative, and that Irving, moreover, frankly acknowledged his source.

[68] *Works,* XXI, 14.

[69] *Ibid.,* p. 370.

[70] O. S. Coad, "The Gothic Element in American Literature," *Journal of English and Germanic Philology,* XXIV (1925), 85.

[71] *Works,* XXI, 466.

[72] Pochmann, *op. cit.,* pp. 1179f.

[73] Grimm, *op. cit.,* I, 384f.

[74] Gottschalck, *op. cit.,* pp. 91–109; in Grimm the basic story is in Vol. I, pp. 174–76.

[75] Thomas Roscoe, *The German Novelists* (London, 1826), II, 157–69, 281f.

[76] *Life and Letters,* II, 214.

[77] Leslie, *op. cit.,* pp. 262f.

[78] *Letters of Irving to Brevoort,* pp. 397ff.

[79] *Blackwood's Edinburgh Magazine,* XVI (1824), pp. 294ff.

[80] *The Examiner,* No. 866 (Sept. 5, 1824), pp. 563f.

[81] *Westminster Review,* II (1824), pp. 334f.

[82] *The London Magazine,* X (1824), pp. 403f.

[83] *Eclectic Review,* n.s. XXIV (1825), pp. 65f.

[84] *Ibid.,* p. 74.

[85] *Atlantic Magazine,* II (1824), pp. 88f.

[86] *Blackwood's Edinburgh Magazine,* XVII (1825), p. 67.

[87] *European Magazine,* LXXXVI (1824), p. 254.

[88] *Letters of Irving to Brevoort,* p. 408.

[89] *New York Mirror, and Ladies' Literary Gazette,* II (Sept. 25, 1824), pp. 70f.

[90] *The Quarterly Review,* XXI (1825), pp. 473–87.

[91] *Blackwood's Edinburgh Magazine,* XVII (1825), p. 59.

[92] See W. A. Reichart, "The Early Reception of Washington Irving's Work in Germany," *Anglia,* LXXIV (1956), 345–363.

[93] The subject of Irving's influence on German literature will be treated in a separate article.

Appendix

A

Dramatic and Musical Performances which Washington Irving Attended During His German Travels.

This compilation of Irving's attendance at theatrical performances is based upon entries in his journals and diaries. References in his correspondence have been utilized, if such performances could be collated with available theatre records. Irving sometimes erred in giving the date of a performance or in identifying titles and authors. Whenever a journal entry conflicts with the date of performance as listed officially, the correction is given in brackets. The spelling in the entries is Irving's.

The large theatre collections in Munich, Vienna, and Dresden were particularly useful, but in some cases the *Tagebuch der deutschen Bühnen,* edited by Karl Winkler (pseudonym Hell), gave more complete information than the programs of the individual theatres. Full identification of author and title, followed by a brief explanatory note, completes each entry. Page references to the Trent-Hellman edition of the *Journals* (J.), S. T. Williams' edition of the *Journal of 1823–1824,* (J. 1823–24) and P. M. Irving's biography, *The Life and Letters of Washington Irving* (L. and L.) are given in parentheses.

Darmstadt, Sept, 20 [*22*], *1822:* "See opera Freischutz" (J., I, 59). C. M. v. Weber's *Der Freischütz.* Berlin, June 18, 1821. Tremendous success which made Weber famous.

Munich, Oct. 10 [*8*]*:* "Theatre—Bettlerstudent—Ballet Wildschutzer—superb theatre" (J., I, 78). *Der Bettelstudent* oder *Das Donnerwetter.* Comedy in 2 Acts by Paul Weidmann. Music by Ritter v. Winter. Vienna, 1776. *Die Wildschützen.* Pantomime and Ballet in 2 parts by Ballet-master Horschelt. This was the Royal Court Theatre, which was completely destroyed by fire, Jan. 14, 1823.

Munich, Oct. 11: "New piece, 'Pilgrim'." (J., I, 83). *Die Pilgerin.* Comedy in 4 Acts by Johanna Franul von Weissenthurn. 1822. A long-forgotten comedy of this prolific writer who was an actress at the Burgtheater at Vienna. Irving saw her productions again in Dresden. Ferdinand Esslair (1772–1840), actor and director of the Court Theatre at Stuttgart, whom Irving saw later in Dresden, played in this performance.

Munich, Oct. 13: "Evening—theatre, Freischütz—the principal part by Mad. Vespermann, who had a delightful voice." (J., I, 84). Weber's *Der Freischütz.* Clara Vespermann (1799–1827), wife of Wilhelm Vespermann, actor and theatre director at Munich, was a popular singer.

Vienna**, Oct. 25: **Raoul, der Blaubart. Opera in 3 Acts from the French. Music by Gretry and Fischer. 1817. Since Irving writes that he was several times at the theatre (L. and L., II, 120) and refers to "Blaubart," it is quite certain that he saw this, the only performance during his visit. Flora Foster's comment (L. and L., IV, 369) that Irving saw *Die Ahnfrau* at this time is probably false. No theatre lists such a performance. Irving noted in his expense account "theatre twice 8 paper florins."

Vienna, Nov. 3: "Evening—opera, Fidelio—music by Beethoven—some parts very good, some rather in the melodramatic taste; strong contrasts and great noise. Beethoven's style is rather out of fashion—Rossini has introduced a different taste. "Mme [Wilhelmine Schröder], an actress with blonde hair has great power of voice, but sings false—acts well—is put in pieces that have strong passion and situation such as the above and Blaubart" (J., I, 104). Beethoven's *Fidelio.* Vienna, 1805. Irving's musical taste or critical judgment was not impeccable. Wilhelmine Schröder (1805–60), married Karl Devrient and came to the Dresden Court Theatre in 1823.

Prague, Nov. 22: "The piece a German translation of the 'Barber of Seville'—the part of Rosina charmingly played by a beautiful actress of the name of Mad. Sontag . . . " (J., I, 121). Rossini's *Barber of Seville.* 1816. One of Irving's favorite operas, which he saw frequently. Henrietta Sontag (1803–54) was just beginning her great career which soon made her world famous.

Prague, Nov. 23: "Saw 'King Lear' . . . translated by Iffland—the part of Lear very well performed, the translation apparently very good and exact. Part of Edgar very well done, as likewise that of Kent—the tender parts of the character of Lear particularly well done and some of the mad passages—a very crowded audience—people much affected and gave great applause—tho' at the battle between Edgar and Edmund, there were tokens of disapprobation." (J., I, 123). Shakespeare's *King Lear.* Actually Schröder's adaptation which Iffland used in his performances. Though the disposition of the realm in the first act was restored, this was still a prose version with a conciliatory ending.

Prague, Nov. 25: "See a tolerable piece in three acts called the 'Alps Röslein' (J., I, 128). *Das Alpen Röslein, das Patent und der Shawl.* Drama in 3 parts by Franz v. Holbein. Vienna, 1820. A trivial piece patterned after a tale of Claurens (Der Kirchhof in Schwytz) by the director of the Prague theatre.

Dresden, Jan. 9, 1823: "Saw part of the 'Wasserträger' " (J., I, 153). *Der Wasserträger* (Les deux Journées). Opera in 3 parts by Cherubini. 1800.

Dresden, Jan. 13: "In the evening go to see Wallenstein's 'Tod'—at such distance from the stage that I could not hear—play was therefore tedious to me" (J., I, 156). Schiller's *Wallensteins Tod.* Weimar, 1799. The first part, *Die Piccolomini,* had been performed the day before, but Irving was probably unaware of its relation to the Wallenstein theme.

Dresden, Jan. 14: "Ev[enin]g theatre—Maske für Maske, and No. 777" (J., I, 157). *Maske für Maske.* Comedy based on Marivaux by J. F. Jünger. Leipzig, 1794. *Nummer 777.* Comedy in 1 Act from the French by Karl Lebrun. Frankfort, 1821. The first is

Le Jeu de l'amour et du hasard of Marivaux, which has remained a popular and representative eighteenth century comedy. Trent-Hellman transcribed "Marke" instead of "Maske."

Dresden, Jan. 15: "Italian opera—a new opera called——, very long, confused and monotonous" (J., I, 157). *Velleda.* Fairy opera in 4 Acts by Josef Rastrelli. Dresden, 1823. This, the first performance of a new work, was poorly received. Irving later met this composer or his father, also a musician.

Dresden, Jan. 18: "Play—to see the Swiss family, music by Winter" (J., I, 157). *Die Schweizer Familie.* Opera in 3 Acts by Joseph Weigl. Vienna, 1809. Based on play of same name (1808) by Ignaz Castelli, a popular Viennese playwright.

Dresden, Jan. 23: "Go to theatre for a short time—see two acts of German play" (J., I, 161). *Das Blatt hat sich gewendet.* Comedy in 5 Acts based on Cumberland's *The Brothers,* adapted by F. L. Schröder. Dresden, 1786. Schröder, the great actor, revised and adapted many English dramas for the German stage.

Dresden, Jan. 27: "Went to theatre" (J., I, 162). *Der Unschuldige muss viel leiden.* Comedy in 3 Acts from the French by Theodor Hell. Dresden, 1823. Hell (pseudonym for Karl Winkler) was editor of the Dresden "Abendzeitung," a member of the "Liederkreis," and intimately associated with the theatre.

Dresden, Jan. 28: "Went to theatre—a drama called 'Kätchen of Heilbronn' " (J., I, 163). *Kätchen von Heilbronn,* with a prologue entitled The Secret Tribunal, by Heinrich v. Kleist, prepared for the stage by Franz v. Holbein. 1822. Irving saw other revisions from the pen of this actor, who was also a playwright and theatre director.

Dresden, Feb. 3: " 'Herbstag' a comedy in five acts by Lessing—full of kissing and crying of old men and ugly women" (J., I, 164). *Der Herbsttag.* Comedy in 5 Acts by A. W. Iffland. Dresden, 1791. Perhaps the best comedy by this prolific writer of middle class drama.

Dresden, Feb. 4: "Go to theatre—Tony, a St. Domingo melodrama—a beautiful little pastoral piece with songs by Goethe called 'Jery und Bätely.' Mad. Haase [Heese] in Swiss costume looked pretty and played delightfully. Sat in same box with Madam de B., who was very gracious" (J., I, 165). *Tony.* Drama in 3 Acts by Theodor Körner. 1812. *Jery und Bätely.* Operetta in 1 Act by Goethe. Weimar, 1780. [Music by J. F. Reichardt.] *Tony* is an adaptation of Kleist's Novelle "Die Verlobung auf San Domingo." Though praised by Goethe and highly successful at the Vienna Burgtheater, it lacks the passionate conflict of emotions of the original story. Goethe wrote the dialogue of *Jery und Bätely* on his return from Switzerland in 1779. Nine musical settings in Goethe's lifetime reflected its popularity.

Dresden, Feb. 6: "Go to theatre—see 'Jery und Bätely' " (J., I, 165). *Jery und Bätely.* Irving was so delighted that he saw it a second time. He did not stay for the other piece, *Die Radikal Kur* by J. F. v. Weissenthurn.

Dresden, Feb. 8: "In the evening to the theatre—the Opera 'L'Inganno Felice' by Rossini and a ballet" (J., I, 166). *L'Inganno Felice.* Comic Opera in 1 Act by Rossini. Venice, 1812. One of Rossini's earliest works.

Dresden, Feb. 9: "In evening go to see 'Hamlet'—the translation of Schiller's. The part of Hamlet very well performed by Julius [Trent-Hellman write Juliers]. He wanted the deep melancholy of Hamlet's character and was rather too cold and dégagé (J., I, 166). Shakespeare's *Hamlet.* Irving no doubt meant the A. W. Schlegel translation published in 1798, which the Dresden theatre adopted in 1820 but cut and modified to replace the completely inadequate Schröder text.

Dresden, Feb. 13: "In ev'g go to see 'Hamlet'—sit in the box of Baron Loewenstein" (J., I, 167). Shakespeare's *Hamlet.* His enthusiasm for the theatre led him to see a second performance; here was a play which he knew and could follow easily.

Dresden, Feb. 17: "After dinner went to the play—staid a short time" (J., I, 168). *Das Portrait der Mutter, oder Die Privatkomödie.* Comedy in 4 Acts by F. L. Schröder. Dresden, 1790. Schröder was primarily a great actor and theatre director. His performances of Shakespeare were a great contribution; his own works are forgotten.

Dresden, Feb. 19: "In evening go to theatre and see the Italian Opera—'Cyrus in Babylon'—one of Rossini's worst" (J., I, 168). *Ciro in Babilonia.* Opera by Rossini. Ferrara, 1812. Called by some critics an oratorio rather than an opera, it was a failure at every performance.

Dresden, Feb. 20: "After dinner go to theatre and see Schiller's tragedy of Piccolomini" (J., I, 168). Schiller's *Die Piccolomini.* Weimar, 1799. Irving had already seen the final part of the *Wallenstein* drama on Jan. 13. Unfortunately he did not attend the next performance of *Wallensteins Tod* on Feb. 23.

Dresden, Feb. 21: "In evening go to theatre" (J., I, 168). No performance is listed anywhere. Possibly Irving's error. He filled in gaps in his diary later. E.g., the lack of entries between March 1–15.

Dresden, Feb. 22: "Go to the play—opera of strolling singers—good scene of the strollers descending from waggon by the roadside, arranging crushed bonnets—woman with squirrel in cage—odd dresses—" (J., I, 168). *I virtuosi ambulanti.* Comic Opera in 2 Acts by V. Fioravanti. Paris, 1807. The libretto by Balocchi was taken from a French comedy of Picard. Such Italian operas could not long compete with Rossini's work.

Dresden, Feb. 27: "Go to play to see the 'Gut Sternberg', a comedy, rather mawkish" (J., I, 170). *Das Gut Sternberg.* Comedy in 4 Acts by Johanna F. v. Weissenthurn. Dresden, 1817. This author's plays were not only popular with the audience but also with the actors because they contained grateful roles.

Dresden, March 1: "Went to theatre and saw part of 'Preciosa'" (J., I, 171). *Preziosa.* Drama in 4 acts by Pius Alexander Wolff. Music by Carl Maria v. Weber. Berlin, 1821. This was an adaptation for the stage of Cervantes' story "La Gitanella." After being revised and provided with some of Weber's finest music, it achieved lasting success.

Dresden, April 5: "In the evening went to theatre—'Matrimonio Secreto'" (J., I, 176). *Il Matrimonio Secreto.* Opera in 2 Acts by D. Cimarosa. Vienna, 1792. Was a tremendous success and still ranks high as an "opéra bouffe."

Dresden, April 8: "Went in the ev'g to theatre—saw a ridiculous German piece about a lighthouse" (J., I, 176). *Der Leuchtthurm.* Drama in 2 Acts by Ernst v. Houwald. Dresden, 1820. A typical "fate drama," popular at the time in spite of Tieck's vigorous criticism.

Dresden, April 14: "Go to theatre—see a German comedy—rather amusing" (J., I, 179). *Künstlers Erdenwallen.* Comedy in 5 Acts by Julius v. Voss. Berlin, 1810. Voss was a talented but careless writer who published over 160 vols. of plays, novels, etc., all completely forgotten.

Dresden, April 21: "Go to theatre to see a translation of 'Merch[an]t of Venice'—theatre crowded. Shylock performed by Wiedy [Werdy] —quite diff't from the English mode of playing it—more in familiar style—Jessica dressed in Jewish costume—the costumes far superior to those on the London boards" (J., I, 182f.). Shakespeare's

Merchant of Venice. In the translation of Schlegel, this comedy had been played since 1821.

Dresden, April 26: "Went to theatre—saw German play of Humboldt—pretty—romantic and extravagant" (J., I, 185). *Der Prinz von Homburg*. Drama in 5 Acts by Heinrich v. Kleist. With music by Marschner. Dresden, 1822. (Performed in Vienna, 1821, as "Die Schlacht bei Fehrbellin".) Irving was apparently unfamiliar with Kleist or his work and referred this drama to Humboldt. This in spite of the appearance in 1821 of Tieck's edition of Kleist's work, and after having seen *Kätchen von Heilbronn,* Jan. 28, 1823.

Dresden, May 6: "Go to theatre to Prince Lippe-Schaumburg's box—see Esslair play Wallenstein in 'Wallensteins Tod'—very excellent actor." (J., I, 190). Schiller's *Wallensteins Tod*. Weimar, 1799. Irving had already seen this play on January 13, 1823. Esslair was one of the foremost actors of the day and Irving had seen him in Munich, October 11, 1822.

Dresden, May 8: "Go to theatre—sit in Prince Lippe's box" (J., I, 191). Weber's *Der Freischütz*. Irving saw every performance he could.

Prague, May 28: "In the evening we see 'Johan of Paris' acted—Madml. Fink makes a first appearance in the part of the Princess of Navarre—very agreeable person, face and voice—very well rec'd" (J., I, 208). *Johann von Paris*. Opera in 2 parts by F. A. Boieldieu. 1812. Extremely popular throughout Europe. Schumann called it with *Figaro* and *Barber of Seville* one of the three best comic operas.

Prague, May 30 [*29*]*:* "Ev'g theatre, 'K[ing] Lear'—tolerable—some parts of Lear well done by Bayer—Schröder's translation" (J., I, 208). Shakespeare's *King Lear*. This was no mere translation but an adaptation by Schröder, who had scored a tremendous success with himself in the title role when he first presented it in Hamburg. Irving had already seen it in Prague, Nov. 23, 1822.

Prague, May 31: "Ev'g play 'The Leper and his Son' and 'Gabriele'—the former amusing—the latter has one or two interesting scenes" (J., I, 208). *Der Lügner und sein Sohn*. Farce in 1 Act based on Collin d'Harleville. *Gabriele*. Drama in 3 Acts based on "Valérie" of Scribe and Mélesville, adapted by Castelli. 1823. Trivial performances of a popular sort that are not even recorded in dramatic history.

Prague, June 4: "In the evening went to theatre for an hour or so. Saw 'Hamlet' played—the part of Hamlet by Bayer—very well done—a pretty Ophelia by Madame Piston [Pistor]" (J., I, 210). Shakespeare's *Hamlet*. No doubt the popular translation and adaptation of Schröder (1777) which dominated all German stages until Schlegel's translation superseded it.

Prague, June 5: "Friday [Thursday] evening a comic piece called the 'Berg-geist—oder Die Drei Wünsche'—very pleasant" (J., I, 210). *Der Berggeist oder Die drei Wünsche*. Operetta in 3 Acts by Josef Gleich. Music by Drechsler. Vienna, 1819. Irving was sufficiently impressed to wish to buy it for the English stage as indicated in a letter to Payne. See note under entry of June 13.

Prague, June 6: "In evenings [Thursday, 5th, Friday, 6th, Saturday, 7th] looked in at theatre" (J., I, 210). *Mittel und Wege, oder Still! ich weiss schon*. Farce in 3 Acts by Karl Lebrun from the English of Colman. 1822. Irving's entries are inexact and supply only two titles for the three evenings. This is a typical and trivial adaptation to satisfy the demand of the theatres.

Prague, June 7: "Saturday, 'Libussa'—so-so" (J., I, 210). *Libussa*. Opera in 3 Acts by J. K. Bernard. Music by C. Kreutzer. 1823. This opera, dealing with the Bohemian legend of the founding of Prague, had its première here on May 21, 1823.

Prague, June 8: "Evening, play—'Freischütz'—very meagrely got up" (J., I, 210). Weber's *Der Freischütz.*

Prague, June 10: "Theatre—'Zauberflöte' in two acts—first act delicious—second very heavy and tedious" (J., I, 211). Mozart's *Die Zauberflöte.* 1791. Irving was no keen critic of music. His judgments are personal reactions of the moment.

Prague, June 11: "Theatre–three pleasant little pieces very well played–viz.– 'Eine hilft der ander'—'Der Schatzgraber'—and 'Ein Stündchen at Töplitz' (J., I, 211). *Ein Mann hilft dem andern.* Comedy in 1 Act by J. F. von Weissenthurn, 1822. *Der Schatzgräber.* Farce in 1 Act by Anton Wall [C. L. Heyne], 1807. *Ein Stündchen in Pyrmont.* Comedy in 1 Act adapted from the French of Scribe by K. Töpfer. 1822. Apparently the place name in the title of this popular piece was adapted to the locality. There are references in play lists to "Eine Stunde in Karlsbad" as well.

Prague, June 13: Though there is no entry for this date, a letter to Payne identifies a drama. On June 13 was the only performance during Irving's sojourn in Prague of *Parteyenwuth oder die Kraft des Glaubens.* Drama in 5 Acts by F. W. Ziegler. 1817. Irving was so interested in this play of the "Covenanters" that he wished to revise it for the English stage. See Thatcher T. P. Luquer, "Correspondence of Washington Irving and John Howard Payne," *Scribner's Magazine,* XLVIII, (October, 1910), 480.

Prague, June 16: "Ev'g play—'Die Holländer', a very tolerable piece and well played—an excellent regimental surgeon play'd by Feistmantel—oil-cloth cocked hat—red underclothes—a long half surtout, half greatcoat with sword sticking out behind and tarnished sword case—pigtail—Mad. Holbein, a very pretty little actress (J., I, 212). *Die Holländer oder Was vermag nicht ein vernünftiges Frauenzimmer?* Comedy in 3 Acts based on Goldoni by Johann C. Bock. 1778. Feistmantel was one of the greatest actors of comic roles.

Prague, June 19: "Ev'g, go to theatre—a comic fairy tale dramatized—'Die Fee aus Frankreich.' Feistmantel played very well in it" (J., I, 212). *Die Fee aus Frankreich oder Liebesqualen eines Hagestolzen.* Opera by W. Müller. 1821. Müller's light operas, said to number over 200, enjoyed enormous popularity at this time.

Prague, June 20: "Theatre—'Freischütz'" (J., I, 212). Weber's *Der Freischütz.* At least the fifth performance that Irving had seen.

Prague, June 21: "Ev'g play–'Fridolin'–interesting German piece" (J., I, 212). *Fridolin.* Drama in 5 Acts by Franz v. Holbein. 1806. A play based on Schiller's poem "Der Gang nach dem Eisenhammer."

Prague, June 22: "Ev'g, 'Brautsmuck,' a very absurd French play" (J., I, 213). *Der Brautschmuck.* Original Drama in 5 Acts by Franz v. Holbein. 1811. Not French at all but a sequel and continuation of *Fridolin.*

Prague, June 23: "Ev'g, play—'Aline'" (J., I, 214). *Aline oder Wien in einem andern Weltteile.* Fairy opera in 3 Acts by A. Bäuerle. Music by W. Müller. Vienna, 1822. Originally a parody of Bertoni's opera, it became the most popular operetta of the time.

Leipzig, July 13: "Evening theatre Mad. Weisserman played the Schone Mullerin—sang charmingly" (J. 1823–24, 5). *Die schöne Müllerin.* (La Molinaria). Opera by G. Paisiello. 1788. This opera was very successful throughout Europe.

Kassel, July 23: "Went to play and saw Das Unterbrockene Opferfest—music by Winter—Madame Arnold played in it, beautiful theatre—Scenery—dresses and numerous chorus" (J. 1823–24, 16). *Das Unterbrochene Opferfest.* Opera in 2 Acts by Peter Winter. 1796. The composer's best work. The program shows no Mme Arnold but a Mme Roland.

B

German Books in Washington Irving's Sunnyside Library

Gespensterbuch. Herausgegeben von A. Apel und F. Laun [Friedr. Aug. Schulze]. Leipzig bei Georg J. Göschen, 1815. Fünftes Bändchen. Der Heckethaler [von F. L.]. Der Liebesschwur [von F. L.]. *Die Ruine von Paulinzell [von A. A.]. *Die Hausehre [von F. L.]. Die Schuhe auf den Stangen [von A. A.]. Legende [von F. L.]. Das silberne Fräulein [von A. A.].

[* pages cut]

Gedichte von Gottfried August Bürger. Neue vollständige Ausgabe. [Herausgegeben von Karl Reinhard]. Wien und Prag bei Franz Haas, 1811. I. Theil, II. Theil.

[pages uncut]

Volks-Sagen, Märchen und Legenden. Gesammelt von Johann Gustav Büsching. Leipzig, 1812. Bei Carl Heinrich Reclam.

Euryanthe von Savoyen. Aus dem Manuscript der Königlichen Bibliothek zu Paris: "Histoire de Gerard de Nevers et de la belle et vertueuse Euryant de Savoye," übertragen von Helmina von Chézy, geb. Freiin Klencke. Berlin in der Vereins-Buchhandlung, 1823.

[pages cut]

Neues Hand-Wörterbuch der Englischen Sprache für die Deutschen und der Deutschen Sprache für die Engländer. Bearbeitet von Johann Ebers. Halle in der Rengerschen Buchhandlung. Erster Theil: Englisch-Deutsch, 1800. Zweiter Theil: Deutsch-Englisch, 1802.

Mährchen der Magyaren, bearbeitet und herausgegeben von Georg von Gaal. Wien, 1822. Druck und Verlag von J. B. Wallishausser.

Goethe's Schriften: Zweyter Band, [Götz von Berlichingen, Die Mitschuldigen] Leipzig bey Georg J. Göschen, 1787. Fünfter Band, [Egmont] [broken volume, only pp. 97–198.]

[pages uncut]

Faust. Eine Tragödie von Goethe. Neue Auflage. Stuttgart u. Tübingen in der J. G. Cotta'schen Buchhandlung, 1821.

[under the title *Faust* is Washington Irving's signature]

Die Sagen und Volksmährchen der Deutschen, gesammelt von Friedrich Gottschalck. Halle bei Hemmerde und Schwetschke, 1814. Erstes Bändchen.

Taschenbuch für Reisende in den Harz von Friedrich Gottschalck. Zweite verbesserte Auflage mit einer Karte. Magdeburg bei Wilhelm Heinrichshofen, 1817.

[on inside cover in Livius's handwriting: "Barham Livius Halberstadt 3 Sep. 1822"]

Kinder- und Haus-Märchen. Gesammelt durch die Brüder Grimm. Berlin in der Realschulbuchhandlung, 1812.

Deutsche Sagen. Herausgegeben von den Brüdern Grimm. Berlin in der Nicolaischen Buchhandlung, 1818. Zweiter Theil.

[at the top of title page in his own handwriting: "W. Irving Dresden 1823"]

Phantasus. Tausend und ein Mährchen, vom Verfasser der grauen Mappe. [J. C. Ludwig Haken]. Berlin 1802. Erster Band.

Zauber-Bibliothek oder von Zauberei, Theurgie und Mantik, Zauberern, Hexen, und Hexenprocessen, Dämonen, Gespenstern, und Geistererscheinungen. Zur Beförderung einer reingeschichtlichen von Aberglauben und Unglauben freien Beurtheilung dieser Gegenstände. Von Georg Conrad Horst, Grossherzoglich-Hessischem Kirchenrathe. Mainz, 1821. Bei Florian Kupferberg. Erster Theil. Zweiter Theil. Dritter Theil. Vierter Theil.

[pages uncut]

Das Buch der Mährchen für Kindheit und Jugend, nebst etzlichen Schnaken und Schnurren; anmuthig und lehrhaftig. Von J. A. C. Löhr. Leipzig bei Gerhard Fleischer d. Jüng. [Erster Band 1818]

Erzählungen und Dialogen von A. G. Meissner. Leipzig bei Johann Gottlob Immanuel Breitkopf. Erster Band 1790. Zweiter Band 1790. Dritter Band 1791 [2. Nachdruck].

Skizzen von A. G. Meissner. Leipzig im Verlage der Dyckischen Buchhandlung. Erste und Zweite Sammlung 1792. Dritte und Vierte Sammlung 1792. Siebte und Achte Sammlung 1792. Neunte und Zehnte Sammlung 1793. Elfte und Zwölfte Sammlung 1796. Dreizehnte und Vierzehnte Sammlung 1796.

[pages uncut]

Vier und zwanzig Bücher Allgemeiner Geschichten besonders der Europäischen Menschheit. Durch Johannes von Müller, 1797. Herausgegeben nach d. Verfassers Tode durch dessen Bruder Johann Georg Müller. Erster Band. Dritter Band—Dritte Auflage. Stuttgardt u. Tübingen in der J. G. Cotta'schen Buchhandlung 1817.

[pages uncut]

Theater von Adolph Müllner. Neueste Auflage. Wien. Bei B. Ph. Bauer. Dritter Theil, 1816: Die Schuld. Vierter Theil, 1817: Die Zweiflerinn, Die grossen Kinder.

König Yngurd; Trauerspiel in 5 Akten von Adolph Müllner. Leipzig bei Georg Johann Göschen, 1817.

Nachgelassene Schriften des verstorbenen Professor Musäus. Herausgegeben von seinem Zögling August von Kotzebue. Leipzig bei Paul Gotthelf Kummer, 1791.

[pages uncut]

Die Deutschen Volksmährchen von Johann August Musäus. Herausgegeben von C. M. Wieland. Gotha, bey Carl Wilhelm Ettinger, 1804. [Die Bücher der Chronika der drei Schwestern. Richilde. Rolands Knappen.]

Rabenhorst's Pocket Dictionary of the German and English Languages in two parts. By G. H. Noehden. London, 1814.

Novellenschatz des deutschen Volkes. Herausgegeben von Ludwig Pustkuchen. Mit einem Vorwort vom Verfasser von Wilhelm Meisters Wanderjahren. Mit Ludwig Tiecks Bildnis. Quedlinburg u. Leipzig, 1822. Bei Gottfried Basse.

[most pages cut]

Don Carlos. A tragedy. Translated from the German of Frederick Schiller. The Third Edition. London. Printed for W. J. and J. Richardson, 1798.

Friedrich v. Schiller. Sämmtliche Werke. Stuttgart und Tübingen, in der J. G. Cotta'-schen Buchhandlung. 1., 2., 3. Band. 1812. 4., 5., 6., 7., 8. Band. 1813. 9., 10. Band. 1814. 11. Band. 1815.

Die Räuber—ein Schauspiel von Schiller. Neue verbesserte Auflage. Tübingen, 1816. Cotta.

[bought in Liverpool; pages uncut]

Schillers Der Geisterseher Eine Geschichte aus den Memoiren des Grafen von O.** Leipzig 1789. Bey Georg Joachim Göschen. Dritter Theil [only pp. 241–322].

Schillers Gedichte. Neueste Auflage, Wien, 1815. Bei B. Ph. Bauer. Erster Theil. [first 80pp. and pp. 83–94 missing] Zweiter Theil. Dritter Theil.

Scenen aus dem Geisterreich von Heinrich Stilling. Frankfurt am Main, bei Varrentrapp und Wenner, 1803 Zweyter Band. Zweyte vermehrte Auflage.

[pages uncut]

Erzählungen von Heinrich Jung genannt Stilling. Frankfurt am Main, 1814 in der Joh. Christ Hermannschen Buchhandlung. Erstes Bändchen.

[pages uncut]

Straussfedern. Berlin und Stettin bey Friedr. Nicolai. Zweyter Band 1790. Vierter Band 1790. Sechster Band 1795. Siebender Band 1797. Achter und letzter Band 1798. [only vol. 4–8 edited by Tieck]

[pages uncut]

Volksmährchen; Herausgegeben von Peter Leberecht [Ludwig Tieck]. Berlin 1797. Bey Carl August Nicolai. Zweiter Band. Dritter Band.

Die Lichtensteiner von C. F. Van der Velde. Zweite verbesserte Auflage; Dresden, 1822 in der Arnoldischen Buchhandlung.

Holzschnitte von Veit Weber [G. P. L. Leonhard Wächter]. Erster Band. [only one published] Die Betfahrt des Bruders Gramsalbus; Berlin bei Friedrich Maurer, 1793. [Included later as vol. VIII of "Sagen der Vorzeit"]

[paper markers at 4th, 5th, and 6th Abentheuer]

Sagen der Vorzeit von Veit Weber. Berlin bey Friedrich Maurer. Erster Band 1787 [Männerschwur und Weibertreue. Der Harfner. Das Ritterwort.] Zweyter Band

1790 Zwote Verbesserte Auflage. [Wolff. Das heilige Kleeblatt. Der Müller des Schwarzthals. Der graue Bruder.] Dritter Band 1792 Zwote Verbesserte Auflage. [Tugendspiegel.] Vierter Band 1791 [Die Teufelsbeschwörung. Die Brüder des Bundes für Freiheit und Recht. Erste Hälfte.] Fünfter Band 1795 [Die Brüder des Bundes für Freiheit und Recht. Zweite Hälfte.] Sechster Band 1795 [Die Heilige Vehme.]

Der Fündling von Egisheim. [von Veit Weber. No date or title page. Really the seventh volume of "Sagen der Vorzeit"; includes "Glaubensmuth" and "Nackt und Bloss."]

Die Abentheuer des Don Sylvio von Rosalva. [Von Christoph Martin Wieland] Erster Teil. Leipzig bey Weidmanns Erben und Reich, 1772.

[bought in Liverpool]

Der Goldne Spiegel oder die Könige von Scheschnian, eine wahre Geschichte. [Von C. M. Wieland] Leipzig bey M. G. Weidmanns Erben und Reich, 1772. Erster, Zweiter, Dritter und Vierter Theil.

Die Abderiten. [Von C. M. Wieland] Erster Theil, Zweiter Theil. [really vols. XIX, XX of Sämmtliche Werke, Leipzig, 1794–1802.]

Erzählungen und Dialogen von Ludwig Wieland. Herausgegeben von C. M. Wieland. Zürich, bey Heinrich Gessner, 1805. Zweiter Band.

[most of "Die Glücksritter" cut]

Teufeleien von Heidelberg bis Weimar und Thüringen von Franz Wildehold. Leipzig bei Wilhelm Rein und Co., 1818.

[about half the pages cut]

Teutsche Lyra ein Taschenbuch für geselliges Vergnügen. Eine Sammlung von Gesängen unserer besten Dichter neuerer Zeit. Mit singbaren Melodien für frohe Gesellschaften gesammelt von einem Freunde des Gesanges. Erstes Bändchen. Leipzig, 1821 in Commission bei C. H. Reclam. Zweites Bändchen. Leipzig, 1822 in Commission bei C. H. Reclam.

[both volumes have Washington Irving's signature on the title page]

Volksmährchen, Sagen und denkwürdige Geschichten aus der Vorzeit Mährens. Eine Sammlung interessanter Erzählungen als Beytrag zu Griems [sic] und Tiek's [sic] Volksmährchen. Brünn und Olmütz. Bey Johann Georg Gastl, 1819.

C

German Titles noted in Irving's Diaries.*

In Notebook of 1818.

[Samuel Christoph] Wagener, Die Gespenster [kurze Erzählung aus dem Reich der Wahrheit. Berlin, 1797, 3. Aufl. 1800.]

* Irving's inadequate and often erroneous titles are completed in brackets as listed in Goedeke or other authoritative bibliographies.

Laun's [Friedrich Aug. Schulze] Erzalungen. [probably ***Kleine Erzählungen,*** Leipzig, 1814–15, 2 Bde.]

Lafontaine [August Heinrich, pseudonym for Miltenberg und Freier] Kleine Romane [und moralische Erzählungen, Berlin, 1799, 6 Bde.]

[Baron Johann Kaspar] Riesbeck's Travels through Germany [in a Series of Letters, written in German . . . and translated by the Rev. Mr. Maty. London, 1787, 2 vols.]

At beginning of notebook covering August–September, 1822.

Dr. Bitter, Denkwürdigkeiten der Stadt Wi[e]sbaden. Schieder 2e edition [Georg Heinrich Ritter, Denkwürdigkeiten der Stadt Wisbaden und der benachbarten Gegend in vorzüglicher Hinsicht ihrer sämtlichen Mineralquellen. 1. Th. Frankfurt, 1799.]

Schiller['s] Maria Stuart [1801.]

10 Band[?] von Wieland [Sämmtliche Werke 1794–1802.]

At end of Notebook covering September 6–October 7, 1822.

Satyros [Goethe's Satyros oder der vergötterte Waldteufel, 1817.]

In Notebook covering October 21–November 15, 1822.

Poetische Sagen der Vorzeit, [als Legenden, Volkssagen, Mährchen u. Schwänke, ernsten und launigen Inhalts, für Freunde der Dichtkunst u. als Stoff für Declamation gesammelt] vom Declamator [Carl F.] Solbrig, Magdeburg, 1817.

Sagen der Vorzeit, oder ausführliche Beschreibung von dem berühmten Salzburgischen Untersberg oder Wunderberg [wie solche Lazarus Gitschner, ein frommer Bauersmann von der Pfarr Berghaim, vor seinem Tode seinem Sohne Johann Gitschner in Gegenwart mehrerer geistlichen und weltlichen Personen geoffenbaret und dieses alles nach seinem Tod bey vorgenommener Inventur schriftlich gefunden worden.] Brixen, 1782.

Franz Sartori: Naturwunder des Östreich. Kaiserthums. Wien, 1807.

Oesterreicher Volksmärchen [Oestreichische Volksmährchen, vom Verfasser der Sagen Oestreichischer Vorzeit. Wien, 1800.]

Volkssagen und Mährchen der Deutschen [u. Ausländer herausgegeben] von Lothar [i.e., Otto Karl von Graeven. Leipzig, 1820.]

Dietrich [E. V.] und Textor [G. A. Weber]: Die Romantischen Sagen des Erzgebirges. [2 Bdchen. Annaberg, 1822.]

Brixener Volksbuch [see entry "Sagen der Vorzeit"]

Fischergedichte [und Erzählungen von F. X. Bronner. Zürich, 1787.]

Das Donauweibchen. [Eine romantische Geschichte der Vorzeit, von Ferdinand Kauer. Wien, 1799.]

Märchen und Sagen von —— [Märchen und Sagenbuch der Böhmen von A. W.] Griesel [Prag, 1820.]

Komisches Theater. [Adolf] Bäuerle. [Pesth., 1820–26]. v. 1, 1820; v. 2, 1820; v. 3, 1821; v. 4, 1821.

Entry of November 22, 1822.

La petite prophete de Böhmisch-Brod by Grimm. [Friedrich M. von Grimm: Le petit Prophète de Boehmischbroda. Paris, 1753.]

End of Notebook covering December, 1822–January, 1823.

Darstellung der Ereignisse in Dresden [im Jahre 1813. Von einem Augenzeugen. Eine Ergänzung (von W. A. Lindau) zu Napoleons Feldzug in Sachsen im Jahre 1813 von Otto von Odeleben. Dresden, 1816.]

Winkel, [G. F. D., Aus dem] Handbuch für Jäger, [Jagdberechtigte u. Jagdliebhaber, mit Musik u. Tabellen. 4 Bde. Leipzig, 1804–1814.]

Sponeck über den Schwarzwald [Karl F. Sponeck: Der Schwarzwald. Ein Handbuch für Forstmänner. Heidelberg, 1819.]

Willdenow, [Karl L.: Grundriss der] Kräuterkunde. [Berlin, 1792. 6 Aufl., 1821.]

Entry of April 17, 1823.

Egmont. [Ein Trauerspiel in 5 Aufzügen. Von Goethe. Leipzig, 1788.]

Entry of April 20, 1823.

Abu Hassan [von Franz Karl Hiemer. Oper in 1 Act. Musik von K. M. v. Weber. Dresden, 1823.]

End of Notebook covering January 20–May 20, 1823.

Der Verbannte Amor by [August v.] Kotzebue [Lustspiel in 4 Acts. Leipzig, 1810.]

Alladin von Oehlenschlagen [Aladdin oder die Wunderlampe. Ein dramatisches Gedicht in zwei Spielen von Adam Oehlenschläger. Amsterdam, 1808; neue verbesserte Auflage in zwei Teilen. Leipzig, 1820.]

Erzalungen von Do. [Märchen und Erzählungen von Adam Oehlenschläger. Stuttgart und Tübingen, 1816–17. 2 Bde.]

Folksglauben von J. Paul. [Friedrich L. F. von Dobeneck: Des deutschen Mittelalters Volksglauben und Heroensagen. Herausgegeben und mit einer Vorrede begleitet von Jean Paul. Berlin, 1815. 2 Bde.]

Jean Pauls Museum. [Stuttgart und Tübingen, 1814.]

Frauendienst by Tieck. [Frauendienst, oder: Geschichte und Liebe des Ritters und Sängers Ulrich von Lichtenstein, von ihm selbst beschrieben. Nach einer alten Handschrift bearbeitet und herausgegeben von L. Tieck. Stuttgart und Tübingen, 1812.]

Arndts Märchen. [E. Moritz Arndt: Mährchen und Jugenderinnerungen. Erster Teil, Berlin, 1818.]

Novalis Schriften by Tieck and F. Schlegel. [Novalis Schriften. Herausgegeben von Friedrich Schlegel und Ludwig Tieck. Berlin, 1802. 2 Bde. Zweite Auflage. Herausgegeben von Ludwig Tieck und Fr. Schlegel. Berlin, 1805. 2 Bde. Dritte Auflage, Berlin, 1815. 2 Bde.]

Menzel Geschichten der Deutschen. [Karl Adolf Menzel: Die Geschichten der Deutschen. Breslau, 1815–23. 8 Bde.]

Selam Sprache der Blumen. [Johann D. Symanski: Selam, oder die Sprache der Blumen. Berlin, 1820. Ohne Verfasser. 2. verb. und verm. Aufl., 1821; 3. verb. und verm. Aufl., 1823.]

Katchen von Heilbronn von Kleist. [Heinrich v. Kleist: Das Käthchen von Heilbronn oder die Feuerprobe. Ein grosses historisches Ritterschauspiel. Berlin, 1810.]

Zerbrochene Krug. [Heinrich v. Kleist: Der zerbrochene Krug. Ein Lustspiel. Berlin, 1811.]

Deutsches Theater von Tieck. [Deutsches Theater. Herausgegeben von Ludwig Tieck. Berlin, 1817. 2 Bde.]

Die sieben Weiber von Blaubart by Leberecht. [Die sieben Weiber des Blaubart: Eine wahre Familiengeschichte, herausgegeben von Gottlieb Färber. Istambul, bey Heraklius Murusi, Hofbuchhändler der Hohen Pforte; im Jahr der Hedschrat 1212. (*i.e.*, Ludwig Tieck, Berlin, 1797.)]

Beginning of Notebook covering May 20–July 11, 1823.

Jean Paul's work. [Probably Der Komet, oder Nikolaus Marggraf. Eine komische Geschichte. Von Jean Paul. 3 Bdchen. Berlin, 1820–22.]

Entry of May 30, 1823.

Der Freyschütz [von Friedrich Kind. Oper in 3 Acts von K. M. v. Weber. Leipzig, 1822.]

End of Notebook covering May 20–July 11, 1823.

Die Höllenfarth. Roman von Klinger où il se moque des usages existants à Frankfurt a/M. [Friedrich M. v. Klinger: Fausts Leben, Thaten und Höllenfarth in fünf Büchern. St. Petersburg, 1791.]

Journal 1823–1824.

November 22, 1823.

Schillers 30 years war. [Geschichte des dreissigjährigen Kriegs. Leipzig, 1793.]

November 25, 1823.

Wallenstein. [von Schiller. Tübingen, 1800.]

December 3, 1823.

Goetz of Berlichingen [Götz von Berlichingen von Goethe. Frankfurt, 1773.]

December 24, 1823.

German work of Grimms. [probably Deutsche Sagen. Herausgegeben von den Brüdern Grimm. Berlin, 1818.]

January 9, 1824.

Partzer Wuth. [Parteyenwuth oder die Kraft des Glaubens. Schauspiel in 5 A. von F. W. Ziegler. Wien, 1817.]

Mullers Genl. Hist. 3 Vols. [Vier und zwanzig Bücher Allgemeiner Geschichten besonders der Europäischen Menschheit. Durch Johannes von Müller 1797. Herausg. nach des Verfassers Tode durch dessen Bruder Johann Georg Müller. 3 Bde. Stuttgart u. Tübingen, 1817.]

January 19, 1824.

Schillers Don Carlos. [A tragedy. Translated from the German of Frederick Schiller. 3d ed. London, 1798.]

February 18, 1824.

Euryanthe. [Euryanthe von Savoyen. Von Helmina von Chézy, geb. Freiin Klencke. Berlin, 1823.]

August 8, 1824.
Peter Schelmel. [Peter Schlemihl's wundersame Geschichte mitgetheilt von Adelbert von Chamisso und herausgegeben von Friedrich Baron de la Motte Fouqué. Nürnberg, 1814; English translation by J. Bowring with 8 plates by G. Cruikshank. London, 1824.]

Journals, II.
Aug. 19, 1824.
Travels in Germany. [Possibly Thomas Hodgskin's Travels in the North of Germany. 2 vols. Edinburgh, 1820.]

January 31, 1825.
Coleridge's translation of Wallenstein [from the German of Fr. Schiller. 2 vols., London, 1800.]

March 25, 1825.
Schuld of Müllner. [Die Schuld. Trauerspiel in 4 A. von Adolph Müllner. Wien, 1816.]

September 17, 1825.
Goethe's Faust. [Eine Tragödie von Goethe. Neue Auflage. Stuttgart u. Tübingen, 1821.]

December 24, 1825.
Klopstock's Messiah. [Der Messias von Friedrich G. Klopstock, 1748–1773; probably Klopstock's Messiah, translated into English verse by G. H. C. Egestorff. Hamburg, 1821.]

Notebook 1824–25 NYPL.
Archenholz' 7 Years War. [Johann W. v. Archenholz: Geschichte des siebenjährigen Krieges in Deutschland. 2 Bde., Berlin, 1793.]

Journals, III.
February 26, 1826.
Bouterweck [Friedrich Bouterwek: Geschichte der Poesie und Beredsamkeit seit dem Ende des dreizehnten Jahrhunderts. 12 Bde. Göttingen, 1801–19. 3. Band: Geschichte der spanischen und portugiesischen Poesie und Beredsamkeit, 1804. Vols. 3 & 4 translated as History of Spanish and Portuguese Literature, London, 1823.]

March 7, 1826.
Schlegel's Remarks on Span[ish] poet[ry]. [Ueber dramatische Kunst und Literatur. Vorlesungen von A. W. Schlegel, 3 Bde., Heidelberg, 1809–11.]

Index

Names in the Notes and the Appendix are not included